MADE HERE, BABY!

The Essential Guide to Finding the Best
American-Made Products for Your Kids

Bruce H. Wolk

American Management Association

New York • Atlanta • Brussels • Chicago • Mexico City • San Francisco
Shanghai • Tokyo • Toronto • Washington, D.C.

Special discounts on bulk quantities of AMACOM books are available to corporations, professional associations, and other organizations. For details, contact Special Sales Department, AMACOM, a division of American Management Association, 1601 Broadway, New York, NY 10019.
Tel: 800-250-5308. Fax: 518-891-2372.
E-mail: specialsls@amanet.org
Website: www.amacombooks.org/go/specialsales
To view all AMACOM titles go to: www.amacombooks.org

This publication is designed to provide accurate and authoritative information in regard to the subject matter covered. It is sold with the understanding that the publisher is not engaged in rendering legal, accounting, or other professional service. If legal advice or other expert assistance is required, the services of a competent professional person should be sought.

Library of Congress Cataloging-in-Publication Data

Wolk, Bruce H.
    Made here, baby! : the essential guide to finding the best American-made products for your kids / Bruce H. Wolk.
        p.   cm.
    Includes bibliographical references and indexes.
    ISBN-13: 978-0-8144-1388-3
    ISBN-10: 0-8144-1388-9
    1. Children's paraphernalia—United States.   2. Manufactures—United States.   3. Child consumers—United States.   I. Title.

HD9970.5.C483U69   2009
649'.1029—dc22

                                                                        2008044340

Printing number

10   9   8   7   6   5   4   3   2

For Samuel Ray Morrison, a teacher from West Virginia

For my uncle, Sy Jaffe, an American who made books with his hands

Contents

☆

Contents

☆
Contents

Acknowledgments

When I started this book, I took a yellow sticky note, wrote the word *Courage* on it, and stuck it to my desk. How could I convince more than 400 companies to share just a bit of themselves with me? Who was I to come barging into their lives and ask questions about their companies?

I was surprised by the incredibly warm welcome I was extended. However, I quickly learned that the true acts of courage had nothing to do with me at all and had everything to do with the companies themselves. It is they who must compete each day against miserable odds.

Every time this project seemed to overwhelm me, one of the manufacturers would reach out and say, *Please don't give up, you're doing a good thing.* Some companies sent me literature, and others sent me samples of their work. Some sent me their wishes, and some their prayers. Many gave me referrals to other American companies, even referrals to their competitors. I began to keep a list of people who were exceptionally "nice." The list grew to hundreds of people. The project had become much larger than myself. My first acknowledgment is to the companies themselves.

I give thanks to Gina Panettieri at Talcott-Notch Literary Agency and to my editors, Stan Wakefield, Barry Richardson, and Mike Sivilli.

Finally, to my support team: to Phil, my brother in Guam; Craig, friend and computer whiz; and Jannette, with my love.

I Hear America Singing

I HEAR America singing, the varied carols I hear; Those of mechanics—each one singing his, as it should be, blithe and strong; The carpenter singing his, as he measures his plank or beam; The mason singing his, as he makes ready for work, or leaves off work; The boatman singing what belongs to him in his boat—the deckhand singing on the steamboat deck; The shoemaker singing as he sits on his bench—the hatter singing as he stands; The wood-cutter's song—the ploughboy's, on his way in the morning, or at the noon intermission, or at sundown; The delicious singing of the mother—or of the young wife at work—or of the girl sewing or washing—Each singing what belongs to her, and to none else; The day what belongs to the day—At night, the party of young fellows, robust, friendly, Singing, with open mouths, their strong melodious songs.

Walt Whitman,
"Leaves of Grass,"
1900

CHAPTER 1

Introduction

My Mom, "Ruthie the Riveter"

She wasn't much more than 23 years old the morning she first stepped onto the manufacturing floor of the Curtiss-Wright airplane factory in Tonawanda, New York. Her jaw dropped at the scale of it all. It was the largest building she had ever seen, with row upon row of aircraft and all the machinery, the noise, and the activity. However, she is quick to explain that she was an inexperienced girl from Buffalo, who hadn't been anywhere and hadn't seen much.

She was tired from too little sleep and very nervous. She was afraid of not being accepted and, worse, of not doing good work. So much was riding on the opportunity. Though it was 1943, the Great Depression hadn't left her family.

There were 10 children, and she was the second youngest. At any given time, at least some of her older brothers and sisters, even those who were married, were out of work. Family meals were potluck. She never knew who would show up. Strangers were fed with the same love as family. You could stretch potato soup. A memory floods my brain. I was a little boy, and my mother, my aunt, and I were walking out of a supermarket. I picked up a shriveled potato that had rolled out of someone's shopping bag a few days before. I threw it to the ground, and my mother yelled at me. I understand now.

She was teased in high school because she would often wear the same dress or ill-fitting hand-me-downs from her older sisters. She

1

sees nothing noble about being poor. It stinks to be poor. Memories of being teased remain with her to this day.

Though she dreamed of going to college and certainly had the stuff to go to college, there was no money to do so. She knew of some in the "other crowd" that had made it through the hard times without a scratch. The Depression wasn't an equal-opportunity era. The girls in the other crowd had dads who were doctors and lawyers; her dad was laid off from the Pullman Company because they no longer needed car-seat upholsterers. He scratched around at all kinds of factory-second sales schemes to bring in money, and almost none of them worked. So the rich girls would get to go to college. Well, good for them. You took what you could get, and you shut up about it.

After high school, Ruth took employment as a sales clerk. She worked her way up to making almost $11 a week at Kobacker's Department Store. She sold nurses' uniforms, aprons, and such. The war was on, and, sadly, nurses were in high demand. The manager praised her work. He said that her department was doing triple the business of any other department. She asked for a nickel an hour raise, and the manager walked away. She quit Kobacker's and took work at another department store. The results weren't much better. The new boss wasn't such a nice man. In today's parlance, they would call it harassment.

Curtiss-Wright was hiring riveters. It was steady work with lots of overtime. The catch was that you would have to go to riveting school for a month without pay. It was worth the chance. Ruth had just gotten engaged to a guy who lived on Long Island. He was in the family tailoring and dry-cleaning business. She wanted to look presentable for his family. She wanted to dress like a woman and not some small-timer who ate potato soup and had two dresses.

Her new boss was a Native American from an upstate New York tribe. He was a big man physically, with a good heart. His job was to make assignments for the different teams. He teamed my mom with a girl named Wanda who was even younger than she.

Ruth, the daughter of Romanian and Russian-Polish Jews, and her partner, a Polish Catholic girl, "clicked." Their job was to rivet the cockpits for the P-40 fighter plane, known in military circles as the Tomahawk or the Kittyhawk. It was the aircraft flown by the Flying Tigers in the Pacific and the Tuskegee Airmen, the Red Tails, in Europe.

There were some who wondered what Ruth was doing there. *You're rich, aren't you? All your people are rich.* She thought about her father, who was now applying for work at Curtiss-Wright as a broom pusher. *What do you think I'm doing here?*

The two young women, 98-pound weaklings, talked of their dreams, sang songs such as *Begin the Beguine*, and leaned into the metal. They finally had real jobs and not small-time work. They became so good at their craft that the bosses assigned them inspection duties to correct the mistakes of other teams. With overtime, working through lunches and inspection work, Ruth pulled down as much as $60 a week. The Great Depression had ended for my mom. I asked her if she ever thought about the pilots sitting in the aircraft she helped build.

Whenever we finished a plane, I touched it, and I prayed that the boys would be safe.

The Curtiss-Wright factory employed nearly 40,000 American factory workers at the peak of its wartime airplane production; more than 80 percent of them were women. During the war years, Curtiss-Wright built nearly 16,000 P-40s. They were built by farm girls, waitresses, and sales clerks.

The nursery rhymes of my childhood were songs of sweat-built aircraft and songs by aunts and uncles who worked as pattern makers, fabric blockers, bookbinders, and car-seat upholsterers. My connection to American manufacturing is genetic. It was no wonder that my first jobs were also in manufacturing. I am drawn to people who like to make things.

We recently honored mom, now 90, with a dinner party. Relatives flew in from all over the country to be with her. At some point during the birthday weekend, she turned to me and unexpectedly asked: *How come we don't make things in America anymore?*

She made the point for this book.

We still make things here, mom, *and we make them well.* They don't always get the credit they deserve—well, hardly ever, really. I don't know if the people who make them touch their products the way you placed your hand against the metal of the plane and prayed for the pilots, but they care just as much. I felt their voices as they talked to me. Many of them will have wonderful nursery rhymes to sing.

Moms and Dads versus "The Globe"

At the start of my professional career, when I was doing R&D for a manufacturing company, I remember workers in the nearby electronics factories getting laid off. I saw them shouting and picketing, then reduced to milling about in front of shuttered doors, and finally, applying for nonexistent jobs at my factory. Whole industries were disappearing, and it was not long before most everyone agreed that American manufacturing was going to join the dinosaurs.

According to the experts, we would buy our products from "somewhere else," and, in turn, Americans would find jobs in fields such as customer service and "computers." My business school professors started to talk about something called the "global economy."

We were delighted; as a freshly minted M.B.A., I envisioned flying to exotic places and dining in Tokyo, Hong Kong, Rome, and Paris.

Imports began to flood our new global economy. "Bargain stores," "super stores," and then the "big box" stores sprang up. They offered everyday cheap prices. Almost everything in those stores was made in that somewhere else place, and that was all right by most of us.

Things seemed fine for a while except for the plant workers losing their jobs; however, economists assured us that "those people" would soon be fixing things, manning call centers, and greeting customers as they walked into the big box stores with their shopping carts.

We began to hear whispers, not much more than a trickle, about products being recalled for safety concerns. It was stuff used by grown-ups, and no one seemed to care. Then there were the disturbing stories about our pets getting sick, and that bothered many more of us. Finally, the media exploded with news bulletins about the products we were buying for our kids. It wasn't just toys but children's games, furniture, room decorations, jewelry, and clothes!

☆
Introduction

In the beginning it was about choking hazards, but then it was about the chemicals on the products themselves.

Whole laws have been created with regard to lead-based paints and the dangers to children; as parents, grandparents, aunts, and uncles, we *know* how dangerous chemicals such as lead can be! In most states, you can't sell a house without signing a lead paint disclosure statement. We were shocked and scared when the first infant products were recalled due to lead contamination!

To our amazement, hundreds of thousands of imported children's products *are still being recalled* because they contain lead-based paints, present choking hazards, or have other safety violations. Most of these products are from that "somewhere else" place. These aren't just fly-by-night brands, either, but brands many of us remember from our own childhoods and even some brands going back to my mom's childhood.

While the media were outraged and the politicians yakked, it was moms who mobilized. Across America, it has been angry moms, and not politicians, who have rallied and led the fight against unsafe imports. Moms are blogging, moms are forming online communities, moms are reviewing products, moms are talking in the workplace, at coffee bars, and at social events. Suddenly, "cheaper" isn't as glamorous a word as it once was; the somewhere else place had come home to haunt us.

However, most moms, dads, and everyone else were convinced that there weren't good alternatives to imported children's products. Who can blame them? For years the only images we'd seen of American manufacturing were chained gates and crumbling factories.

Wouldn't we consider American-made choices if they were available? According to the experts, moms and dads are willing to at least look at American-made products—*if they can find them!* In most cases, we *can* find excellent American-made children's products, and that is why we wrote *Made Here, Baby!*

What American Manufacturers Have Taught Us

A few years ago, we began a journey to rediscover American manufacturing. As the problems with imported children's products began to surface, we focused our efforts on American manufacturers of children's products.

Friends shook their heads and laughed: *There's no one left! Who's going to want a three-page book?* We are happy to report that the pessimists would have been wrong. Let's visit some of the findings from our journey:

There are more of us than you might think, but it doesn't mean we're easy to find.

Web searches can be tricky if you don't look beneath the surface. Just because a manufacturer has "USA" in its name or appears on a list doesn't necessarily mean any part of its products are manufactured or even assembled in America. A well-known brand name whose product line *used* to be manufactured in America does not guarantee that it is *still* being produced in America.

On the other hand, many companies can't be easily found by typing keywords into a search engine. Though they are true American manufacturers, several of these businesses have such small advertising and marketing budgets that they can't get the word out about how good they are or how committed they are to making their products in the United States.

It took a lot of research, interviews, referrals, and sometimes *luck* to find the fine companies listed in this book. We list more than 400 companies that manufacture children's products in the United States.

We haven't lost our skills, but . . .

American manufacturers still produce excellent products in wood, plastic, fabric, and fine metals. The American-made wooden toys shown on these pages, the fine pewter baby spoons, the fun plastic wagons, the incredible keepsake jewelry, and even the dresses for your little girl hold their own in terms of quality and manufacturing integrity against any products produced *anywhere* in the world.

However, the bad news is that we can't always buy American no matter how hard we might try. All of the flag waving in the world won't revive an electronics industry that was allowed, even encouraged, to leave our shores. This book, sadly, doesn't list American-made bottle warmers or baby-room monitoring systems.

Nor is it possible to find a new, American-made baby stroller or even a new, American-made glass baby bottle, for that matter. These types of products have been outsourced to distant shores.

We must do the best we can with what we have left and try to build upon that base. We need to look to the future.

We know where we live, and that's good enough.

It is surprising that, among American manufacturers, we found relatively little import bashing. It is easy to put down another country. It is easy to whine. Instead, here is what our manufacturers told us: *Don't buy from us just because we're Americans or because you feel sorry for us. Buy our products because they are better and we can make them better.*

We make our products in America because it makes sense to make them here.

Some of the companies we detail started out *wanting* to import or were *actually importing* but didn't like what they were getting from "over there." Several companies we interviewed brought production back to the United States because of the poor quality of the products they had made overseas.

Shipping costs have gone through the roof, as well. Savings from making things overseas were being eaten up by what it cost to put those items in a container and ship them halfway around the world.

Inflation has also become a problem, even in the Third World. Several manufacturers we interviewed that used to produce overseas reported that what was once very cheap to make in places such as China is getting more and more expensive.

In many cases, it was too difficult to correct manufacturing defects long distance, especially when there were language barriers. Many American manufacturers find it easier to walk out onto the manufacturing floor and make an on-the-spot improvement than to wait three months to see a production result.

I am an American. Don't define me!

The face of American manufacturing has changed. Many of the organizations are now founded, cofounded, run, or owned by women. A few companies are second-generation women-owned. There are many minority-owned businesses. There is no common political orientation. The manufacturers we spoke with represent nearly every state in the nation, not just the so-called Rust Belt.

Many businesses are owned by grandparents tired of retirement or by young people barely out of their teens. Some companies were started by dropouts from the high-tech rat race, while founders of other companies were lifelong friends with common dreams shared over a latte and an initial business plan sketched, yes, on a napkin.

We found manufacturers that revived businesses that had been shut down decades before and companies that have been in continuous operation for more than two centuries.

We live here.

Most companies are committed to recycling programs or to reforestation or "green manufacturing." Several companies use organic fabrics, especially when the products are intended for infants, while other companies find ingenious ways to reuse fabrics or reclaim wood or to make novel products from waste plastic. American companies are also exploring new sustainable fibers such as bamboo and hemp or are working with fibers that have almost disappeared, such as linen. Some companies power their operations with energy derived from the wind, while others have rebuilt their factories to allow for the natural warmth and beauty of sunshine.

Many organizations actively support causes in order to give back to their communities, or to children, or to help cure disease, or to nurture the arts, or even to honor the animals they've rescued. We are a generous nation, and, despite how tough it is to manufacture competitively, it is heartwarming to see the way in which we still reach out to those who are less fortunate.

Commitment to customer service.

The dedication to customer service, customization when it is possible, and on-time delivery is also a common thread. Every one of the manufacturers deeply understands that it has foreign competition. Every one of these manufacturers wants your business.

Do You Know of a Company?

The listings in *Made Here, Baby!* represent a snapshot in time. Every effort has been made to find as many American manufacturers as possible that make children's products. In a country as large as ours, we have probably missed a few companies. We will do our best to include those companies in the future. Please let us know if there is a company that should be included (www.madeherebaby.com).

It is also a possibility that some of the companies we have listed may go out of business or that the ownership may retire or may even elect to manufacture overseas. Those listings will be dropped.

We are aware that there are legal differences between "Made in the USA" and "Assembled in the USA." The rules are confusing. At this critical time, when American manufacturers are fighting to maintain their toeholds, indeed, *any* toehold, our stand is that if a children's product manufacturer has an American manufacturing operation using American labor and most of its raw materials or parts are sourced from domestic sources, then it is made here.

In some cases, companies based in America have told us that most of their product line is made in the USA but that some of their products are imported. In that case, we will inform you which items are made in America, or we will direct you to the part of their Web site devoted to American-made items.

We don't penalize a company if it is small in size. A two-person company gets equal footing with a 500-person company. We honor the commitment of two stay-at-home moms with small children or a husband-and-wife team or a grandfather-and-grandson partnership that decides to manufacture a product and then acts on the idea by setting up a manufacturing operation. Bill Gates, Henry Ford, and Thomas Edison, not to mention the Wright Brothers, were not exactly conglomerates when they started out.

If a company only has an administrative office in America but does absolutely no production in this country of any kind, it is not included.

The good news: almost every company is exactly what it says it is. Every company we interviewed strives to source all of its parts or materials in America. The hundreds of interviews revealed a collective honesty and openness. No company claimed to be manufacturing in America if it wasn't. We have seen small but unmistakable signs that the trend is beginning to reverse itself; American manufacturing is slowly returning to life. We must help nurture its return.

CHAPTER 2

How to Use This Book

We have designed *Made Here, Baby!* to be as easy as possible to use. Our biggest challenge is to help the reader understand that most companies make more than one kind of product. For example, a company that makes baby rattles may also make children's furniture; a company that makes baby bibs may also make tee shirts for your teenage daughter; a company that makes backpacks for your school-age son may also make baby carriers for new moms.

To help solve the challenge, we use three different ways to help you find and buy American-made products for your child: *chapters, symbols,* and *listings by product line.*

1. The *Chapters* place the American manufacturer in the group of products that is its main focus. For example, if a company makes mostly baby clothes but also produces a few pieces of clothing for preschoolers, it will fall into the "Mom, Dad, and Baby" section.

2. The *Symbols* help to guide your search. Let's say you are in the "American-Made Toys & Games" section, and you are reading about a company that makes wooden toys for preschool and school-age children. If you look to the right of the company name, you may also see this symbol ↓ , which tells you that the company makes products for even younger children.

3. The *American-Made Children's Products Cross Reference* is the third way to find an American manufacturer. For example, some companies

that make children's bedroom furniture also make baby cribs. By going to the listing for "Baby Furniture," you will be able to find all of the companies that make baby furniture, no matter what other sections they may also appear in. The *American-Made Children's Products Cross Reference* may be found in the index section at the back of this book.

The Chapters

Made Here, Baby! company listings are divided into the five following chapters:

Chapter 3: **Mom, Dad, and Baby**

- ✢ Nursing and Feeding My Baby: Includes bottle wraps, nursing clothes, and nursing pillows

- ✢ Traveling with My Baby: Includes baby slings, pouches, carriers, car seats, and accessories

- ✢ Diaper Bags, Totes, Changing Pads, Diapers, and Diaper Organizers

- ✢ Baby's Breath: Includes American-made baby's-room air purifiers

- ✢ Baby's Safety and Wellness: Includes first-aid kits, thermometers, sound conditioners, natural "heating pads," safety barriers, identification systems, and special needs products for autistic children

- ✢ Precious Baby Keepsakes: Includes mommy and baby jewelry, pottery, pewter and silver, beautiful keepsake albums, personalized books, quilts, and other items

- ✢ Baby Furniture: Includes cribs, bassinets, changing tables, high chairs, bonding benches, beds, and bedroom furniture

- ✢ Baby's First Mattress

- ✢ Baby's Blankets and Bedding: Includes blankets, sheets and pillowcases, quilts, bumpers, and room decorations and accessories

- ✢ Baby Clothing: Includes bibs, burp cloths, snappies, tees, pants, baby outerwear, and costumes

☆
Made Here, Baby!

- Baby Footwear
- Baby Fun! Includes baby-safe dolls, rattles, and pacifiers

Chapter 4: American-Made Children's Clothing and Accessories

- Clothing and accessories for toddlers through teens
- Our Little Baby Is Changing!: Includes clothing for toddlers and preschool children
- Mostly for Girls: Includes clothing for school-age girls to 'tweens and beyond
- Girls' Jewelry and Hair Accessories
- Mostly for Boys: Includes clothing for school-age boys to 'tweens and beyond
- For Girls and Boys: Includes companies that make products for both boys and girls, generally from school age to 'tweens and beyond
- Children's and Infants' Footwear and Socks

Chapter 5: American-Made Children's Furniture

- Furniture for children from toddler to teens
- Outdoor Furniture
- Indoor Furniture: Includes furniture for any room of the house
- Children's Carpeting: Includes playroom and bedroom carpeting
- Educational and Play Furniture

Chapter 6: American-Made Sports and Fitness Equipment

- Sports-related products from school-age children to 'tweens and beyond
- Sports and Fitness Clothing: Includes clothing for all sports
- Fitness Equipment: Circuit training equipment specifically made for children

❄ Sporting Goods: Includes a broad range of items, from soccer goals to baseball bats to jump ropes

❄ Anything on Wheels: Includes skateboards, bicycles, roller skates, scooters, and many other products

❄ Water Sports: Includes canoes, kayaks, and water exercise equipment

❄ Winter Sports: Includes snowshoes, ice skates, sleds, and snowboards

❄ Hiking, Traveling, or Going to School: Includes backpacks and small carrying cases

Chapter 7: **American-Made Toys and Games**

❄ American Classic Toys: Includes American handcrafted wood toys

❄ Let's Build This Together: American model making and dollhouses

❄ Puzzles and Games for All Ages: Includes building sets

❄ Fantastic American Plastic Toys: The world of plastic toys

❄ Arts and Crafts

❄ Everything Plush and Cuddly

❄ Just Plain Fun: Includes kazoos, garden gnomes, and flying saucers

❄ Outdoor Play: Includes swing sets and sandboxes

What Will the Company Listings Tell Me?

Each section lists those companies specializing in children's products that most closely match the heading.

We have tried to include the following information about each company:

Company or brand name. Sometimes the company name may be different from the brand name. Usually, the manufacturers prefer that we list them by their popular brand name.

Address. This may be a physical address or a post office box depending upon the information the company wishes to share. Sometimes you will see the term "Company is an online business," or sometimes the listing will state that the company is in a certain area. This means that the company prefers that all transactions take place over the Internet or does not want sales solicitations at its factory location.

Telephone number. This is generally the customer service number. It may or may not be a toll-free number. Sometimes you might see the term "Prefers e-mail," which means the company would rather answer questions over the Internet.

Web site. This is the main Web site of the company.

Description of products. This is to help the reader learn about the products a company manufactures. We will tell you about the general age range of the product line, whether the production is limited or customized, and other useful information, such as whether the company imports any of its products or uses organic materials.

Interesting fact. We try to tell a story about each company or provide interesting information about how the company got started or even facts about the technology. Most often, these stories are based on interviews with company owners or executives.

How to find. This section will help you find and buy the company's products. In some cases, the companies don't sell direct but go through store chains or distributors. We don't list the exact brick-and-mortar store locations or online stores, but we will tell you how to find those stores.

What Do the Symbols Mean?

Symbols are used to give the reader additional information about a company. The symbols appear to the right of each company's name or its well-known brand name.

> **T—** The company is an American manufacturing treasure. This is usually a company that has been manufacturing in America for more than a century.

↓ —The company also makes products for children in a younger age group. For example, a company that makes dresses for school-age girls might also make layettes and receiving blankets for infants.

↑—The manufacturer also makes products for children in an older age group. For example, a company that makes rattles for babies might also make pull toys for toddlers.

✿— This symbol honors companies that are owned, cofounded, or managed by women.

☺— This recognizes companies' commitment to "green," manufacturing through recycling, the use of organic materials, local sourcing of raw materials, sustainable forestry methods, use of alternative energy sources, or promotion of employee programs that foster environmental responsibility.

✈— The company imports part of its product line. In this case, we will detail the products still manufactured in this country.

✂—The company customizes to order or is a company with limited production, and there may be a wait for delivery of your product.

★— The company makes products for children with special needs, such as children who are visually impaired or are autistic.

⌸— The company allows factory or studio tours. Please call ahead.

●—The manufacturing company sells its products only to distributors and you must call or e-mail the distributor. Sometimes you may call the company to get a list of the nearest distributor.

CHAPTER 3

Mom, Dad, and Baby—American-Made Products for Infants

Walk into just about any library in the world and ask to see the section that has the books about mommies and babies. The librarians won't call it that, of course, but you know what we mean.

In the bigger libraries, you will find hundreds of important books on the subject of raising good babies to be good people. Psychologists, teachers, social workers, and medical doctors have spent lifetimes studying what most of us should already know: the bond between moms and dads and their babies is beautiful, sometimes fragile, and very, very precious.

Our book can't do much to add to all the knowledge about the mommy–baby bond. However, we can point to one interesting fact: of the more than 130 American manufacturing companies we list in this chapter, 95 percent of them are owned, co-owned, or founded by women. These aren't just small companies, either; the list includes companies with sales in the many millions of dollars per year.

Are all of these women-owned American manufacturing companies also "Mommy-owned"? It's difficult to say. The topic of motherhood and manufacturing did come up in many of our interviews with these companies, and it seems that, in most cases, the women-owned companies that make baby products are also mommy-owned.

How did this happen? Wasn't the face of American manufacturing always a cigar-chomping man sitting behind a mahogany desk? Yes, that was the face, but it wasn't always the truth. This book contains several examples of women who took on active roles in the management of manufacturing companies going well back into the 1950s, but, starting in the 1970s with the women's movement, things really began to change. That is when a lot of confusion began to set in, as well.

Remember those romantic comedies in the 1980s and 1990s about the hard-charging career woman who was suddenly "forced" to make serious life decisions after becoming pregnant? She would be doing something important like dictating a memo, when the call would come in from the doctor. *I'm what? Are you sure there isn't a mistake?* The rest of the movie would be devoted to watching our executive deal with the "problem."

As women settled into the new millennium, a kind of comfort began to settle into place. For some, "the better way" has become the understanding that when all is said and done, *they prefer* to be home with their babies; it is OK to be a mommy.

However, these moms also want to use their talents. They were well respected in their careers, rose in the ranks, and contributed to their organizations; why should that stop? These women don't want a life where the most exciting event of the day is separating light and dark socks! Offices became home offices, and then home offices started to become home office nurseries.

It was not long before women in home offices with nurseries began reaching out to one another and, after reaching out, formed business as well as social partnerships. There are many great stories about how these new moms met. Some moms met while watching their kids at play, or perhaps they had known each other in the corporate world, or they were lifelong friends, or they were even strangers who met by e-mailing through a Web site devoted to women entrepreneurs who, like them, were writing business plans that were covered with thrown baby food!

These smart and savvy moms talked over their problems and priorities. It's no great news flash that we live in pretty hectic times. We want the products we use to stand up to use; we want our products to save us time and to be well designed. The moms studied the products they were using for their babies and thought about how they could make them better. Some even wondered if it would be possible to manufacture in America, where they could maintain quality and better oversee operations and, well, give jobs to other Americans.

Frequently, it has been moms who have also coaxed their husbands from high-stress careers in order join together to build a small manufacturing business. Of course, it's a leap of faith. America was built on such faith—then and now.

Many of these mom companies or mom-and-dad manufacturing teams don't just want to make better things; they want to make things better. They don't want to build factories where pollution is dumped into the environment but to leave the environment in better shape than they found it. They want workers treated fairly. They want to donate to the causes they love. Most of all, they want children to be safe.

If there is any single factor responsible for motivating moms and dads to create American manufacturing companies for baby products, we believe it is the anger all of us felt when the news stories first appeared about the brands that we once trusted. Unfortunately, the recalls still continue. Fortunately, mom, dad, and baby are making their voices heard.

This section of *Made Here, Baby!* is devoted to American manufacturing companies, both small and large, that have dedicated themselves to making quality, safe products for your baby.

Mom, Dad, and Baby

This chapter has been divided into several sections to best describe the products made by these manufacturers for your baby. Please keep in mind that most of the companies in this book make products for several age groups. An "American-Made Children's Products" index appears in the back of the book to help you locate all companies that may make a certain type of product.

❋ Nursing and Feeding My Baby (includes bottle wraps, nursing clothes, and nursing pillows)

❋ Traveling with My Baby (includes baby slings, pouches, carriers, car seats, and accessories)

❋ Diaper Bags, Diapers, and Diaper Organizers

❋ Baby's Breath (includes American-made baby's-room air purifiers)

❋ Baby's Safety and Wellness (includes items such as first-aid kits, thermometers, sound conditioners, safety barriers, and identification systems)

❋ Precious Baby Keepsakes (includes mommy and baby jewelry, objects in pottery, pewter, and silver, keepsake albums, personalized books, and quilts

❋ Baby Furniture (includes cribs, bassinets, changing tables, bonding benches, beds and bedroom furniture, and high chairs)

❋ Baby's First Mattress

❋ Baby's Blankets and Bedding (includes blankets, sheets and pillowcases, quilts, bumpers, and room decorations and accessories)

❋ Baby Clothing (includes bibs, burp cloths, snappies, tees, pants, baby outerwear, and costumes)

❋ Baby Footwear

❋ Baby Fun! (includes baby-safe dolls, rattles, and pacifiers)

Nursing and Feeding My Baby

The closest of all nurturing occurs between mom and baby during the first weeks and months of life, and especially in nursing and feeding. These American manufacturers make products to assist nursing moms to better care for their newborns during this period.

BOTTLE BLANKIE™, INC.

3453 Ingraham Street, San Diego, CA 92109
Telephone: 888-285-2565
Web site: www.babybottleblankie.com

Bottle Blankie™, Inc. makes baby bottle wraps in unique colors and designs.

Interesting Fact: The unique design of this product was based on a newborn's parents' wish to give their baby a better tactile sensation than he would get from holding a glass or plastic bottle.

How to Find: You may order directly from the company through its Web site or contact customer service to determine if there are retailers in your area.

CAYDEN CREATIONS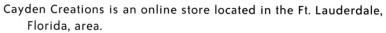

Cayden Creations is an online store located in the Ft. Lauderdale,
Florida, area.
Telephone: 954-648-0304
Web site: www.caydencreations.com

Cayden Creations makes the Peek-a-Boo Nursing Cover™ for women who wish to discreetly nurse their babies in public. Available in six different colors.

Interesting Fact: Cayden Creations is a company founded by women. Cayden Creations supports the La Leche League and other women's organizations.

How to Find: The nursing covers are available for purchase through the company's Web site, or the company can refer moms to independent dealers and lactation consultants.

LEACHCO™, INC.

P.O. Box 717, Ada, OK 74821
Telephone: 800-525-1050
Web site: www.leachco.com

Leachco™, Inc. manufactures an extensive selection of pregnancy pillows, nursing pillows, bathing pillows, safety straps, grocery shopping cart protection, crib pillows, and travel accessories.

Interesting Fact: The inspiration for Leachco™ came after the founder's baby nearly fell from a high chair. Realizing there were very few safety devices on the market to prevent such falls, the new mom designed the very first product in the Leachco line in her kitchen with makeshift materials.

How to Find: Leachco's products are found in major retailers, juvenile specialty shops, catalogs, and online stores. Call customer service if you can't find the products, and a representative will assist you in finding a retailer.

OZARK MOUNTAIN KIDS ↑ O

1125 N. 20th Street, Ozark, MO 65721
Telephone: 417-485-4279
Web site: www.ozarkmountainkids.com

Ozark Mountain Kids handcrafts a wide selection of products for baby, mom, and 'tweens. Their products include nursing pillows, diaper bags, stuffed toys, infant bedding, and furniture.

Interesting Fact: Founded in 1980, Ozark Mountain Kids specializes in handcrafted items reminiscent of designs your grandmother might have used.

How to Find: Ozark Mountain Kids primarily sells to retailers. You may e-mail or call customer service for the name of the nearest retail location.

ZENOFF PRODUCTS, INC. ✿ O

177 Post Street, San Francisco, CA 94108
Telephone: 415-421-5300
Web site: www.mybrestfriend.com

Zenoff Products, Inc. manufactures the My Brest Friend® nursing pillow.

Interesting Fact: Andrew Zenoff, the founder of the company, was visiting a friend who was the mother of a newborn. The mother explained that breast feeding was difficult for her because she found it hard to comfortably position the baby. Realizing that there might be some potential in developing a pillow for new moms, Andrew started to design prototype pillows. After 60 prototypes, he found the perfect pillow! The company has now sold more than a million pillows.

How to Find: The company does not sell directly to the public. There is a store locator page on the Web site, or you can search for online retailers.

Traveling with My Baby

In this section, moms and dads will find all kinds of baby carriers to fit all kinds of situations, whether they are traveling by foot, bicycle, or car, along with carrier accessories such as stroller and car-seat covers. The American manufacturers listed in this section are always pleased to offer assistance and any answer any questions you might have on the best way to carry your baby and the safest way to use their products. Please refer to the American-Made Children's Products Cross Reference in the index section for all companies that make products for traveling with baby.

BELLE ORGANIC BABY CARRIER ❀ ☺
97 Benthaven Place, Boulder, CO 80305
Telephone: 303-482-2752
Web site: www.bellebabycarriers.com

Belle Organic Baby Carrier manufactures baby carriers.

Interesting Fact: The inventor of the Belle Baby Carrier is an avid outdoorsman who has two degrees in engineering. The carrier was designed to allow parents to hike with their babies. As the company takes a strong stance on environmental issues, the material used in the Belle Baby Carrier is organic. The company employs a network of home sewers to help make its products.

How to Find: The Belle Organic Baby Carrier may be purchased at retailers across the United States, or you may order directly from the company through its Web site.

··

BRITAX™ USA
13501 S. Ridge Drive, Charlotte, NC 28273
Telephone: 888-409-1700
Web site: www.britaxusa.com

Britax™ USA manufactures a wide selection of car seats, all of which include side impact protection. Britax manufactures infant seats, convertible seats, and combination harness booster seats. A few products may be imported.

Interesting Fact: Though part of an international company, Britax™ might make the only car seat sold in America that is actually manufactured in America. Britax has been in Charlotte, North Carolina, since 1996. Britax assembles most of its car seats in its Charlotte factory, with about 90 percent of the components coming from vendors within a 250-mile radius of Charlotte. The Britax car seats are noted for what the company calls True Side Impact Protection®, which is a proprietary design technology that helps to transfer the energy from a side impact collision away from the child in the car seat.

How to Find: Britax USA has a detailed store locator on its Web site. If you don't have a computer or can't find a retail location nearby, please call Britax customer service for assistance.

··

CORNPATCH CREATIONS ⊛ ✂
Cornpatch Creations is an online business located in Wisconsin.
The company prefers e-mail.
Web site: www.cornpatchcreations.net

Cornpatch Creations handcrafts car seat covers out of 100 percent cotton flannel. There is a large selection of fabrics. The company also makes children's clothing to order. Limited production.

Interesting Fact: Angela, the founder of Cornpatch Creations, was taught to sew by her mother when she was 12. She has been working with fabric and patterns since that time. One day, while Angela was watching a mom carry a baby in a car seat, the wind kicked up and blew the baby's blanket into the mud. Angela knew that there must be a better way to make a car seat cover; after several months of experimenting, she had developed the Cozy Carseat Cover.

How to Find: Angela states: "I like to receive emails and hear what people want. I like people to know that I'm just another mom on the other side of the computer." Please e-mail Angela with questions.

• •

DITTANY BABY

Dittany Baby is an online business.
Telephone: 877-843-3398
Web site: www.dittanybaby.com

Dittany Baby is a manufacturer of baby slings that are available in organic and nonorganic fabrics. The company also makes baby clothing, such as skid pants, leg warmers, and baby bottle wraps.

Interesting Fact: Shannon Krieger, the president of Dittany Baby, has made a commitment to helping others. In addition to slings and clothes, the company makes a unique bottle wrap designed to assist babies with special needs who have difficulty grasping objects. The company supports cerebral palsy research and therapy. Dittany Baby is introducing a Hero's Skid Pant Collection, with proceeds helping to support the Wounded Warrior Project, a charity that assists veterans in overcoming physical and emotional injuries.

How to Find: The company has wide distribution through online retailers and is in some retail outlets. If you need assistance, please call the customer service number.

• •

GOZO USA™ ⊛

7585 W. 66th Avenue, Arvada, CO 80003
Telephone: 303-424-9750
Web site: www.gozousa.com

GoZo USA™ manufactures a unique baby carrier that rests on the hip, a diaper bag with built-in changing pad, and women-friendly backpacks used for hiking or carrying baby supplies.

Interesting Fact: GoZo USA™ is a woman-owned and -operated company that was founded in 2004. The company is very committed to the support of women's networking events.

How to Find: GoZo Products are available through the company Web site. It also sells its products at many women-friendly events.

HOTSLINGS® ✿ ☺

10606 Shady Trail, Dallas, TX 75220
Telephone: 214-350-4160
Web site: www.hotslings.com

Hotslings® produces a wide selection of slings in many fabric options, including organic fabrics. There is a detachable pocket option available. The company also makes a kid-size play sling as a way for children to emulate their parents.

Interesting Fact: Hotslings® wanted to create a sling that not only allowed closer bonding between parent and child but also made a fashion statement. The unique print fabrics are exclusive to the company.

How to Find: The Web site has a retail store locator for your convenience, or you can find the products by searching the sites of online stores. If you need assistance, please call the customer service number.

iBERT, INC. ✿

1733 W. 12600 Street, Riverton, UT 84065
Telephone: 801-440-4024
Web site: www.ibertinc.com

iBert, Inc. makes a unique, front-mounted bicycle safety seat along with mounting hardware and tools to enable moms and dads to better carry their babies on bicycle trips.

Interesting Fact: The iBert Safe-T-Seat© is the dedicated result of a husband-and-wife team working together for six years to develop a unique, front-mounted bicycle baby carrier. The company feels that it is much easier for parent and baby to interact in the front-mounted position and also much safer for both baby and rider.

How to Find: The iBert Safe-T-Seat may be ordered through the company Web site. The product is also sold through bike shops and sporting goods retailers.

....

MY KARMA BABY™ ❀ ☺
3667 Iris Avenue, Boulder, CO 80301
Telephone: 303-443-1834
Web site: www.mykarmababy.com

My Karma Baby™ manufactures a wide selection of baby slings and carriers in organic fabrics.

Interesting Fact: Stacey Potter was inspired to start her company after completing a master's thesis in Transpersonal Psychology. She committed herself to helping moms better bond with their babies. Stacey learned how to sew from her mother-in-law. She started to make slings for her friends, and people loved them. The slings are now sold in more than 100 stores worldwide. Though trained as a psychologist, Stacey realized she was as interested in business as she was in psychology. In fact, she has just started another company.

How to Find: E-mail or call the company for the nearest retail location, or, if you wish, you may order directly from the company through the My Karma Baby Web site.

....

NEW NATIVE® BABY ❀ ☺
135 Aviation Way, Watsonville, CA 95076
Telephone: 800-646-1682
Web site: www.newnativebaby.com

New Native® Baby manufactures products primarily for infants and their moms, including baby carriers, organic cotton wash cloths, burp pads, receiving blankets, hooded blankets, children's doll carriers, and diaper bags.

Interesting Fact: Founded in 1992 by Nancy Main, the mother of three children, New Native® Baby takes as its guiding principle a strong commitment to community outreach and community events. The company makes most of the items in its product line from organic cotton.

How to Find: The best way to order New Native Baby products is through the company Web site. If you need further assistance, please call the customer service number.

PEANUT SHELL, THE®

55 W. Angela Street, Pleasanton, CA 94566
Telephone: 925-931-0947
Web site: www.thepeanutshell.com

The Peanut Shell® specializes in nursing wraps, baby slings, and baby wraps.

Interesting Fact: The company began business in 2004, shortly after the birth of Alicia Shaffer's son. She searched for a comfortable way to carry her baby and nothing met her needs, so she developed her own sling, brought it to a commercial seamstress with a selection of designer fabrics, and soon realized she had also given birth to a company. The Peanut Shell® initially manufactured all of its baby slings overseas, but, in late 2008, production was moved to the United States to ensure better quality.

How to Find: Please go to the company Web site for a retail store locator.

ROCKIN' BABY SLING

5048 Eagle Rock Boulevard, Los Angeles, CA 90041
Telephone: 888-645-BABY
Web site: www.rockinbabysling.com

Rockin' Baby Sling handcrafts baby slings and pouches in many different fabrics to enable moms to keep their sense of style.

Interesting Fact: Rockin' Baby Slings was founded in 2002 by two friends, Lisa and Natasha. The women were both employed in the entertainment business in costume design, but they wanted to create something for themselves and for their children. Their philosophy is that slings and pouches more closely bond babies with their moms, as opposed to car seats and carriers that are difficult to carry and separate mom and baby.

How to Find: The company has a factory store in Los Angeles; however, its products are also sold in more than 100 retail outlets, including some in Japan and in Europe. You may also order through the Web site. If you need assistance finding a retail location, please call the customer service number.

....

SWEET FLETCHER DESIGNS ⚜ ↑
19 E. 53rd Street, Savannah, GA 31405
Telephone: 912-507-6721
Web site: www.sweetfletcher.com

Sweet Fletcher Designs produces pouch-style slings in four different sizes. Slings are made without rings, buckles, or clasps and can accommodate children from infancy through 30 pounds. The company also makes baby quilts, Grab-n-Go clutches made of laminated fabric, and tee shirts for children 6 months to 5T.

Interesting Fact: Ashley Waldvogel Gaddy, the founder of Sweet Fletcher Designs, is an artist. One of the reasons she started her company was that she wasn't pleased with the aesthetic quality of most of the baby slings on the market. Sweet Fletcher slings are reversible, with prints on one side and solid colors on the other, to better coordinate with mom's apparel.

How to Find: Sweet Fletcher's Web site has a retail store locator or you may order through the customer service number.

....

TOUGH TRAVELER® ⚜ ↑ ⌑
1012 State Street, Schenectady, NY 12307
Telephone: 800-GOTOUGH
Web site: www.toughtraveler.com

Tough Traveler® manufactures a selection of carriers and backpack products for parents and infants. For mom and baby, the company manufactures baby carriers, diaper bags, diaper backpacks, and infant carry-alls. Many of the backpacks and carriers are available in special ergonomic designs. The company has a large selection of backpacks for kids from preschool through the teen years.

Interesting Fact: Tough Traveler® has been in business for about 40 years and has not wavered in its mission to remain an American manufacturer. It welcomes visits from customers at its manufacturing plant in upstate New York.

How to Find: You may place an order directly through the Web site or call customer service if you need additional assistance.

ZOLO WEAR® ❀ ☺

321 W. Ben White Boulevard, Austin, TX 78704
Telephone: 888-285-0044
Web site: www.zolowear.com

Zolo Wear® produces baby slings in several different fabrics.

Interesting Fact: Zolo Wear® was founded in 2000 by Darien and Joe Wilson. Ms. Wilson first learned to sew in college when she was a theater major specializing in costume design. Zolo Wear received the iParenting Media Outstanding Products of 2007 Award for its stretch cotton ring slings. The company recommends that customers go to its local retail store to get fitted for a sling. It feels it is important to try several slings on for size to find one that is comfortable.

How to Find: The Web site has a store locator of both online and brick-and-mortar retailers. If you don't have a computer or need assistance, please call the customer service number.

Diaper Bags, Diapers, and Organizers

Diaper bags really aren't hidden anymore, and these are not your grandmother's diaper bags! Not only are these bags made in all kinds of beautiful fabrics to coordinate with mom's outfits, but designers are always experimenting with the fabrics themselves, such as recycled or sustainable materials. Please see the product listings in the index for a complete listing of diaper bag and diaper products.

☆
Made Here, Baby!

. . . .

BUM GENIUS™

5165 Lemay Ferry Road, St. Louis, MO 63129
Telephone: 888-332-2243
Web site: www.bumgenius.com

Bum Genius™ manufactures fitted cloth diapers made of cotton and woven bamboo, as well as woven wipes made of bamboo and flannel.

Interesting Fact: The founders of the company were victims of the dot.com crash of the late 1990s. As new moms, they wanted to spend more time with their babies, as well as to use their marketing skills in a stay-at-home business setting. They started a baby products company using natural, sustainable fabrics.

How to Find: Please see the company's Web site for a detailed list of retail and online stores that carry its products.

. . . .

BUMKINS® FINER BABY PRODUCTS

7802 E. Gray Road, Scottsdale, AZ 85260
Telephone: 866-286-5467
Web site: www.bumkins.com

Bumkins® Finer Baby Products manufactures a wide range of USA-made cloth diapering products and selection of USA-made waterproof bibs for children from newborn to 2 years, including its best-selling SuperBib®. Bumkins waterproof line also includes USA-made waterproof smocks and aprons for children 2 to 12 years old. Other products may be imported.

Interesting Fact: Founded in 1989 by a mother who created cloth diapers for her children, Bumkins® Finer Baby Products is recognized as one of the pioneers in the "Green Parenting Movement." For example, its line of SuperBibs is made of a proprietary material that is free of PVC, lead, phthalates, and BPA.

How to Find: Bumkins Finer Baby Products® is sold at major children's store chains throughout the United States as well as at children's specialty stores. You may also order directly through the company Web site.

30

. . . .

CLAIREBELLA, INC. ✿

Telephone: 770-751-0921
Web site: www.clairebella.com

Clairebella, Inc. handcrafts diaper clutches, bibs, burp cloths, blankets, and moses basket sets.

Interesting Fact: Kathy Denness, founder of Clairebella™, began designing baby items soon after her children were born. While living in Sydney, Australia, Kathy used her art background to create handpainted children's furniture. However, her first love was fabrics, and when she returned to the United States, she realized her dream and launched a fashion line of products for moms and babies.

How to Find: The Web site has a store locator for your convenience, or you may order directly from the company.

. . . .

DIAPEES & WIPEES® ✿

P.O. Box 270661, Flower Mound, TX 75027
Telephone: 817-506-5136
Web site: www.diapeesandwipees.com

Diapees & Wipees® manufactures a unique selection of diaper bags in numerous colors, as well as chenille baby blankets.

Interesting Fact: Founded in 2004 by Christie Rein, Diapees & Wipees® was created to help moms find a better alternative to the traditional diaper bag. The Diapee & Wipee bag is made to hold a travel pack of wipes along with 2–4 diapers.

How to Find: Please see the company's Web site for a detailed list of retail and online stores that carry its products. If you don't have a computer, please call the company for assistance in locating a nearby retailer.

. . . .

POSH™ BY TORI ✿

POSH by Tori is an online store in the Austin, Texas, area.
Telephone: 512-659-6328
Web site: www.poshbytori.com

POSH™ **by Tori** manufactures diaper bags and totes in many different colors and fabrics.

Interesting Fact: Tori Tinnon, the founder of POSH™ by Tori LLC, is an Austin-based designer. Tori has built a strong following with her unique ability to interpret the latest fashion looks into fun and functional diaper bags and toddler totes. The proud mom of two boys, Tori is not content to rest on the success of just one business; her latest under-taking is a chocolate truffle business named Baby Cake Truffles!

How to Find: Please see the company's Web site for a detailed list of retail and online stores that carry its products. Orders may also be placed through customer service on the company Web site.

· ·

PRINCE LIONHEART® ✿ ✈

2421 S. Westgate Road, Santa Monica, CA 93455
Telephone: 800-544-1132
Web site: www.princelionheart.com

Prince Lionheart® manufactures diaper organizers, including the Diaper Depot™ and the Dresser Top Diaper Depot™, the Click 'n Go Stroller Accessory System™ for holding baby bottles onto strollers, Infant and Toddler Dishwasher Baskets™ to help you avoid losing baby bottle parts, and the Universal Food Organizer for kitchens. Other prod-ucts in the line may be imported.

Interesting Fact: The company was founded in 1973, and the first product the company manufactured was a rocking horse.

How to Find: Please see the company's Web site for a detailed list of retail and online stores that carry their products. Orders may also be placed through the customer service center or the company Web site.

· ·

QUEEN BEE CREATIONS™ & CHICKPEA BABY™ ✿ ⌑

1847 E. Burnside Street, Portland, OR 97214
Telephone: 503-232-1755
Web site: www.queenbee-creations.com

Queen Bee Creations™ **& Chickpea Baby**™ handcrafts diaper bags, diaper totes, and changing pads in several different colors and styles.

Interesting Fact: Founded in 1996 by Rebecca Pearcy, the company has grown from a cluttered corner in Rebecca's bedroom to a full-fledged studio with several highly skilled artisans.

How to Find: You may order directly through the company Web site or call customer service for information. If you are in the Portland area, visit the studio to pick out your own bag!

....

RETHREDS, INC. ❀ ☺ ✂
383 Meadowbrook Road, North Wales, PA 19454
Telephone: 215-661-1726
Web site: www.rethreds.com

ReThreds™ manufactures unique, one-of-kind diaper bags, work totes, school bags, and gym bags that are made from recycled jeans. The founder of the company, Mary Beth, observed that with today's fashions, many women no longer have pockets. The idea behind using pieces of jeans and incorporating them into the design is to allow for pockets to store things as well as loops on which to put key chains. Limited production. In the fall of 2008, the company is introducing baby booties that will be made from the yarn of recycled sweaters.

Interesting Fact: The founder is the mother of three children. She began ReThreds™ both for environmental reasons and to allow her the flexibility to create unique designs while still caring for her children at home.

How to Find: Customers may order ReThred items directly through the Web site. If you wish to order a diaper bag and have questions, please use the customer service number.

Baby's Breath

Contrary to popular opinion, America has not lost the ability to manufacture superior electrical appliances, nor have we forgotten how to take the most up-to-date technology and to incorporate the technology into our products. The following manufacturers make air purification systems that are ideal for baby's room or for any room of the house.

....

AIR OASIS™ ↑

3401 Airway Boulevard, Amarillo, TX 79118
Telephone: 800-936-1764
Web site: www.airoasis.com

Air Oasis™ manufacturers air purifiers for both large and small spaces. For home use, it makes a "mini" model that is said to be good for use in baby's room.

Interesting Fact: The company was originally a distributor of air purifiers. In 2002, it was informed that the products it was distributing would be discontinued and, therefore, it would be forced out of business. In an act of great courage, the father-and-son team decided to start its own company. The two developed their own technology, and the company now fabricates nearly every part it needs in its own factory.

How to Find: There are several ways to order. You may call customer service, place orders directly through the company Web site, or go to the retail locator on the company Web site to find stores that carry the company's products.

....

AUSTIN AIR SYSTEMS, LTD. ↑

500 Elk Street, Buffalo, NY 14210
Telephone: 800-724-8403
Web site: www.austinair.com

Austin Air Systems, Ltd. manufactures many purification systems to remove allergens from the air. For children's rooms, the most popular models are in The Baby's Breath™ series, which is available in pink or blue. The children's models also feature a white-noise technology that helps babies sleep better.

Interesting Fact: Based in Buffalo, New York, Austin Air Systems claims to have one of the largest manufacturing facilities in the world for the production of air purification systems. The company feels that one of its strengths is that it creates simple, easy-to-use, and effective systems, rather than loading each system with a lot of unecessary gadgetry.

How to Find: Austin Air has a dealer locator on its Web site, or you may call customer service for assistance in finding the nearest retailer to your location.

BETTER LIVING–SUN AIRE™ PRODUCTS

P.O. Box 3133, Holiday Island, AR 72631
Telephone: 800-684-8253
Web site: www.betterair.com

Better Living–Sun Aire™ Products produces air purifiers and ductless furnaces.

Interesting Fact: This small manufacturing company started because of the vision of a husband-and-wife team to build a safe "photon process" air purifier. The first models were housed in recycled materials; in fact, the company builds purifier cabinetry from recycled pallet lumber and sheet metal taken from discarded steel doors. It has expanded its line to include area heaters enclosed in cabinetry built by Mennonite cabinetmakers.

How to Find: You may order directly from the company through its Web site or contact customer service to learn more about their products.

CALUTECH®, INC.

15536 S. 70th Court, Orland Park, IL 60462
Telephone: 888-932-0380
Web site: www.calutech.com

Calutech®, Inc. manufactures a variety of ultraviolet (UV) air purification systems for large spaces down to rooms of 500 square feet. For the nursery, Calutech recommends its original Blue UV Lights model 9002CB.

Interesting Fact: Calutech® is a leader in ultraviolet air purification technology. The Web site has several interesting air safety studies and research papers on air purification.

How to Find: You may directly purchase from the company through its Web site or search for Calutech on the Internet for online stores. For further information, call the customer service number.

··

ORECK CORPORATION ↑ ✈

565 Marriott Drive, Nashville, TN 37214
Telephone: 800-289-5888
Web site: www.oreck.com

Oreck Corporation manufactures the following USA-made, labor-saving products for moms, in addition to its well-known USA-made vacuums: Oreck XL® Tower Professional Air Purifier, the cordless Zip Vac®, and the cordless Electrikbroom® for picking up after babies and toddlers. Other products may be imported.

Interesting Fact: Oreck's story is inspiring and honors the commitment of the company to its workers and to this country. The company's headquarters were located near the worst devastation of Hurricane Katrina. The manufacturing plant was badly damaged. Yet the company reopened *within 10 days* of the disaster. Two years later, the company decided to move to Tennessee, taking many of its original employees. Since the hurricane, despite the temptation to outsource manufacturing, the company still produces the majority of its products in the USA.

How to Find: Orders may be placed directly through the Oreck Web site, by calling the Oreck customer service number, or by visiting one of the hundreds of Oreck Clean Home Centers.

Baby's Safety and Wellness

The following American companies devote themselves to the health and safety of your baby and toddler. Products range from traditional products rooted in the very beginnings of our country to the most modern technologies available. Please don't hesitate to e-mail or call these companies if you have any questions.

··

CORNBAG CRITTERS ✹ ↑

Cornbag Critters is an online company based in Pennsylvania. The company prefers e-mail.
Web site: www.cornbagcritters.com

Cornbag Critters handcrafts traditional cornbags, which are a natural alternative to the electric heating pad. The cornbags are fashioned in the shapes of dogs, bears, pigs, and ducks, and are made of 100 percent cotton chenille that holds whole-kernel Deer Corn.

Interesting Fact: Aimee Jones has carried on in the tradition of her grandmother, who gave her a cornbag when she was a little girl. The cornbag is placed in a microwave for about a minute, and the bag retains its heat for one to two hours. It is perfect for any aches, pains, and cramps that a mom might normally treat with a heating pad. The cute designs make the product a lot more attractive to a child than a heating pad, as well. It also makes a great foot warmer during the winter.

How to Find: The best way to order Cornbag Critters is directly through the Web site. Please e-mail the company if you have any questions.

COVER PLAY YARD® COVERS ✿
The company is located in the Los Angeles, California, area.
Telephone: 877-475-2992
Web site: www.coverplayard.com

Cover Play Yard® manufactures an ingenious slipcover liner for play yards that is especially valuable when parents are traveling with their baby and must use the play yards provided by the hotels. The item is also perfect for home use, as well. The product is available in boys' or girls' colors, or several different designer fabrics perfect for any room décor; fabrics include chenille, cotton lycra, and denim.

Interesting Fact: Allison Costa is the mother of twin boys who used to do a lot of traveling with her family. On one vacation she requested a play yard for the room, and the play yard was so filthy that she sent it back—and then another, and another! As she was waiting for the hotel to clean the "best of the worst" play yards, she wondered why no one had designed a slipcover liner that could be taken off a play yard, washed, and then used again. A furniture designer by avocation, Allison realized she had already made a prototype at home for another piece of baby furniture. When she returned home with her family, she designed the first Cover Play Yard®, then she applied for patents, and a successful company was born.

How to Find: The best way to order the Cover Play Yard is directly through the company Web site. If you don't have a computer or need additional assistance, please call the customer service number.

CREATIVE FRONTIER, THE/RETRACT-A-GATE® ↑
624 Spring Street, Galena, IL 61036
Telephone: 312-546-4702
Web site: www.retract-a-gate.com

The Creative Frontier/Retract-A-Gate® manufactures a retractable safety gate called Retract-A-Gate for children and pets.

Interesting Fact: The company's founder explains that Retract-A-Gate® started from a personal need and not a fancy marketing plan. He and his wife had just purchased a puppy and couldn't find a gate to their liking. He made the first gate simply out of necessity and then realized they had developed a unique solution to a child safety challenge.

How to Find: You may order directly from the company through its Web site or contact customer service to determine if there are retailers in your area.

EXERGEN THERMOMETER ↑
400 Pleasant Street, Watertown, MA 02472
Telephone: 800-422-3006
Web site: www.exergen.com

Exergen Thermometer manufactures the Temporal Scanner™, a device that reads the temperature of the body by scanning the temporal artery of the forehead.

Interesting Fact: Exergen was founded in 1980 by Dr. Francesco Pompei, a brilliant scientist. He literally started product development in his garage.

How to Find: Exergen scanning thermometers are sold at all major drug and general merchandise retailers throughout the United States.

LUCASWORKS ™ ⊛ ★

808 Evergreen Road, Magnolia, DE 19962
Telephone: 302-698-5352
Web site: www.lucasworks.org

LucasWorks ™ manufactures a unique thermometer, made by disabled workers, that has three different "regional faces." In addition to helping autistic children, the thermometers assist all children in learning how to properly dress for the climate. Autistic children don't often have a sense of outside temperature. The workers also make placemats, lanyards, and unique pieces of jewelry to create better awareness of autism.

Interesting Fact: LucasWorks ™ was started by Lauren Padgett, mother of two children, one of whom (Lucas) is autistic and mentally retarded. Lauren feels that so many parents of disabled children don't really understand how much their children can do if only given the proper training and a chance. LucasWorks wants to create awareness that children with autism and similar needs can become integrated into society and can lead meaningful lives.

How to Find: Orders for these items may be placed directly through the Web site. The Web site also has many links to autism resources and information on the disease.

MARPAC CORPORATION ↑

P.O. Box 560, Rocky Point, NC 28457
Telephone: 800-999-6962
Web site: www.marpac.com

Marpac Corporation manufactures several sound conditioners, including the Lifesounds® 440, a model made specifically for infant rooms to simulate womb sounds and many other sounds.

Interesting Fact: The Marpac Corporation, founded in 1962, is the only sound conditioner company that still makes its products in the United States. According to the company, pediatricians recommend sound conditioners to help babies fall asleep faster and stay asleep longer. Just as these machines are said to reduce stress levels in adults, the company states it will also help to reduce stress for children and infants.

How to Find: You may order Marpac's products directly through the company Web site. There are several online retailers as well, and they can be accessed by searching for "Marpac." If you need further assistance or lack a computer, call the customer service number.

. . . .

ME4Kidz™, INC. ❀ ☺ ↑
P.O. Box 73200, Phoenix, AZ 85050
Telephone: 480-444-2332
Web site: www.me4kidz.com

Me4Kidz™ manufactures the Medibag for Kids™, a home first aid kit, and the Medibuddy™, which is a smaller version of the kit and is meant for travel or camping trips.

Interesting Fact: The idea for the company was sparked very soon after the son of the parent-founders was stung by a bee. The parents realized that they had to scramble throughout the house to find the things they needed to give aid to their child. They designed a kit so that everything could be found in one place and then brought to the child. All of the components for the kits are made in Phoenix. The case is made of 100 percent recycled plastic, and Me4Kidz employs physically challenged workers to assemble its products.

How to Find: Order directly from the company's Web site or check local retailers through the Web site.

. . . .

MY PRECIOUS KID™ ❀
P.O. Box 550, Cornelius, OR 97110
Telephone: 503-693-2832
Web site: www.mypreciouskid.com

My Precious Kid™ produces the Child Safety Kit© by My Precious Kid, which is a child identification system containing identification cards for displaying vital information about the child.

Interesting Fact: Kay Green, the founder of My Precious Kid™, is extremely concerned about the issue of child safety. She developed the kit not only to help protect babies but to provide identification for children and teenagers who have disabilities.

How to Find: Orders may be placed directly through the Web site or by calling customer service.

. . . .

NEAT SOLUTIONS, INC. ☺ ✿ ✈

The company is based in the Huntersville, North Carolina, area.
Telephone: 888-888-4779
Web site: www.tabletopper.com

Neat Solutions, Inc. manufactures the Table Topper®, a disposable stick-in-place place mat for parents to bring to restaurants, to cover high chairs, or to stick on top of airline tray tables. The table toppers are available in many different designs. A new eco-friendly, biodegradable version has just been introduced. Other products in the product line are imported.

Interesting Fact: Neat Solutions®for Kids was started in 1996, when the company's founder took her baby to a restaurant. The baby threw the place mat to the floor and then started to eat the finger food off the restaurant table.

How to Find: The table topper is widely available in major retail stores throughout the United States. Please view the store locator on the Web site.

. . . .

NORTH STATES INDUSTRIES, INC. ✈

1507 92nd Lane NE, Blaine, MN 55449
Telephone: 763-486-1754
Web site: www.northstatesind.com

North States Industries, Inc. produces a wide selection of safety gates for use anywhere in the home and yard. Twelve of the 20 varieties of gate, including the most popular gate, the Supergate III, is manufactured in the United States; other gates may be imported. The American-made gates are clearly marked.

Interesting Fact: North States Industries also specializes in manufacturing bird houses and bird feeders.

How to Find: The gates are available at retailers throughout the United States. If you need a part, you may place an order through the Web site

or call customer service. Customer service can also help you locate a retailer in your area.

....

POOL BARRIER™, INC. ↑

1313 S. Killian Drive, Lake Park, FL 33403
Telephone: 888-551-0400
Web site: www.poolbarrier.com

Pool Barrier™, Inc. produces a complete line of pool barriers.

Interesting Fact: Based in Florida where swimming pools are plentiful, the company feels its mission is to safeguard babies and toddlers from an accidental tragedy. The Web site contains information on how to better safeguard pool areas from young children.

How to Find: Please see the company's Web site for a detailed list of retailers and distributors that carry its products, or you may call customer service if there is no distributor in your area.

Precious Baby Keepsakes

It is traditional for many of us to want to capture the time when a new baby is welcomed into our families. Keepsakes are a way for us to celebrate the future as well as the past, and, because of that, we choose keepsakes that can be handed down from generation to generation. The companies listed in this section make products that can be serious heirlooms or just plain fun. In this section you will find the best of traditional American craftsmanship in silver, pewter, and semiprecious stones; or perhaps you want a beautiful keepsake album or quilt. In any case, these keepsakes help us to remember who we are, as we connect one generation to another. Most of these companies customize upon request and have a strong commitment to customer service.

....

BABY'S FIRST BALL ✿ ✂

Baby's First Ball is located in the Cape Cod, Massachusetts, area.
Telephone: 508-540-7104
Web site: www.babysfirstball.com

Baby's First Ball handcrafts handmade fabric balls to develop baby's grasping ability along with matching quilts in the same fabrics. The company can customize. Limited production.

Interesting Fact: Founded in 1973, Baby's First Ball is a true American cottage industry; it employs local seamstresses who produce these unusual and often one-of-a-kind gifts.

How to Find: You may buy directly from the company through its Web site or call for more detailed information on the products.

BELLE PEARL™ ✿ ↑ ✄ ✈
Belle Pearl is an online store that is based in Maine.
Telephone: 877-PEARLS-9
Web site: www.bellepearl.com

Belle Pearl™ handcrafts jewelry for babies and toddlers. The company offers name bracelets, pearl bracelets and necklaces, earrings, rings, and hair accessories. Many of the pieces match with jewelry made for mom. The company can customize upon request. According to the company, 90 percent of the jewelry is made in the USA. Some pieces may be imported.

Interesting Fact: Angela Apon founded Belle Pearl™ in 2006. Angela was trained and worked as a dental hygienist before starting her company, and she is the mother of five. Initially the company designed pieces exclusively using freshwater pearls, but the line expanded to include semiprecious stones.

How to Find: Customers can buy products directly through the Web site, through authorized online retailers, and from fine gift and fashion boutiques catering to children and adults. Please call customer service for additional assistance.

BRAG-E-LET'S® ✿ ↑ ✄
300 Woodside Road, Harvard, MA 01451
The company prefers e-mail.
Web site: www.braglets.com

Brag-e-let's® manufactures a unique collection of baby and mom name jewelry. The company can customize.

Interesting Fact: The company has changed ownership three times since it was founded in 1992, each time being sold by a woman to a woman.

How to Find: You may order directly from the company through its Web site.

....

CAROLINE & COMPANY™ ❀ ↑ ✄

2368 Brook Hollow Cove, Memphis, TN 38119
Telephone: 901-821-0601
Web site: www.carolinecompany.com

Caroline & Company™ handcrafts personalized pottery baby tea sets, baptism crosses, plates and cups, tiles, picture frames, trinket boxes, and many more keepsake items. The company can customize.

Interesting Fact: Karen Hoff has been hand decorating pottery for nearly 15 years. After many years of working for the company, she was finally able to purchase the business and changed the company name to the name of her baby girl.

How to Find: Orders may be placed directly through the company Web site, or call Caroline & Company™ for the nearest store location.

....

CHLOE EMMA DESIGNS ❀ ↑

The company is located in the Denver, Colorado, area.
Telephone: 720-984-9923
Web site: www.chloeemma.com

Chloe Emma Designs manufactures high-end keepsake jewelery for girls, from newborns to age 12. Most pieces feature sterling silver and are meant for occasions such as christenings, communions, and special events. Chloe Emma makes bracelets, necklaces, and earrings. The company also makes matching products for moms, grandmothers, and godmothers.

Interesting Fact: Jennifer, the founder of Chloe Emma, named her company after the last of her four children. She had been designing jewelry most of her life, but with the birth of Chloe Emma, she wanted to do something to honor her child. Her desire to give a keepsake to her child has blossomed into a serious business.

How to Find: You may purchase Chloe Emma products directly through the Web site. The company also distributes to approximately 200 retail outlets throughout the United States. Call for the nearest retail location.

CUSTOM MADE FOR KIDS™ ✿ ↑ ✂

Custom Made for Kids is an online store located in the Chicago, Illinois, area.
Telephone: 866-360-4546
Web site: www.custommadeforkids.com

Custom Made for Kids™ produces a customized keepsake book and special gift that takes personalization to a higher level than other offerings on the market. The company's first book, entitled *The First Adventures of Incredible You*, is appropriate for children ages 0 to 8. By having customers complete a detailed, online fact sheet, the company is able to make to order a highly detailed book specific to the child.

Interesting Fact: While Sarah Riley Headrick and Sarah Foreman Rivera, the founders of Custom Made for Kids™, are accomplished professionals, they met not in the workplace but in a playgroup for their young children. One day, while discussing all of the gifts and presents they were buying for their babies, they realized that none were truly personalized or could grow and foster the bond between the child and her or his parents. They decided to produce books in which opportunities could be created to personalize a high-quality cloth book.

How to Find: As each book is customized with the child's information, customers must go to the Web site in order to fill out the form. If you don't have a computer, call customer service.

HAMPSHIRE PEWTER ↑ ⌗

43 Mill Street, Wolfboro, NH 03894
Telephone: 800-639-7704
Web site: www.hampshirepewter.com

Hampshire Pewter is a manufacturer of baby cups and spoons, christening keepsakes, bowls, and nursery lamps.

Interesting Fact: According to the company, Hampshire Pewter makes its pewter products the old-fashioned way. Every keepsake in the collection is handcast and then finished by hand.

Made Here, Baby!

How to Find: Hampshire Pewter is dedicated to customer service. When you call the company, you may talk directly to the president. Hampshire Pewter is available in retail outlets nationwide.

• •

METAL MORPHOSIS®
1030 Grant Street SE, Atlanta, GA 30315
Telephone: 404-607-8307
Web site: www.metalmorphosisinc.com

Metal Morphosis® handcrafts heirloom-quality gifts in pewter and silver to include baby spoons, tooth fairy boxes, soap dishes, candle holders, goal charts, and wall hooks. The designs are unique and fun for children.

Interesting Fact: Kacey Binns started her company with a vision and a dream. An art student, she was waiting on tables in order to support herself while developing ideas for a company that would manufacture keepsakes. She made her first baby spoon for a friend in the basement of her home. Since that time, the company has made more than 75,000 baby spoons. The product line is quite large and diverse. To this day, Ms. Binns remains the sole designer.

How to Find: You may buy directly from the company through its Web site. The product line is also distributed through a nationwide network of retail stores. For more information please call the customer service number.

• •

SALISBURY PEWTER ↑
29085 Airport Drive, Easton, MD 21601
Telephone: 410-770-4901
Web site: www.salisburypewter.com

Salisbury Pewter manufactures heirloom baby gifts in sterling and pewter, including baby rattles, cups, spoons, and other keepsakes.

Interesting Fact: Each piece in the collection is handmade or hand finished by fine metal craftspeople.

How to Find: The Salisbury product line is available only through a network of nationwide dealers. Please e-mail the company for the nearest retailer, or see the store locator on the company Web site.

••

SIMPLY TIFFANY TAITE™ ✿ ↑

The company is located in the Seattle, Washington, area.
Telephone: 425-432-PINK
Web site: www.simplytiffanytaite.com

Simply Tiffany Taite™ handcrafts fine jewelry for children and moms
and features precious elements such as pearls, semiprecious stones,
crystal, and sterling silver. The jewelry is meant to establish special
moments between mom and daughter, and, according to the company,
they are designed as symbols of time to reflect special moments. Other
keepsake items made by the company include miniature tea sets,
rattles, and piggy banks.

Interesting Fact: Tiffany Whitchurch-Taite began her business in a most
innocent way; she needed to string a pearl bracelet for one of her five
children. The result was so beautiful that people encouraged her to
launch a business. Over time, her unique, high-end jewelry and gifts
have won national acclaim. Her story has been an inspiration for many
aspiring "inventor moms," and, in fact, she was named Mrs. Washington—Business Woman of the Year for 2006–2007. The company is
dedicated to sourcing as much of its jewelry components in America as
possible.

How to Find: The Simply Tiffany Taite™ company has its products in
more than 1,000 stores nationwide. Please see the company Web site
for the store locator, or call customer service if you lack a computer or
need more information.

••

TERRA TRADITIONS® ✿ ↑ ✂

4920 W. Pico Boulevard, Los Angeles, CA 90019
Telephone: 323-954-1404
Web site: www.terratraditions.com

Terra Traditions® handcrafts beautiful, artisan-inspired baby books,
photo albums, journals, candles, and other keepsakes. These items are
made to order by Terra Traditions artisans. Each piece is handcrafted
from domestic and imported materials.

Interesting Fact: Terra Traditions® describes itself as an "Italian-style
artisan studio." No product is taken from stock; products are all custom

made. In 2007, *iParenting* named the Terra Traditions Baby's Journey Book the best baby book.

How to Find: There is a store locator on the Web site, or customers may call customer service. The best way to gain an appreciation for this product line is to request a catalog, as the decorative possibilities of the keepsakes are endless.

....

WOODBURY PEWTER ⊛
860 Main Street South, Woodbury, CT 06798
Telephone: 800-648-2014
Web site: www.woodburypewter.com

Woodbury Pewter makes a collection of keepsake baby gifts in lead-free pewter, including bowls, porringers, cups, cutlery, and plates.

Interesting Fact: The company was founded in 1952 in a small blacksmith shop near the center of the quaint town of Woodbury, Connecticut. The company remains a family-owned and -operated business, with several second- and third-generation employees.

How to Find: The product line is available through a network of nationwide dealers and online catalog stores. The company store, in Woodbury, Connecticut, is open to the public.

Baby Furniture

The American baby furniture manufacturers listed here take immense pride in their work and traditions. Many craftspeople who work to create these beautiful pieces have done so only after years of apprenticeship. In some cases, the companies listed in this section have revived skills thought to be almost lost; they apply these skills to fine woodworking, shaping wrought iron, even crafting in materials such as sail canvas. The artisans derive much pride from working at these crafts and also from realizing that they are making baby furniture for their friends and neighbors.

••

A NATURAL HOME ☺ ↑ ✂

109 N. Main Street, Fredericktown, OH 43019
Telephone: 866-239-4142
Web site: www.anaturalhome.com

A Natural Home manufactures an extensive line of what the company calls "organic furniture," including cribs, basinettes, changing tables, baby dressers and armoires, and baby toys such as cherry and maple rattles. A Natural Home also produces baby mattresses and baby bedding made of organic materials and furniture for older children and adults.

Interesting Fact: A Natural Home is a cooperative effort within the Amish community. The Amish craftspeople use sustainable woods, organic cotton, and environmentally-friendly manufacturing processes.

How to Find: You may buy directly from the company through its Web site, or call for more detailed information on the products. The product line is also distributed through a limited network of retail stores.

••

AMISH VALLEY OAK ↑ ✂

3700 Massillon Road, Uniontown, OH 44685
Telephone: 330-630-1185
Web site: www.amishvalleyoak.com

Amish Valley Oak handcrafts heirloom-quality high chairs and cribs, as well as kid-size tables, chairs, and rockers.

Interesting Fact: The company, established in 1996, is a retail representative for the Amish community. Amish Valley Oak calls upon more than 50 Amish craftspeople handcrafting a selection of products. According to the company, everything it sells is handcrafted from solid wood and not veneer. It can customize.

How to Find: To order, you may contact Amish Valley Oak customer service through its Web site to get more information. To purchase, visit the company's retail location or order online.

☆
Made Here, Baby!

....

CHILDWOOD BABY CRADLES & ROCKING HORSES ↑ ✂

24454 Orange Cove, Verdigris, OK 74019
The company prefers e-mail.
Web site: www.childwoodproducts.com

Childwood Baby Cradles & Rocking Horses produces Victorian-style baby cradles utilizing several different finishes. A mattress and cover are provided with each cradle. It also makes a Victorian-style rocking horse that is based on a rocking horse on display at the Philadelphia Art Museum.

Interesting Fact: Dick McGuire, the founder of Childwood Products, spent most of his career in the aerospace industry. In fact, he worked in the space shuttle program. His passion, however, was fine woodworking and, beyond that, Victorian woodworking design. On his frequent business trips to the East Coast, he found himself driving through old neighborhoods noting the Victorian structures. It is no wonder that in his new career, he handcrafts heirloom-quality Victorian-style baby cradles.

How to Find: Please contact Childwood Products directly through the Web site if you have an interest in its products.

....

COMMUNITY PLAYTHINGS® ☺ ↑ ✈

P.O. Box 2, Ulster Park, NY 12487
Telephone: 800-777-4244
Web site: www.communityplaythings.com

Community Playthings® produces an extensive line of wood products for children from infants through school age and beyond, including cribs, high chairs, changing tables, cots, desks, gliders, role-play toys, riding toys, sand and water tables, rocking chairs, art equipment and easels, blocks, and storage. A very limited number of items are imported from the U.K.

Interesting Fact: Community Playthings® makes solid maple furniture and toys for early childhood and elementary-age children. The company philosophy is to create environments that welcome children into a space of beauty, simplicity, and stability, where they can explore, discover, and learn through play. Community Playthings works only in wood and has done so for more than 50 years. It primarily works in red maple, which grows fast and reforests well. It is harvested in the Northeast, near the workshops, to minimize the carbon footprint that typically comes from long-distance transportation.

How to Find: You may order directly from the company through customer service or fax the order.

CORSICAN FURNITURE COMPANY/ CORSICAN.COM™ ↑

1933 S. Broadway, Los Angeles, CA 90007
Telephone: 800-421-6247
Web site: www.corsican.com

Corsican Furniture Company/corsican.com™ manufactures a wide selection of baby cribs and cradles using traditional wrought iron techniques. The company also produces beds for older children and adults.

Interesting Fact: The company has been in business for more than 40 years. Many people are interested in the Victorian period and the traditions of bed-making from that period. The company's products remain faithful to the era.

How to Find: The product line is available through a network of nationwide dealers and online retailers. Please e-mail or call the company for the nearest retailer.

DCM PRODUCTS ✿

P.O. Box 83, Okarche, OK 73762
Telephone: 405-263-4570
Web site: www.dcmproducts.com

DCM Products handcrafts a selection of wooden baby-quilt holders.

Interesting Fact: The owner of the company is a shop teacher and expert woodworker who has taught woodworking to hundreds of students. The company is well known for its handcrafted saddle-racks, which are used for displays at historic and agricultural museums.

How to Find: You may order directly from the Web site or call customer service.

· ·

DUC DUC™ ☺ ↑
524 Broadway, New York, NY 10012
Telephone: 212-226-1868
Web site: www.ducducnyc.com

Duc Duc™ produces cribs, mom-and-baby bonding benches, children's playtables, and bedroom furniture for older children.

Interesting Fact: The Duc Duc factory is located in a reclaimed factory building in Connecticut that was built in 1897. The building was just renovated with more than 200 new windows that allow employees to work in natural light and fresh air. The renovations also reduce electrical usage, which in turn lowers the carbon footprint, and the building design lessens fatigue, as well. The company is very committed to American manufacturing. Opening the factory in Connecticut has brought needed jobs to the area. Duc Duc has a strong commitment to the sustainable harvesting of wood used in its products. The company actively supports several charitable organizations.

How to Find: Please see the company's Web site for a detailed list of retailers who carry their products or you may call customer service for the nearest retail location.

· ·

LITTLE MISS LIBERTY ROUND CRIB CO.™ ❀ ↑ ✂
10309-1/2 W. Olympic Boulevard, Los Angeles, CA 90064
Telephone: 800-RND-CRIB
Web site: www.crib.com

Little Miss Liberty Round Crib Co.™ is a manufacturer of round and heart-shaped cribs and bedding. The company has the ability to customize.

Interesting Fact: The company was co-founded by the husband-and-wife team of Jeannie and Casey Kasem. Ms. Kasem played Loretta Tortelli in the *Cheers* TV sitcom, and Mr. Kasem is widely known as the "Countdown King" in radio and television.

How to Find: You may order directly from Little Miss Liberty through its Web site, or call customer service.

....

PACIFIC RIM WOODWORKING ☺ ↑

The company is located in the Eugene, Oregon, area.
Telephone: 541-342-4508
Web site: www.pacificrimwoodworking.com

Pacific Rim Woodworking produces handcrafted, solid maple baby cribs.

Interesting Fact: Founded in 1982, Pacific Rim Woodworking has a deep commitment to green manufacturing and environmental responsibility. In addition to following green manufacturing practices within its own shop, it donates any excess wood to local schools and community centers for woodworking classes or to low-income families for heat during the winter months. Even the sawdust is recycled into compost.

How to Find: Please see the company's Web site for a detailed list of retailers that carry its products, or you may e-mail customer service.

....

PENOBSCOT BAY PORCH SWINGS

14 Maine Street, Brunswick, ME 04011
Telephone: 207-729-1616
Web site: www.penobscotbayporchswings.com

Penobscot Bay Porch Swings produces handcrafted canvas cradles for infants, as well as swings for adults and bigger kids. The company can customize.

Interesting Fact: After being fascinated for years by the old canvas porch swings that once hung from nearly every porch in Maine and were most probably the remnants of old sailing vessels, Sarah Bloy began to consider the possibility of turning her interest into a company. She went back to school to train at the Marine Canvas Training Institute to learn the art of working with canvas. With hard work, and through the dedication of employees who also have a love of canvas making, Sarah has realized her dream of bringing back a feature of Maine life that was almost lost.

How to Find: Please contact the company through the Web site if you have an interest in its products, or call customer service. Please note that it takes two to three weeks to produce a canvas swing.

....

ROCHELLE FURNITURE COMPANY

P.O. Box 649, Ludington, MI 49431
Telephone: 800-223-6047
Web site: www.rochellefurniture.com

Rochelle Furniture Company manufactures high chairs in four different styles. You may also order replacement parts and high chair safety accessories.

Interesting Fact: Rochelle Furniture was established in 1942 and remains an American company. The high chairs are made of either maple or ash and come in a variety of finishes and models.

How to Find: You may order directly from Rochelle Furniture through the Web site or call customer service for additional information.

Baby's First Mattress

The traditions of American mattress manufacturing continue to this day. Despite the popular belief that all of our mattress manufacturing has been outsourced, there are still many great companies that continue to make mattresses for babies and older children as they have done for many, many years. As with all of the companies we interviewed, these manufacturers have an absolute dedication to customer service. They are always happy to answer your questions.

....

COLGATE JUVENILE PRODUCTS T

779 Fulton Terrace SE, Atlanta, GA 30316
Telephone: 404-681-2121
Web site: www.colgatekids.com

Colgate Juvenile Products manufacturers crib mattresses, mattress covers, mattress pads, and accessories.

Interesting Fact: An American manufacturing treasure, the Colgate Mattress Company was established in 1907 on Colgate Avenue in the Bronx, New York City. In 1935, the company started to make mattresses for children, and, as a result, it is the oldest crib mattress manufacturer in the United States. Recently, the management of Colgate Mattress was honored by the Georgia House of Representatives for its commitment to American manufacturing and its support of the Georgia economy.

How to Find: The company has a store locator on its Web site, or, if you don't have a computer, please call the company for the nearest retail location.

HEART OF VERMONT ™   ❁ ☺ ✂

P.O. Box 612, Barre, VT 05641
Telephone: 800-639-4123
Web site: www.heartofvermont.com

Heart of Vermont ™ manufactures bassinet futons, bassinet futon covers, organic flannel sheets, baby blankets, and receiving blankets. All of its products are made to order. It can ship out to customers within a week of placing the order. The company can customize.

Interesting Fact: The founder of Heart of Vermont ™ was motivated to start her company as a result of her newborn baby being sensitive to its bedding. Frustrated at not being able to find organic bedding that could be customized to their baby's crib, the parents launched a company that makes organic bedding to order.

How to Find: You may buy directly from the company through its Web site or call for a product catalog.

LIFE KIND PRODUCTS ™   ☺ ↑

P.O. Box 1774, Grass Valley, CA 95945
Telephone: 800-284-4983
Web site: www.lifekind.com

Life Kind Products ™ manufactures organic crib mattresses, organic juvenile mattresses, and organic mattresses for adults.

Interesting fact: Life Kind Products ™ owes its beginning to Walt Bader, a man who has severe chemical sensitivities. The sensitivities led him

55

to found a company that makes organic mattresses for babies. The process of how Life Kind Products™ makes these mattresses is fascinating. The company claims to be the largest manufacturer of organic mattresses in the country and that its mattresses are 100 percent biodegradable. It is Mr. Bader's contention that chemicals in our home environments will become a major health issue in the years ahead. In 2007, he wrote a book entitled *Toxic Bedrooms* on the topic. The manufacturing facility is organically certified by a third-party agency.

How to Find: Life Kind Products sells directly to customers through its Web site, or you can call customer service for more specific information. If you wish to purchase a Life Kind mattress at a retailer, go to: www.omifactory.com, where there is a store locator.

• •

NATUREPEDIC® ☺
4370 Cranwood Parkway, Cleveland, OH 44128
Telephone: 800-91-PEDIC
Web site: www.naturepedic.com

Naturepedic® manufactures organic crib and children's mattresses and mattress covers.

Interesting fact: The founder of Naturepedic® wasn't a marketer or a retailer but a widely published, board-certified environmental engineer. When his first grandchild was born, he didn't want the child to sleep on a mattress made of synthetic materials or even on an organic mattress that was a cut-down version of an adult mattress. He decided to design his own product. The new grandfather convinced his two sons to join him in establishing a manufacturing business.

How to Find: The company has a store locator on its Web site, or, if you don't have a computer, please call the company for the nearest retail location.

• •

SIMMONS KIDS® ↑ T
One Concourse Parkway, Suite 800, Atlanta, GA 30328
Telephone: 877-399-9397
Web site: www.simmonskids.com

Simmons Kids® produces three broad product lines for children: Simmons Kids®, mattresses for babies, teens, and in-betweens; SlumberTime® bedding, a line of value-priced children's mattresses that includes a traditional open-coil design; and the Beautyrest Beginnings™ collection of premium children's mattresses, which feature the company's signature Pocketed Coil construction. All three product lines are manufactured in the United States.

Interesting Fact: An American manufacturing treasure, Simmons was established in Kenosha, Wisconsin, in 1870. Simmons is the only *major* bedding manufacturer that actually owns and operates its own baby mattress manufacturing facilities. Many of the Simmons Kids® products carry a seal that states "Made in the USA by Simmons, trusted by moms for more than 100 years."

How to Find: The company has a store locator on its Web site, or, if you don't have a computer, please call Simmons Customer Service for the nearest retail location.

VIVETIQUE™, INC. ☺

Vivetique, Inc. is based in the Arcadia, California, area.
Telephone: 800-365-6563
Web site: www.vivetique.com

Vivetique™, Inc. manufactures organic crib mattresses, organic crib innerspring mattresses, organic comforters, bumper pads, and bumper pad covers, as well as a bedwetting moisture barrier.

Interesting Fact: The company traces its origins to the founding of Crown City Mattress, in 1917, in the City of Pasadena. In 2004, the company underwent a significant change of focus to produce organic mattresses using natural latex cores. Today, this third-generation family business is one of the nation's leaders in organic bedding products.

How to Find: Vivetique™ has a dealer locator on its Web site. If you don't have a computer, please call customer service for information.

Baby's Blankets and Bedding

In this part of the book, we are able to capture some of the very earliest beginnings of American manufacturing. In talking with some of these manufacturers, we were able to imagine days when farmers and ranchers delivered wagonloads of wool or cotton to factory loading docks and to imagine merchants delivering silk and linen from the great sailing ships to the men and women who were making things for a young and growing America. Whether you buy from a relatively new company or from one that has been in business for more than a century, rest assured your baby will be wrapped in a tradition that is as old as America itself. Every one of these manufacturers also has another commitment, and that is to safety. Some of the most dedicated supporters of tough child safety laws may be found in these listings; they make things that are beautiful but also products that are safe.

AMANA® WOOLEN MILL ❀ ↑ T

800 48th Avenue, Amana, IA 52203
Telephone: 800-222-6430
Web site: www.amanawoolenmill.com

Amana® Woolen Mill manufactures cotton and wool baby blankets and embroidered blankets.

Interesting Fact: The Amana® Woolen Mill is a true piece of America's manufacturing history, with roots going back to a religious community that fled Germany in the 1700s. At first, the community members settled on estates in the Midwest, where they could be protected and sharpen their skills as fabric makers. Their first commercial mill was established in the 1840s, but they were forced to move due to religious intolerance. They reestablished the mill in 1857 in Iowa and have been in continuous operation at that location since that time.

How to Find: You may buy directly from the company through its Web site or call for more detailed information on the products. The product line is also available at retail outlets, and customer service can direct you to those stores, as well.

AMENITY™, INC. ❀ ☺ ↑ ✈

453 S. Spring Street, Los Angeles, CA 90013
Telephone: 213-624-7309
Web site: www.amenityhome.com

Amenity™, Inc. produces baby blankets, pillows and floor pillows, crib sheets, bumper covers, and inserts. It also makes bedding for older children and adults.

Interesting Fact: Founded in 2004, Amenity™ is owned by a group of friends from similar rural backgrounds. They wanted to run a company with products that were both natural and eco-friendly. Since its inception, Amenity has placed an ever-increasing emphasis on sustainable and eco-friendly fabrics. Some, but not all, of the fabric in Amenity's line may be imported; however, all of the sewing and production on those products are done in the USA.

How to Find: You may buy directly from the company through its Web site or call for more detailed information on the products. The product line is also available at retail outlets. See the store locator on the company Web site.

....

BÉBÉ CHIC, INC.® ✿ ↑
115 River Road, Edgewater, NJ 07020
Telephone: 201-941-5414
Web site: www.bebechic.com

Bébé Chic, Inc.® produces baby and child bedding and accessories for infants to early teens. The products include crib bedding, bumpers, dust ruffles, mobiles, valances, duvets, sham pillows, toy bags, pillows, quilts, and stuffed animals.

Interesting Fact: Prior to buying Bébé Chic®, the founder of the company was in the computer consulting field. She decided she liked fabrics and furnishings far more than computers!

How to Find: There is a store locator on the Web site for your convenience. If you don't have a computer or need assistance, please call the customer service number.

....

BLANKETS BY CAROL ✿ ✂
Blankets by Carol is an online store located in the Tampa, Florida, area.
Telephone: 813-689-3424
Web site: www.blanketsbycarol.com

Blankets by Carol handcrafts children's blankets and throws in many different designs. The company also makes matching baby room curtains and bedskirts. Blankets by Carol will monogram any item in its product line, or, if you prefer, it will take your fabric and make your baby blankets and throws to order. The company will customize. Limited production.

Interesting Fact: Blankets by Carol, a mother-and-daughter business, began as a hobby. In the beginning, they made their blankets as gifts for family and friends, and then the business snowballed. They now ship blankets, throws, and room decorative items throughout the United States.

How to Find: Customers may buy directly from the company through its Web site, e-mail the company, or call for more detailed information on the products.

BRAHMS-MOUNT TEXTILES, INC. ❀ ↑
19 Central Street, Hallowell, ME 04347
Telephone: 800-545-9347
Web site: www.brahmsmount.com

Brahms-Mount Textiles, Inc. weaves heirloom-quality baby blankets in many different colors and weaves.

Interesting Fact: The founder of Brahms-Mount, Noel Mount, emigrated to America from Northern Ireland, where he was trained as a weaver through the classic European apprenticeship system. He and his wife, Claudia Brahms, also a weaver, built a manufacturing space in a beautifully renovated building that was originally constructed in 1866. Brahms-Mount is the last weaver in the United States to weave in linen as well as cotton. The couple is very committed to encouraging young craftspeople to enter the weaving profession. They are active in their support of local artists organizations.

How to Find: The best way to order baby blankets from the company is through the Web site. If you need additional assistance, please call the toll-free customer service number.

CINDY'S THROWS ❀ ☺ ↑
93 Cherry Creek Road, Thompson Falls, MT 59873
Telephone: 877-684-7694
Web site: www.cindysthrows.com

Cindy's Throws produces cable-knit blankets and tapestry throws for infants. It makes several of its children's blankets in organic cotton. The company has embroidery machinery on-site and can personalize to a much greater extent than other manufacturers. For example, it can embroider baby's name, parent's names, birthdate, and weight, or virtually anything. The company can customize.

Interesting Fact: Founded in 1993 by a husband-and-wife team, the company had a vision to design a full line of cotton throws and blankets that could be embroidered and personalized. The cotton used in the company's products is 100 percent preshrunk and is grown in the USA.

How to Find: You may buy directly from the company through its Web site or call customer service for more detailed information on the products.

··

COTTON MONKEY

P.O. Box 570526, Dallas, TX 75357
Telephone: 214-367-0719
Web site: www.cottonmonkey.com

Cotton Monkey produces collections of organic baby bedding for conventional and round cribs, bibs, hooded towels, and baby gift sets.

Interesting Fact: Michelle Meyer, the president of Cotton Monkey, has a background in design and architecture and an interest in organic fabrics and green manufacturing. While expecting her son, she wanted to further explore her interests in designing products made from organic materials that would be good for the earth as well as fashionable. Michelle's pursuit of these interests led her to start a company.

How to Find: The company has a store locator on its Web site, along with listings of online retailers. If you don't have a computer, please call the company for the nearest retail location.

··

FARIBAULT MILLS™

1819 2nd Avenue NW, Faribault, MN 55021
Telephone: 800-448-9665
Web site: www.faribaultmills.com

Faribault Mills™ manufactures baby blankets and throws in cotton or cotton-acrylic blends. The company also makes blankets for older children and adults. Faribault Mills can monogram upon request.

Interesting Fact: Faribault, Inc. was established in 1865 and is another one of America's national historic manufacturing treasures. According to the company, Faribault is the last of the vertically integrated weavers, which means that it undertakes all the steps in making a woven product, going from raw wool to woven blanket under one roof. The steps involved in this process, including dyeing, spinning, and weaving, have been all but lost in our country's commercial production.

How to Find: Customers may buy directly from the company through its Web site or call for more detailed information on the products. The company also has a retail outlet.

GLENNA JEAN MANUFACTURING ✿

230 N. Sycamore Street, Petersburg, VA 23803
Telephone: 804-861-0687
Web site: www.glennajean.com

Glenna Jean Manufacturing offers an extensive selection of bedding for infants and toddlers in many different fabrics and coordinated collections. The Web site gives you an excellent idea of the selection.

Interesting Fact: Established in 1977 as a family-owned business, Glenna Jean has actually been *increasing* its workforce of American workers. More than 98 percent of the collections are made in America.

How to Find: Please go to the Web site to view the listing of authorized retailers. If you don't have a computer, call customer service for assistance.

GO MAMA GO DESIGNS ✿

2520 N. Chambliss Street, Alexandria, VA 22311
Telephone: 888-466-2621
Web site: www.snugandtug.com

Go Mama Go Designs manufactures Snug & Tug®, a swaddling blanket that helps babies, and thus parents, get a better night's sleep. The product is made so that babies can't wiggle out. The Snug & Tug is available in seven color options and in two sizes.

Interesting Fact: According to this women-owned company, the Snug & Tug® by Go Mama Go Designs was recently chosen by *Parents.com* as "a product parents can't live without!"

How to Find: You may purchase the Snug & Tug directly through the Web site. If you don't have a computer or need information, please call the customer service number.

....

HOLY LAMB ORGANICS

4431 Boston Harbor Road, Olympia, WA 98506
Telephone: 360-402-5781
Web site: www.holylamborganics.com

Holy Lamb Organics makes an extensive line of products utilizing locally sourced wool and organic fabrics. Baby products include the Cozy Buns™ bedding system for crib, cradle, and bassinet. Elements of the system are mattresses and mattress toppers, comforters, bumpers, pillows, sheets, and crib skirts. Holy Lamb Organics also makes jumpers, tee shirts and bibs, hooded towels, and nursing pillows.

Interesting Fact: A woman-owned company, Holy Lamb Organics specializes in bedding and clothing made from organic wool. The company has a deep commitment to environmentally friendly manufacturing. The inspiration for the company came as the founders of the company were walking in the redwood forests of Northern California.

How to Find: Customers may purchase through the Holy Lamb Organics Web site or view the store locator list. If you can't locate a store or lack a computer, please call customer service.

....

LAMBS & IVY®

2040 E. Maple Avenue, El Segundo, CA 90245
Telephone: 800-345-2627
Web site: www.lambsivy.com

Lambs & Ivy® manufactures quilts, pillows, bedding, slipcovers, and valances for windows in nurseries in many different styles. The bedding is also available in toddler sizes. The bedding and accessories are arranged by collection on the Web site.

Interesting Fact: Founded almost 30 years ago, Lambs & Ivy® remains an American manufacturer of infant bedding and accessories.

How to Find: Please see the store locator list on the company Web site, or call customer service for information on the store nearest to your location.

. . . .

LITTLE GIRAFFE®, INC. ⊛ ↑

6940 Valjean Avenue, Van Nuys, CA 91406
Telephone: 818-782-8803
Web site: www.littlegiraffe.com

Little Giraffe®, Inc. manufactures baby blankets, blankies, bumpers and pillows, crib bedding, baby outfits for infants to toddlers 18 months old, as well as products for older children and adults.

Interesting Fact: The company was established in 2000 and specializes in luxury "lifestyle" bedding and clothing and accessories for children and adults. Though Little Giraffe has been quite successful, its origins were humble; a new mother and grandmother decided to make a blanket for the newborn child.

How to Find: Little Giraffe does not sell directly to the public; however, go to the Web site and, if you see products that you would like to purchase, call customer service for the retail store nearest to you.

. . . .

MR. BOBBLES BLANKETS ⊛ ↑ ✂

This is an online company based in the Baltimore, Maryland, area.
Telephone: 301-540-0633
Web site: www.mrbobblesblankets.com

Mr. Bobbles Blankets handcrafts receiving blankets, security blankets, playpen sheets, toddler pillows, supersized toddler blankets, burp cloths, wash cloths, and nap sheets for children to take to school to cover nap mats.

Interesting Fact: After giving birth to her second child, Renee Sirulnik decided to leave the computer business to pursue her dream of running a baby products company. The company name is based on the nickname she gave to her baby. The company is committed to helping children learn needlecraft skills. As part of its outreach, it donates cloth remnants from blanket manufacturing to a local school so that the students can learn to sew.

How to Find: You may buy directly from the company through its Web site. The product line is also available through online stores and in limited retail outlets.

· ·

MY BLANKEE™, INC. ↑ ★

742 S. Hill Street, Los Angeles, CA 90026
Telephone: 213-955-4516
Web site: www.myblankeeinc.com

My Blankee™, Inc. manufactures blankets, car-seat covers, bibs, burp cloths, hooded towels, jackets, warmers, pajamas, and many more products for babies, kids, and adults with sensitive skin.

Interesting Fact: My Blankee™ owes its existence to a two-month-old child named Luca who was born with eczema. The infant was allergic to nearly all fabric. Luca's father, Serge, had been in the textile business for 20 years, and he made it his mission to find hypoallergenic clothing for his son. The result of Serge's efforts is a line of products for infants, children, and adults that is made in the USA and that features hypoallergenic fabric.

How to Find: My Blankee™ products may be purchased through the company Web site and in select boutiques. You may call customer service if you require additional information.

· ·

MY LITTLE BLANKIE ✿ ✂

6839 Herron Place, Dayton, OH 45424
The company prefers e-mail.
Web site: www.mylittleblankie.com

My Little Blankie handcrafts quilted blankets that are approximately 15" × 20." You can create your own blanket from the choices on the Web site, or you can customize blankets in any fabric you desire. The company can customize. Limited production.

Interesting Fact: Melissa Blair, the founder of My Little Blankie, first started to make security blankets for her own children, and then she began to make extra blankets for her friends for their baby showers.

How to Find: You may order blankets directly through the company Web site. If you desire a custom-made blanket, please e-mail the company.

PATCH KRAFT® ORIGINAL DESIGNS ✿ ↑

70 Outwater Lane, Garfield, NJ 07026
Telephone: 201-833-2201
Web site: www.patchkraft.com

Patch Kraft® Original Designs manufactures coordinated bedding sets for infants, juveniles, and teens. Items include crib bedding, quilts, bumpers, sheets, dust ruffles, window valances, cushion covers, and lamps.

Interesting Fact: Paula Markowitz founded Patchkraft® Original Designs more than 30 years ago after she sewed a crib bumper for her new baby and realized the potential for coordinated baby bedding. As the company grew, Ms. Markowitz steered her organization to take a leadership role in the area of child safety. The company considers the two most important elements of its products to be that they are fashionable and safe.

How to Find: The company has a store locator on its Web site, or, if you don't have a computer, please call the company for the nearest retail location.

QUALITY FLEECE ✿ ○

407 Pleasant Street, Fall River, MA 02722
Telephone: 508-947-1853
Web site: www.qualityfleece.com

Quality Fleece is a manufacturer of baby blankets and scarves.

Interesting Fact: A woman-owned company, Quality Fleece sells exclusively to large baby stores and chains and not to private consumers.

How to Find: The company strictly sells to retailers. When you are shopping for fleece blankets, if you find something that was made in the USA, there is a good chance that Quality Fleece made the item.

ROBBIE ADRIAN™ ✿ ☺

2222 Francisco Drive, El Dorado Hills, CA 95762
Telephone: 916-570-3775
Web site: www.robbieadrian.com

Robbie Adrian™ manufactures certified organic baby blankets in fleece or velour trimmed in natural silk trim and in many different colors.

Interesting Fact: Robbie Adrian™ is a mom-owned company, founded by two former executives who wanted something completely different for their careers. They liked organic fabrics but felt that in order to break through to the mainstream, it was necessary for the designs and colors to have wider appeal to customers who were used to buying more attractive and more colorful products. The result of this philosophy was a beautiful line of certified organic upscale blankets made of U.S.-grown cotton.

How to Find: You may buy directly from the company through its Web site or call for more detailed information on the products.

••

SNUG FLEECE WOOLENS® ↑

2740 Pole Line Road, Pocatello, ID 83201
Telephone: 800-824-1177
Web site: www.snugfleece.com

Snug Fleece Woolens® manufactures fleece infant mattress covers and also makes larger sizes for beds for older children and adults.

Interesting Fact: The company sources all of its wool from American sheep ranchers. According to the company, American wool has more crimp and curl, and, as a result, it resists compression.

How to Find: Please see the company Web site for a list of distributors of its products. If you're ever in Pocatello, please visit the company store.

••

THREE WEAVERS ✿ ✂

3532 Coleman Court, Lafayette, IN 47905
Telephone: 765-447-4700
Web site: www.weaversthree.com

Three Weavers handcrafts woven baby blankets in acrylic and cotton.

Interesting Fact: Three Weavers is more than simply three weavers! A reading of the history will show the intertwining of five weaving companies that have come together in one manufacturing facility in Lafayette,

Indiana. The company weaves its products by hand in the traditions of the great American craftspeople. The techniques it uses have their origins in the spirit of the early weavers of this country.

How to Find: You may buy directly from the company through its Web site, or call customer service for more detailed information on the products.

Baby Clothing

The manufacturers of baby clothing understand that their clothes are not only meant to be durable and safe but also meant to reflect your taste and your desire to show off your baby! The designs run from traditional to retro to edgy and are often the creation of men and women who spent many years working in classic designer studio settings. Several of these companies will customize upon request.

··

APPALACHIAN BABY DESIGN ✿ ☺ ✂

17481 Seneca Trail, Maxwelton, WV 24957
Telephone: 304-497-2213
Web site: www.appalachianbaby.com

Appalachian Baby Design handcrafts layette gown and bonnet sets, sweaters, blankets, and hats for ages newborn to 24 months. They work in natural and organic fibers. Other products include locally made wooden baby keepsake spoons, fabric clutch toys, and baby gifts. The company also sells sweater kits to enable home knitters to make many of the sweater designs.

Interesting Fact: Appalachian Baby Design started its life as a women's economic development cooperative. In 2006, the organization went private. The company has a simple, yet beautiful philosophy: to capture the beauty and tradition of Appalachia with classic American styles.

How to Find: Please order through the Web site or call customer service for more information.

. . . .

BABY BEAU & BELLE ❀ ↑

7817 Skansie Avenue, Gig Harbor, WA 98335
Telephone: 866-228-6969
Web site: www.babybeauandbelle.com

Baby Beau & Belle handcrafts high-end "take me home" layettes, christening and baptism wear, and clothing for other special events in a baby's life. In 2009, the company will be introducing flower girl and communion wear.

Interesting Fact: Baby Beau & Belle has been in business for close to 20 years. The husband-and-wife team and the wife's sister are fashion designers strongly influenced by fashions that evoke an era when women wore long, flowing gowns. The company's inspiration flows from a great-aunt who was also a fashion designer. The feel of the baby products reflects a vintage heirloom tradition.

How to Find: Baby Beau & Belle is sold in finer children's clothing stores, or customers may order directly through the Web site. If you don't have a computer or need special assistance, please call the customer service number.

. . . .

BABY BURPEES ❀ ✂

517-1/2 Carnation, Corona del Mar, CA 92625
Telephone: 949-307-5667
Web site: www.babyburpees.com

Baby Burpees handcrafts custom-made burp cloths for girls and boys in all kinds of designs. The company can customize. Limited production.

Interesting Fact: Lindsay McVey started her business after handcrafting a burp cloth for her cousin's baby. The company likes customization, and customers can pick any color scheme they want. Customers who don't have a specific preference can generalize and order "brights," "pastels," or "browns" and the company will create a design. Lindsay can even make burp cloths in the team colors of your favorite school.

How to Find: Customers are welcome to order through the Burpee Baby Web site or by calling the customer service number.

☆
Made Here, Baby!

··

BABY KNITS AND MORE ⊛ ✂ ↑
121 Delay Road, Harwinton, CT 06791
Telephone: 866-485-0146
Web site: www.babyknitsandmore.com

Baby Knits and More handcrafts personalized and monogrammed sweaters as well as hats, baby clothes, baby layette, baby blankets, and baby gifts. The size range of the products goes from preemies through children's sizes 8, 10, 12, and 14. Larger sizes are also available. The company offers free gift wrapping on all items. The company can customize.

Interesting Fact: Colleen Baldwin has been fascinated by yarn her entire career. After working for more than 10 years as a production manager for a New York City sweater manufacturer, she decided to launch her own company. Baby Knits & More has been in business for 25 years.

How to Find: The company is an online business. If you don't have a computer or need assistance, call the customer service number.

··

BABY GO RETRO® ⊛ ✂ ↑
The company is located on Whidbey Island, Washington State.
Telephone: 360-321-2342
Web site: www.babygoretro.com

Baby Go Retro® makes handcrafted clothing for babies, toddlers, and preschoolers in vintage and fanciful designs. Products include dresses, tees, pants, bottoms, and two-piece sets. Limited production.

Interesting Fact: Sheila Steicek, Baby Go Retro®'s founder, is a former costume designer who did work for several television shows. She employs home sewers in the community to handcraft her unique designs and to support the economy of the local community.

How to Find: Ordering is done through the Web site. If you find yourself on Whidbey Island, you are welcome to make an appointment to stop by and visit.

. . . .

BIG BELLIES BIBS™

Big Bellies Bibs is located in the Maple Glen, Pennsylvania, area.
The company prefers e-mail.
Web site: www.big-bellies.com

Big Bellies Bibs™ manufactures starter bibs for infants, such as cotton/ terry teether bibs, and bibs with cotton print fronts in many patterns, as well as burp cloths. It also manufactures pocket bibs for toddlers. Big Bellies also produces bibs for older, special-needs children in adult colors.

Interesting Fact: Lisa Quinn, the president of Big Bellies Bibs, was a schoolteacher who taught kindergarteners and fourth and fifth graders, as well as special-needs children. The company plans to introduce more products for little boys, as Lisa feels that the clothing market is currently very skewed toward girls.

How to Find: The product line is sold through numerous retail outlets, or you can download the company catalog. Please e-mail the company for more specific information if you are unable to locate its products at a nearby retailer.

. . . .

BOSSY BABY

Bossy Baby is located in the Sarasota, Florida, area.
Telephone: 941-925-0036
Web site: www.bossybaby.com

Bossy Baby produces several collections of clothing for infants and toddlers. The products employ organic cotton, hemp, and recycled fibers. Baby clothes include snappies, bibs, gowns, blankets, caps, and rompers.

Interesting Fact: Tina Bossy was working as a fashion designer in Los Angeles when she gave birth to her baby. She realized that she needed to rearrange the priorities in her life and decided to start a small business that would enable her to spend more quality time with her new daughter. The company produces everything in the USA, including fabric and trim.

How to Find: The Bossy Baby Web site has a retail store locator. Please e-mail or call the company if you need help finding a retail store.

☆
Made Here, Baby!

CHARLES CRAFT®, INC. ↑
P.O. Box 1049, Laurinburg, NC 28353
Telephone: 910-844-3521
Web site: www.charlescraft.com

Charles Craft® produces a broad selection of craft fabrics and prefinished craft items ready for embroidery and other needlecraft talents. The infant and baby selection includes bibs, receiving blankets, burp towels, bath mitts, caps, mittens, booties, and bathing sets.

Interesting Fact: Charles Craft, Inc., founded in 1967 by Charles Buie, Jr., has grown to become one of the country's leading manufacturers and distributors of fabric craft products for home sewers and embroiderers.

How to Find: Charles Craft products may be found in craft and needlecraft shops throughout the United States. A retail shop locator list may be viewed on the company's Web site. If you don't have a computer, please call customer service for the name of the store nearest to you.

COLORGROWN CLOTHING, INC. ✿ ☺
Colorgrown Clothing is an online store located in the Eugene, Oregon, area.
Telephone: 541-683-6092
Web site: www.colorgrown.com

Colorgrown Clothing, Inc. manufactures sunhats, ribbed knit hats, and receiving blankets.

Interesting Fact: Colorgrown Clothing Co. is a mother-owned business that uses U.S.-grown organic cotton materials. In the manufacturing of the clothing, no glues, dyes, or other chemicals are ever used. The name of the company comes from the fact that different types of cotton have different colors.

How to Find: There is a store locator on the Web site, or you may call customer service to inquire about ordering directly from the company.

DOWNTIME™ BABY ✿
Downtime is an online business, based in New York, New York.
Telephone: 646-862-6115
Web site: www.downtimebaby.com

Downtime™ Baby manufactures a sleep mask solution for babies that is safe and comfortable. It also serves as a hat. The product comes in two different sizes and three colors.

Interesting Fact: Andrea Verity, the founder of Downtime™ Baby, was on a long road trip with her newborn. She was having all kinds of trouble getting the baby to sleep because of the glare of oncoming carlights and other stimulation. As the weather had turned cold, she placed a knit cap on the baby to keep him warm. For fun, the mom pulled the hat down over the baby's eyes, and he immediately fell asleep. The idea led to numerous prototypes, and, over time, the Downtime™ Baby hat was born.

How to Find: Though Downtime Baby products are sold in a limited number of retail stores, the easiest way to buy the hat is through the company's Web site. Customers can also call customer service for assistance.

EDEN'S BOUQUET ⊛ ✂ ↑ ✈

P.O. Box 429, Yacolt, WA 98675
Telephone: 800-940-2086
Web site: www.edensbouquet.com

Eden's Bouquet produces heirloom infant gowns, hats, layettes, slippers, headbands, rompers, and receiving blankets. The company can customize. A few items are imported. Limited production.

Interesting Fact: Based in Washington State, this company was founded by a mother of eight children who has a love of design and especially of Victorian-era children's clothing. There are several collections of higher-end clothing for toddlers and preschool girls as well as couture services if a one-of-a-kind item is desired.

How to Find: Clothing may be ordered through the Web site or by calling customer service. Select retail locations also carry some of the collection.

ESPERANZA THREADS ⊛ ☺ ↑

1160 Broadway Avenue, Bedford, OH 44146
Telephone: 800-397-0045
Web site: www.esperanzathreads.com

Esperanza Threads manufactures products from organic fabric including baby wraps, baptismal gowns, bibs, dresses for babies and toddlers, jackets, nightgowns, snappies, rompers, socks, tee shirts, and tote bags. The company also makes baby bedding.

Interesting Fact: Esperanza Threads was founded in 2000, in part because of the vision of a Catholic nun, Sister Mary Eileen, who wanted to facilitate the development of a community-based cooperative. The cooperative seeks to help those who need a second chance in life by making them self-sustaining and building community pride.

How to Find: You may order directly through the Web site. Should customers need assistance, they are welcome to call the customer service line.

HAND PICKED PUMPKIN™ ⊗ ☺ ✂

The company is an online store based in the Oak Park, Illinois, area.
Telephone: 708-524-1812
Web site: www.handpickedpumpkin.com

Hand Picked Pumpkin™ manufactures custom and limited-edition baby clothes and accessories. Size ranges include 3–6 months, 6–12 months, 12–18 months, and 18–24 months. The Hand Picked Pumpkin™ has a large selection of products that can all be customized in every customer's limited-edition style. Items include reversible hoodies, rompers, overalls, shorts, pants, shirts, hats, blankets, and gifts. The company can customize.

Interesting Fact: Allison Case, founder and president of Hand Picked Pumpkin™, began her career in architectural engineering. After the birth of her second child, this stay-at-home mom decided to launch a babywear line featuring comfortable knit clothing. What makes the product line unique is that the company enables customers to pick their item and then to have it customized from a wide selection of fabrics and styles.

How to Find: Though some of the products may be found at trunk shows and in boutiques, the best way to order is through the Web site, where customers can view the entire selection.

. . . .

HAPPY PANDA® BABY ✿

3610 Greenwood Place, Deer Park, TX 77536
The company prefers e-mail.
Web site: www.happypandababy.com

Happy Panda® Baby produces a variety of styles of lap tees, snappies, pants, and hats. What makes the company different is that it caters to bigger babies. It has altered its size chart to make shopping easier when shopping by age. If you would like to buy a product on the Web site but you don't have a bigger baby, it can help you find the right size.

Interesting Fact: Pamela Kramer, the president of Happy Panda® Baby, is an advocate for work-at-home moms. She is part of a new wave of creative and visionary women who share in the possibilities of the American manufacturing dream. The company organizes many events for women and is involved in working with other companies that have online businesses. Happy Panda Baby often acts as the hostess of what it calls "cyber baby showers." It organizes the gathering of many companies that make their products for moms and offers reviews of new baby products.

How to Find: Orders may be placed through the company Web site. Please e-mail the company if you would like to find a retail location in your area that may carry the product line.

. . . .

KIDIOMS™ ↑

Kidioms is a company based in Gloucester, Massachusetts.
Telephone: 877-630-2010
Web site: www.kidioms.com

Kidioms™ makes infant snappies, lap tees, and jersey tees and produces clothing for children from newborns to 4T. Kidioms offers snappies and tee shirts with many different expressions in several colors.

Interesting Fact: Kidioms™ was founded by three fathers: a creative director, a vice president of marketing, and a bankruptcy lawyer! They wanted to create children's clothing that did not fall into the super-sweet or super-edgy categories and preferred rather whimsical clothing that was fun and creative. Their motto for the clothing line is "Words you can grow on."

How to Find: Orders may be placed through the company Web site. At present there is limited retail distribution, but it is expanding. Call customer service for store locations or for further information.

KIWI INDUSTRIES ❀ ☺ ✈ ↑
3 Juniper Hill Road NE, Albuquerque, NM 87122
Telephone: 505-332-9090
Web site: www.kiwiindustries.com

Kiwi Industries manufactures infant and toddler clothing. The organic and natural fabric lines are all made in the USA. The knitwear is imported.

Interesting Fact: A women-founded company, Kiwi Industries is making a major commitment to organic fabrics. Interestingly, the company has recently moved organic production from overseas to the United States to maintain its high-quality standards.

How to Find: The company has a store locator on its Web site, or you may order online directly through the Web site as well. If you don't have a computer, please call the company for the nearest retail location.

KUMQUAT BABY ❀ ↑
969 Colorado Boulevard, Los Angeles, CA 90041
Telephone: 626-296-3537
Web site: www.kumquatbaby.com

Kumquat Baby manufactures many collections of children's clothes for preemies through to preschool. For infants, the company makes snappies, hats, bibs, hoodies, wash cloths, blankets, and gift sets.

Interesting Fact: Kumquat is a woman-founded company.

How to Find: Kumquat Baby is widely distributed throughout the United States and may be found online at numerous online stores or at numerous retail locations. Please view the retail locator for more information.

M GROUP, THE/BAMBOOSA® ❀ ☺ ↑

P.O. Box 1239, Andrews, SC 29510
Telephone: 800-673-8461
Web site: www.bamboosa.com

The M Group manufactures products for children made from woven bamboo from sizes 0 through to 18 months. This diverse product line includes shirts, blankets, towels, body suits, bibs, booties, pants, beanies, and crib sheets. The company also produces products for older children and adults. For men and older boys, the company produces bamboo polos and cotton/bamboo tees; for women and older girls, the company produces hoodies, V-necks, tank tops, and sleep-slips.

Interesting Fact: The Bamboosa® story reflects the true meaning of the American entrepreneurial spirit. The founders had been working at a tee shirt screen printing company early in their careers when they were laid off due to overseas outsourcing. They vowed to create a company that would bring sewing back to their community and help rehire many of the experienced workers who had lost their jobs. Their second motivation was to do something good for the planet by making products from sustainable materials. They chose to make clothing of woven bamboo, a unique and renewable material, and they have kept their promise by bringing jobs back to their community.

How to Find: All of the products on the Web site may be ordered online through the company Web site. Bamboo Baby also has a retail store locator so that you can shop in a store near to your location. If you don't have a computer, call the company for additional information.

MON AMIE ❀ ✂

P.O. Box 1052, Douglas, MI 49406
Telephone: 616-433-2538
Web site: www.mon-amie.com

Mon Amie handcrafts baby bibs, blankets, burp cloths, and diaper clutches. Mon Amie gift-wraps its products so that they can be given as presents. Limited production. The company can customize.

Interesting Fact: Amie Shanahan was frustrated by the quality of the clothing she was buying for her growing family. No matter how much money she paid, the items always seemed to fall apart. Realizing she wanted to be at home with her family as well as to do something to give back to her community, she launched a clothing company specializing in baby items. She employs local home sewers to help with her production. About 80 percent of the orders that come in are from repeat customers.

How to Find: Mon Amie has limited retail distribution. Customers may order directly through the Mon Amie Web site. If you don't have a computer, call customer service for more information about the products.

· ·

MY GOODNESS DUDS
410 Allentown Road, Yardville, NJ 08620
The company prefers e-mail.
Web site: www.mygoodnessduds.com

My Goodness Duds manufactures organic and nonorganic clothing for babies. It makes fabric tops and body suits, organic clothing collections, clothing for twins, baby blankets, and a novelty product line of baby holiday outfits for Christmas, Thanksgiving, Halloween, Valentine's Day, and Easter. The company also designs clothing for toddlers.

Interesting Fact: My Goodness Duds is a woman-owned company.

How to Find: My Goodness Duds sells products through its Web site. Please e-mail the company if you have questions.

· ·

NANNY GRAM ™ ❀
Nanny Gram is an online company that is based in Massachusetts.
Telephone: 508-397-2399
Web site: www.nannygram.com

Nanny Gram™ handcrafts baby booties, hand-crocheted heirloom layettes, knit hats, and sweaters. Age range is from 0 to 6 months. The items are produced by a network of independent knitters in New England and are gift wrapped as ready-to-give presents for baby showers. The sweaters are hand knit of a cashmere-merino blend. Limited production.

Interesting Fact: The inspiration for Maureen Flaherty's company comes from her mother ("Nanny"), who was an immigrant from Ireland. Her mother began a new life here at the age of 17. Mom had a great passion for her new country and also for the art of knitting. Maureen learned to appreciate the value of handmade, heirloom knit products. This appreciation eventually led her to start a company.

How to Find: Orders may be placed directly through the company Web site. If you don't have a computer, please call customer service.

OUTSIDE BABY   ⚜ ↑ ✈

2149 Cascade Avenue, Hood River, OR 97031
Telephone: 541-387-4554
Web site: www.outsidebaby.com

Outside Baby is a manufacturer of outerwear for children. The company makes two-layer, windproof bunting, several styles of jackets and pants, hats, and mittens for babies ranging in size from 0 to 6T. Other products may be imported.

Interesting Fact: Outside Baby was started around 2004 by a husband-and-wife team who are avid outdoor enthusiasts.

How to Find: The company Web site has a store locator or customers can call the customer service number for more information.

PANHANDLE BABIES™   ⚜ ↑

3307 Wimberly Road, Amarillo, TX 79109
Telephone: 806-467-1472
Web site: www.panhandlebabies.com

Panhandle Babies™ manufactures clothing for micro-preemies to children's size 7. In addition to making clothes, the company also has a line of rocking animals, toy boxes, and benches for toddlers.

Interesting Fact: Panhandle Babies™ was founded by a grandmother because she was having trouble finding American-made products for her grandkids.

How to Find: Please see the Web site for a listing of retail locations that carry Panhandle Baby products, or you can order through the company

Web site. If you don't have a computer, please call the company for additional information.

••

PREEMIE-YUMS©/NU BABY ⊛
2260 Gibsonwoods Court, Salem, OR 97304
Telephone: 503-370-9279
Web site: www.preemie-yums.com

Preemie-Yums©/Nu Baby is a manufacturer of clothing for premature babies. The company also makes clothing for infants under the Nu-Baby label.

Interesting Fact: A woman-owned company, Preemie-Yums proudly manufactures all of its baby clothing in the USA.

How to Find: Preemie-Yums sells its clothing through numerous retail locations. The products are frequently carried by gift shops associated with hospitals. Please e-mail the company if you need additional information or the location of a nearby retail store.

••

SAGE CREEK USA, INC./SAGE CREEK NATURALS® ⊛ ☺ ↑
18321 Ventura Boulevard, Tarzana, CA 91356
Telephone: 877-513-2183
Web site: www.sagecreeknaturals.com

Sage Creek USA, Inc. manufactures layettes for ages 0–24 months, and toddler girl and boy playwear for sizes 2T–4T. In addition to clothing, the company makes bedding and towels. According to the company, all items in the Sage Creek Naturals™ line are certified organic by EcoCert®, an international organic registering body.

Interesting Fact: Sage Creek Naturals™ is a family-run business that was founded on an inspiring story. After 13 years of marriage, the owner's daughter was delighted to learn that she had finally conceived. Unfortunately, she learned soon after that she had thyroid cancer. The baby was born two and one-half months premature. The mom's sickness, along with the baby's struggle, led the mom to conclude that "going organic" was essential for her family's health. Sage Creek Naturals became a mission as well as a company.

How to Find: Sage Creek USA has a store locator on its Web site to enable you to find the nearest retail location.

....

SERENDIPITI-DO-DA

5116 E. 88th Street, Tulsa, OK 74137
Telephone: 918-289-6025
Web site: www.serendipiti-do-da.com

Serendipiti-Do-Da handcrafts personalized burp cloths, nap mats, bibs, hooded towels, baby outfits, and child-sized aprons. Limited production. The company can customize upon request.

Interesting Fact: The owner founded her company just after the birth of her first daughter. Initially, she started making her gifts for friends, but then she was encouraged to turn her hobby into a business.

How to Find: Please contact or order directly through the Web site if you have an interest in the company's products.

....

SLICK SUGAR™

Slick Sugar is based in Iowa.
The company prefers e-mail.
Web site: www.slicksugar.com

Slick Sugar™ manufactures the following products in the USA: layettes, infant sets, and sweatshirts. For preschool girls, the company makes the T-shirt Peace Dress and A-line Black Dress/Flare Pants. For preschool boys, the company makes the Drummer tee and Purple Guitar tee. Other products are imported.

Interesting Fact: Slick Sugar™ describes its products as "Clothing for Kids Who Were Born to Rock." The company reflects the love of music shared by the women who founded it, Michelle Hanson and Dana Steele. In fact, a portion of the sales of the company is donated to a music foundation that supports music education by providing musical instruments to schools where there is a lack of funding.

How to Find: There is a store locator on the Slick Sugar Web site with both brick-and-mortar and online stores. Customers may also order directly through the Slick Sugar Web site.

☆
Made Here, Baby!

....

SOLAR ECLIPSE® ⚙
20235 N. Cave Creek Road, Phoenix, AZ 85024
Telephone: 800-878-9600
Web site: www.solareclipse.com

Solar Eclipse® manufactures sun protective clothing for infants, toddlers, and children with a 50 + protection in the weave that doesn't wash out. For infants, the company makes hats, bonnets, stroller covers, and rompers. For older children, Solar Eclipse makes shirts, surf suits, tops, and pants.

Interesting Fact: Mary K. McCormick was motivated to start Solar Eclipse® in 1996, after her athletically active husband was diagnosed with a melanoma-related skin cancer. She searched for a sun-protective product that would make a real difference in the lives of others who also loved the great outdoors. Her mission led her to create a line of products that would be both attractive and functional.

How to Find: Customers can purchase Solar Eclipse clothing through the Web site or by calling the customer service number.

....

U.S. SHEEPSKIN ↑
450 Fawcett Avenue, Tacoma, WA 98402
Telephone: 800-766-9665
Web site: www.ussheepskin.com

U.S. Sheepskin manufactures baby mittens and booties, baby caps, baby travel pillows, infant seat covers for car seats, baby-size sheepskin rugs, a baby "sleeping sack" made of sheepskin, and sheepskin infant toys.

Interesting Fact: U.S. Sheepskin manufactures a diverse line of sheepskin products for babies, children, and adults. The company points out that the sheepskin it uses is a by-product of food production. No sheep are raised specifically to make these products.

How to Find: U.S. Sheepskin has retail partners throughout the United States. Please go to its Web site to find the nearest dealer to your location, or call customer service.

WILD CHILDWEAR ✽ ☺ ↑

The company is based in the Greater Los Angeles, California, area.
Telephone: 310-659-1177
Web site: www.wildchildwear.com

Wild Childwear manufactures apparel for babies, toddlers, school-age, and older girls. The Visionary baby products include tunics, tank tops, and leggings.

Interesting Fact: The woman-owned company has two broad apparel lines for children: Wild Child Wear and Visionary. The Visionary products, launched in 2007, use organic fabrics and reflects the eco-consciousness of the organization.

How to Find: Customers may order through the Web site, or there is a retail store locator. In 2008, the company opened its flagship store in the Los Angeles area.

YIKES TWINS ✽

Yikes Twins is an online business based in Virginia.
Telephone: 540-659-9695
Web site: www.yikestwins.com

Yikes Twins produces hooded towels, hairwraps, towel wraps, and soap pockets.

Interesting Fact: Wendy Carter founded her business about the time she learned she was pregnant with twins. She knew the birth of her children would lead to a change in lifestyle. Around that time, Wendy became fascinated with a worn hooded towel she had received as a present for her first child. She wondered if she could improve upon the design of the hooded towel and maybe start a little company selling them. She began her venture by going to street fairs and selling her small inventory. She did so well that she realized she could expand her little venture into a full-blown company.

How to Find: Customers can place orders directly through the Web site.

Baby Footwear

The great shoemaking companies of America were some of the first to shutter their doors and outsource to foreign manufacturers. Certain parts of our country have never quite recovered from this exodus. Nevertheless, it is nice know that we have a handful of American companies that still work at this craft. Please refer to index E, and look under Baby and Children's Products: Booties, Footwear, and Socks for companies that make baby booties in addition to other product lines.

· ·

FOOTWEAR BY FOOTSKINS®

110 E. Main Street, Spring Grove, MN 55974
Telephone: 507-498-3703
Web site: www.footwearbyfootskins.com

Footwear by Footskins® handcrafts infant booties and moccasins from deerskin or sheepskin. For toddlers and older children, the company makes booties, moccasins, shoes, and slippers. Children's sizes range from newborns to size 8. Footskins also produces shoes for teenagers and adults.

Interesting Fact: A true American shoe company, Minnesota-based Footwear by Footskins® works in both cowhide and sheepskin. In addition to stock sizes, the company also has the ability to customize. It receives many requests to customize shoes for those who have special needs and sensitive skin.

How to Find: Orders may be placed directly through the company Web site, or the company can send you a catalog. Call customer service for special-order assistance.

· ·

ITASCA MOCCASIN ⊛ ↑

37144 U.S. Highway 71, Lake George, MN 56458
Telephone: 218-699-3978
Web site: www.itascamoccasin.com

Itasca Moccasin handcrafts shoes for infants and older children. For infants, the company makes the Papoose in elk, buckskin, and suede and in sizes from small to extra large. It also makes Teepee Boots in children's sizes 7–13 and 1–3 in suede and full-grain leather.

Interesting Fact: Itasca Mocassin specializes in handcrafted shoes in several different types of leather including deerskin, elk, cowhide, and sheepskin. The product line for babies is large and features moccasins dyed in many different colors.

How to Find: Orders may be placed through the company Web site. Please visit the retail store if you are in the area.

· ·

SOFT STAR SHOES™

521 SW Second, Corvallis, OR 97333
Telephone: 866-763-2525
Web site: www.softstarshoes.com

Soft Star Shoes™ handcrafts soft-sole shoes for children, including sheepskin-lined moccasins, baby booties, sandals, sheepskin boots, and street shoes. Age range goes from infant through to children's size 13. There is a complete product line for older children and teenagers and for adults.

Interesting Fact: Established nearly 25 years ago, Soft Star Shoes is a family-owned business. It makes soft leather shoes with fleece inner-soles in a variety of styles for infants, toddlers, and older children. As serious as it is about making quality shoes, it is equally serious about minimizing the environmental imact of its operation and has incorporated a number of programs to be responsible manufacturers.

How to Find: All of the products on the Soft Star Web site may be ordered directly through the Web site. If you don't have a computer or need information, please call the customer service number.

Baby Fun!

It is hard to imagine a less political or controversial item than a baby rattle. However, it was the baby rattle and similar items that were at the very center of American anger toward imported children's products. The objects our babies were putting in their mouths were found to contain lead and other harmful chemicals. We won't go any further on the topic except to say that American manufacturers, working in wood and plastic, give parents wonderful alternatives to imported items. In a similar fashion, there are many American manufacturers of plush toys and dolls that are also safe for babies. The plush toys contained here have no pieces or parts that can come off in baby's mouth. Please refer to the American-made Children's Product Index for a list of all companies making plush toys and dolls for older children as well as for babies.

CAMDEN ROSE
221 Felch Street, Ann Arbor, MI 48103
Telephone: 734-99-1400
Web site: www.camdenrose.com

Camden Rose handcrafts the following products for babies: maple teethers, cherrywood rattles, and wooden bowls and spoons. The company also makes wooden toys and games for toddlers and preschool children, which include dollhouse toys, children's aprons, playstands, and musical instruments. There are craftspeople at Camden Rose who also make woolen items for baby.

Interesting Fact: About six years ago, Jason Gold, a Waldorf teacher and craftsperson, set out to create a company based on the principles of what he calls "organic design." He did what any other entrepreneur might do: he sat on a rock, watched a stream, and came up with an idea! His observations of how things flow led him develop products that exist to create imagination-based feelings within children. He and his business partner, Judy Alexander, have a strong commitment to the environment, and, as a result, the company has a major focus on green manufacturing and recycled packaging.

How to Find: There are three ways to find Camden Rose products: through the Web site, at online retailers, or at brick-and-mortar stores that appear on the Web site in a store locator section. Call customer service if you need additional information.

EMBEARS
P.O. Box 402, Hannawa Falls, NY 13647
Telephone: 315-268-1227
Web site: www.embears.com

EmBears handcrafts baby-safe bears with embroidered eyes, noses, and mouths, as well as stuffed animals for older children. The company can customize. Limited production.

Interesting Fact: Ellen MacMaster personally creates each stuffed animal, so no two are ever exactly the same. Each has its own unique expression. The founder states that her business began in her childhood as a hobby and that the bears still bring her joy. EmBears uses a quality synthetic fur to make its animals, rather than a cheaper hohair. The company will customize. Limited production.

How to Find: You may order directly from the company through its Web site or call for more detailed information on the products.

HONEYSUCKLE DREAMS

1613 Auburn Avenue, Rockville, MD 20850
Telephone: 301-217-0546
Web site: www.honeysuckledreams.com

Honeysuckle Dreams handcrafts dolls and stuffed animals, blankets, quilts, and pillows. The company can customize. Limited production.

Interesting Fact: The colors given to the organic cotton fabrics, dolls' hair, and embroidery yarns are hand dyed by Diana Yun in her home studio using natural dyes. These dyes come from flowers, roots, barks, fruits, berries, and leaves, some of which were home grown or hand gathered.

How to Find: Please call or e-mail the company for more information.

HUGG-A-PLANET®

7A Morse Drive, Essex Junction, VT 05452
Telephone: 802-878-8900
Web site: www.peacetoys.com

Hugg-A-Planet® handcrafts the Foundlings®, which are stuffed animals made from organic materials that are appropriate for infants and older children; Hugg America® pillows, which show all of the states, parks, rivers, mountains, and other geographic features; and the Hugg-A-Planet® Line of Earth-shaped pillows. Foundlings® and Hugg America® are made in the USA. Hugg-A-Planet is manufactured in the USA using domestic and imported materials.

Interesting Fact: Founded by Robert Forenza more than 25 years ago, the company was launched on the basis of an idea suggested by Robert's mother. She thought that a pillow in the shape of the Earth would be a great idea. It was! The company now makes a wide selection of stuffed toys and pillows that are as educational as they are comfortable.

How to Find: The best way to place an order is through the company Web site; however, customers can call customer service for more information or to order through an operator.

• •

LOTS 2 SAY BABY™ ⊛

P.O. Box 762, Snoqualmie, WA 98065
Telephone: 425-444-3746
Web site: www.lots2saybaby.com

Lots 2 Say Baby™ manufactures infant pacifiers featuring funny sayings and in several colors.

Interesting Fact: Erin Wilson had her baby decked out in an Easter outfit, and she realized that the orange pacifier clashed with the baby's clothes. She decided then and there to develop a line of unique pacifiers. The company feels that its mission is to honor children, and it is very concerned about any product that a baby will ultimately put in its mouth.

How to Find: The company has a store locator on its Web site to help you find the nearest retail location. If there are no stores nearby, the company invites you to order through customer service.

• •

NORTHSTAR TOYS ⊛ ☺ ↑

Box 617, Questa, NM 87556
Telephone: 800-737-0112
Web site: www.northstartoys.com

Northstar Toys manufactures wooden toys for babies and toddlers. Baby toys include "Baby's First Toy," a rattle made from birch and maple. For toddlers and older children, the toy line includes airplanes, boats, jungle and sea animals, wooden cameras, cars, and people movers. Northstar Toys also makes pull toys such as a duck and puppy, magic wands, and nativity sets.

Interesting Fact: Established in 1979, this family business specializes in nontoxic wooden toys in walnut, oak, alder, and other fine woods. The wood is rubbed with a nontoxic oil to allow the natural beauty to shine. Recycled materials are used whenever possible, and top priority is given to environmental sustainability. Even the leftovers from manufacturing are recycled. The wood scraps are donated to schools for art projects, and the sawdust is used to supplement compost.

How to Find: You may buy directly from the company through its Web site or call for more detailed information on the products.

TURNER TOYS, INC.
1958 Elmore Road, Morrisville, VT 05661
Telephone: 800-955-4097
Web site: www.turnertoys.com

Turner Toys, Inc. manufactures My Very Own® wooden baby rattles.

Interesting Fact: Established in 1974, Turner began life as a company that produced fine wood-turned bowls and candlesticks that were sold at crafts fairs. As the company began to explore other product possibilities, it developed a unique solid maple baby rattle using rock maple, incredibly made out of one piece of wood; these are still handcrafted in the original wood shop and are now considered a classic American baby toy.

How to Find: Please note that the baby rattle is also available on other online stores as well as through retailers. Other products on the Web site are distributed and not made by the company.

TWINKLE BABY® ✿ ☺ ✂
P.O. Box 731, Santa Cruz, CA 95061
Telephone: 831-419-1265
Web site: www.twinklebaby.com

Twinkle Baby® handcrafts bonding dolls in various fabrics, including organic cotton. The company also makes aroma blankets and baby blankets.

Interesting Fact: The founder of Twinkle Baby®, Lara Pebbles, has created a company whose product line is designed to soothe baby. The bonding dolls were fashioned after nurses explained to Lara that for premature babies especially, sight was not as important as mother's scent. As it is difficult for premature babies to bond with moms because they are confined to incubators, Twinkle Baby's bonding dolls are made to help with the bonding process. When a mom sleeps with the doll, the doll takes on the mother's scent, and then the doll is placed with baby.

How to Find: You may purchase the dolls directly from the company through its Web site or call for more detailed information on the products.

CHAPTER 4

American-Made Children's Clothing and Accessories

My father's father was a tailor, and my father's mother was a seamstress. They were trained in the European way, in the last years of the nineteenth century.

We are not able to reconstruct what their lives might have been like in what was then Russo-Poland. We only know they left as quickly as they could. Around 1903, Grandpa Phillip, his older brother Morris, and his younger sister Rose found their way to New York City through Ellis Island. He was 17 years of age. Grandma Seley was 15 when she made the crossing with her two older sisters.

There are several conflicting stories as to how they met. The story I like is that they met on New York's Lower East Side, maybe in some type of social club or through an intermediary such as a matchmaker. While my grandfather had a reputation for being somewhat flamboyant and a man who never met a horserace he didn't like, my grandmother would always remain a staid, proper, and closed woman.

The couple courted and then married around 1907. They moved to Hempstead, New York, and found a cheap apartment on Hilton Avenue. They were loaned or they scraped up enough cash to buy a second-hand sewing machine and set up shop in their living room.

Around 1914, Phillip and Seley moved into an attached home

in Hempstead, at 55 Kellum Place. By then the couple had built the business to the point where they could afford the rent on a small tailor shop in the village of Garden City. They had three boys between 1915 and 1923.

There is a picture of grandma and grandpa at the Kentucky Derby. He is in a finely tailored white linen suit and Panama hat. They stand near a shiny Packard with spoke wheels. A man who dresses like that has very big American Dreams. Just before World War II, Grandpa took out a new lease on a retail store near the tailor shop. He wanted to go into the dry cleaning business. At first, the store was a "drop-off" store. After the war, he would add machinery and become independent from the wholesale cleaners. Who knows what other plans they made?

The oldest son, Morris, married my mother, Ruth, and, not long after, I was born.

Grandpa had his first heart attack when I was four, and he died of heart disease when I was five. I can't remember *enough* about him. Yet I have always missed him. While he left me almost no memories, he did leave me a sailor's suit. You see, grandpa was not educated much beyond grammar school, but he could cut a three-piece suit or an overcoat from a bolt of cloth. It was his craft, he loved it, and he was good at it. Fabric had given him an American life.

There is another faded picture. I am about two years old and am standing in the doorway of the tailor shop, wearing a custom-made sailor suit. I can only imagine grandpa placing his tailor's measuring tape across my shoulders and around my little waist. Grandma decorated the suit with full-sized naval patches and official-looking gold buttons. I look across time. The little boy smiles at me.

I can't help but wonder what my grandfather might have felt as he was sewing my sailor suit. I imagine that it is dusk on a Saturday evening, sometime in late spring. He is sitting at his tailor's bench. It has been a long day, yet he looks around the shop and sees that it is full of work.

He was not a religious man, yet I am sure he gives thanks that his sons have safely returned from the war. One of his sons came back as a hero, highly decorated as a belly gunner on a B-24 that had flown several missions over Germany. Grandpa is thankful that he was financially able to sponsor what was left of his Russo-Polish family and bring them to America from the displaced persons camps. He could not allow himself any more sadness. He had undoubtedly pleaded with his remaining sister in Poland and her husband and children to flee while they had the chance. Now there was nothing to do but light candles.

He would soon leave the shop for an evening in a new home, and maybe there would be a family gathering. He looks at the little boy's sailor suit, a suit for his first-born American grandson. It will make a nice present for the boy's birthday. Grandpa gently folds the sailor suit, wraps it in tissue paper, and smiles.

In speaking with the American clothing manufacturers listed in the pages to follow, I realized that nearly every one of them was started by the owner making a piece of clothing for a child, usually the owner's child.

What were my grandfather's hopes and dreams? I had convinced myself I would never know. I was wrong. I heard his voice every time I spoke with one of the clothing manufacturers mentioned in this chapter.

American-Made Children's Clothing and Accessories

- ❊ Our Little Baby Is Changing! (includes clothing for toddlers and preschool children)

- ❊ Mostly for Girls (includes clothing for school-age girls to 'tweens and beyond)

- ❊ Girls' Jewelry and Hair Accessories

- ❊ Mostly for Boys (includes clothing for school-age boys to 'tweens and beyond)

- ❊ For Girls and Boys (includes companies making products for both boys and girls, generally from school-age to 'tweens and beyond)

- ❊ Children's and Infant's Footwear and Socks

Our Little Baby Is Changing!

The listings in this part of the chapter cover American clothing manufacturers that meet the needs of babies as they become toddlers and then as they go on to the preschool years. It is that time in a baby's life when parents or grandparents might suddenly look at each other and ask: "Where did our little baby go?" There are many companies that make clothing for babies who are "in transition." Some companies specialize in clothing for toddlers, some for infants and toddlers, and still more make clothing for toddlers to preschool. Please refer to the American-Made Children's Products Cross Reference index for additional companies that make toddler and preschool clothing.

....

BABY NAY®

2863 E. 11th Street, Los Angeles, CA 90023
Telephone: 323-780-4949
Web site: www.nayetal.com

Baby Nay® manufactures toddler and preschool clothing for both boys and girls, as well as clothing for infants. Items include rompers, snappies, hats, tunics, dresses, shorts, pants, tees, bibs, and accessories.

Interesting Fact: More than 80 percent of the girls' line is made in the USA. The boys' products are imported.

How to Find: The Web site has a store locator for your convenience. If you don't own a computer or need information, please call customer service for assistance or for the nearest store location.

....

BEARY BASICS™

2 N. Central Avenue, Upland, CA 91786
Telephone: 909-920-6620
Web site: www.bearybasics.us

Beary Basics™ manufactures baby clothes, including hooded towels, burp cloths, blankets, and quilts. For toddlers and older, the company makes kimono dresses, wrap dresses, rompers, and tops.

Interesting Fact: Though Beary Basics™ products are made in the United States, the company sells only to boutiques and not to individual customers. The brand is widely distributed.

How to Find: Look for the Beary Basics label at your local children's boutique.

....

BÉBÉ MONDE, INC. ⊛ ↓
6 Journey, Aliso Viejo, CA 92656
Telephone: 949-362-1213
Web site: www.bebemonde.com

BÉBÉ MONDE, INC. manufactures layettes for boy and girl infants, plus an extensive line of fashions for toddler and preschool girls. The age range of the Bébémonde® product line goes from infant to approximately age 6.

Interesting Fact: Founded by a husband-and-wife management team more than 20 years ago, Bébémonde® has a deep commitment to manufacturing its clothing line in America. The company specializes in clothing for toddlers and preschool children.

How to Find: The Web site has a store locator for your convenience. There you will find a listing of both brick-and-mortar and online stores, or call customer service for assistance in finding the nearest store location.

....

CHARLIE ROCKET ↑
2861 W. 7th Street, Los Angeles, CA 90005
Telephone: 213-251-9952
Web site: www.charlierocket.com

Charlie Rocket manufactures clothing for both boys and girls, from infancy through to school age. Products include pants in denim, twill, and fleece, screen-printed tee shirts, and thermal tee shirts.

Interesting Fact: Founded in 1995, Charlie Rocket USA manufactures virtually all of its clothing in the USA.

How to Find: The Charlie Rocket Web site has a store locator for your convenience. If you don't have a computer, please call customer service for the store nearest you.

CLOTH & NEEDLE

Cloth & Needle is an online company located in Pennsylvania.
Telephone: 866-288-1917
Web site: www.clothandneedle.net

Cloth & Needle produces jumpers for infants, along with outerwear and hats for toddlers, preschool, and school-age children.

Interesting Fact: Cloth & Needle is a woman-owned business that hand-crafts its clothing. Limited production.

How to Find: You may order directly through the company Web site, or, if you don't have a computer, call customer service for more information about the product line.

CLOTHES MADE FROM SCRAP, INC. ☺ ↑

14 Grandview Drive, Palm Coast, FL 32137
Telephone: 386-447-6656
Web site: www.clothesmadefromscrap.com

Clothes Made from Scrap manufactures tees from recycled materials for infants and children, youth caps, and visors. For teens, it makes recycled jackets and vests. The tees are made either from 100 percent recycled materials or from a 50/50 blend of postconsumer poly (made from soda bottles) and recycled cotton or are 100 percent organic cotton. The other products are made primarily from recycled poly from soda bottles.

Interesting Fact: Founded by Graham Jarrett in 1994, the company specializes in marketing and manufacturing products made from Earth-friendly materials.

How to Find: Normally, Clothes Made from Scrap sells not directly to the public but to municipalities, amusement parks, and organizations that buy in quantities. However, it will accept orders from consumers if orders are placed over the telephone or by e-mail. Please note that, in these cases, stock may or may not be available depending on whether there are orders from larger customers.

EARTH WEAR® ORGANIC COTTON ORIGINALS ☺ ↑

1007 Swallow Lane, Chattanooga, TN 37421
Telephone: 423-894-3674
Web site: www.earth-wear.com

Earth Wear® Organic Cotton Originals manufactures certified organic cotton baby and children's clothing. For infants to toddlers, the selection includes creepers, diaper sets, bibs, tees, infant dresses, jeans, bloomers, and jumpers. The company also makes knit dresses for girls in sizes 4–10.

Interesting Fact: Earlier in his career, the founder of Earth Wear® Organic Cotton Originals worked for a large chemical company and witnessed the mishandling of toxic waste. An avid outdoorsman with young children at the time, he decided he wanted to create a company where he could give back rather than detract from the environment.

How to Find: Customers may order directly through the Web site or call customer service for assistance.

EIGHT3ONE™ ☺

The Eight3One company is based in the Seattle, Washington, area.
Telephone: 949-697-0542
Web site: www.eight3one.com

Eight3One™ produces two collections: Urban Pop and Tot Couture. The size range goes from age 3 months to about six years. The company offers infant snappies, tee shirts, and pants. The nonorganic products are completely made in the United States of USA-sourced fabric. The organic products are finished in the United States but use imported organic fabric.

Interesting Fact: Eight3One™ derives its unusual name from a secret code that one of the founders used when she was a little girl. The name stands for "Eight letters, Three words, and One meaning." In other words, it stands for "I Love You."

How to Find: The Web site has a store locator showing both brick-and-mortar and online stores. Customers may also order directly through the Web site.

FORTUNE TEE

1702 Micheltorena, Los Angeles, CA 90028
Telephone: 888-358-2598
Web site: www.fortuneteeshirt.com

Fortune Tee manufactures tops, long pants, and zodiac tees for toddlers and preschool children, as well as tops, diaper covers, burp cloths, and hats for babies.

Interesting Fact: Fortune Tees owner Carla O'Brien found that, as she traveled across the USA, everyone seemed to love fortune cookies and everyone, it seemed, wore tee shirts. She decided to combine the two and launched a line of baby clothes with fortune cookie messages on all of the shirts. The shirts are all gift packaged inside take-out boxes.

How to Find: Fortune Tees has a store locator on its Web site, or you may order through the Web site or call customer service for the store nearest to your location.

GREEN BABIES ☺

28 Spring Street, Tarrytown, NY 10591
Telephone: 800-603-7508
Web site: www.greenbabies.com

Green Babies manufactures three different organic fabric product lines for children from ages 0 months to about 5 years. Baby items include snappies, separates, baby bags, hats, and bibs. Toddler to school-age clothing includes rompers and dresses.

Interesting Fact: Green Babies is a woman-founded company that was established in 1994. The company is proud of its large selection of USA-made certified organic clothing for children.

How to Find: There is a store locator on the Web site where customers may find the nearest retail location, or customers may order online directly through the Web site. Call customer service for assistance if you have questions or lack a computer.

KANDLE KIDS WEAR

The company is based in the Austin, Texas, area.
The company prefers e-mail.
Web site: www.kandlekidswear.com

Kandle Kids Wear handcrafts toddler-size shirts and infant snappies. The company can customize by request.

Interesting Fact: The business creation of two Texas moms, Kandle Kidswear specializes in hand-sewing felt designs onto organic cotton shirts. The company is transitioning to a 100% recycled-felt product that uses felt made entirely from used plastic bottles.

How to Find: There are three ways to order: online by directly ordering through the Web site, through online stores, or by visiting children's boutique retailers in the Austin area.

LILIPUTIANS NYC™ ✿ ✄
The company is based in New York, New York.
Telephone: 917-796-3472
Web site: www.liliputians-nyc.com

Liliputians NYC™ manufactures a collection for toddlers that features vintage looks, bright colors, and whimsical themes. The company offers "initial shirts," birthday dresses, birthday shirts, holiday outfits, summer sets, and appliqued jeans. In addition to girls and boy's clothing, there are also mother-daughter and brother-sister outfits and infant clothing. The clothing is produced in limited quantities, and many of the items are one of a kind. The company can customize.

Interesting Fact: Heather Flottman founded Liliputians NYC in 2004. She named the company after her daughter, Lily Belle, who was born on May 12 of that year. Liliputians NYC is an "indie," or independent design firm. The indie firms are helping to reshape American manufacturing with innovative and often breakthrough concepts and designs.

How to Find: Customers may also order directly through the Web site. If you have additional questions or lack a computer, please call the customer service number.

LOLLIPOP ZEN™ ✿ ☺ ↑
10624 S. Eastern Avenue, Henderson, NV 89052
Telephone: 702-796-1313
Web site: www.lollipopzen.com

Lollipop Zen™ manufactures baby and toddler clothes and matching mother-child tees. Most products are made of cotton, some using organic cotton.

Interesting Fact: Ronee and Nicole, the mother-and-daughter team that founded Lollipop Zen, want their collection to be more than an apparel line. They want their clothing to nurture mother and baby mind and spirit and to be an expression of peace.

How to Find: There is a store locator on the Web site. Customers may also order directly through the Web site. If you need additional assistance, please call the customer service number.

....

NEPTUNE ZOO ™

The company is based in the Los Angeles, California, area.
Telephone: 949-480-1227
Web site: www.neptunezoo.com

Neptune Zoo ™ produces uniquely designed long- and short-sleeve tee shirt collections for boys and girls. The company also makes tees and snappies for infants.

Interesting Fact: A woman-owned company, Neptune Zoo makes all of its clothing from 100 percent cotton.

How to Find: There is a store locator on the Web site, and the line is also carried by several online stores. Please type "Neptune Zoo" into a search engine, and several online retailers will appear. For further assistance, please call customer service.

....

RED PRAIRIE, THE

The Red Praire is located in the Baltimore, Maryland, area.
Telephone: 443-622-1598
Web site: www.redprairiepress.com

The Red Prairie handcrafts infant and unisex snappies in organic fabrics and a selection of organic cotton toddler tee shirts, as well as clothes for teens.

Interesting Fact: Rachel Bone, founder of The Red Prairie, was educated as an artist. She became very interested in print making and over summers apprenticed to companies that did silk screening. She graduated with degrees in print making. She and her husband, also an artist, launched their company about five years ago. They are part of the wave of cottage artists and manufacturers that make up the emerging "indie" movement.

How to Find: Orders are taken through the Red Prairie Web site. Online retailers are also beginning to carry the product line.

··

SWEET T BABY ❀ ☺ ↓
650 Brownwood Avenue SE, Atlanta, GA 30316
Telephone: 678-358-7768
Web site: www.sweettbaby.com

Sweet T Baby handcrafts tees, caps, bibs, blankets, diaper bags, pants, and dresses. The size range of Sweet T Baby products is infant size 0 through 4T, with clothing for both boys and girls.

Interesting Fact: Erica was always a creative person, and she always appreciated handcrafted clothing because she sensed the passion behind the creation. A social worker by trade, she gave up her profession in order to stay at home with her children; however, she soon realized she needed the stimulation of the workplace. She began Sweet T Baby in her home, using her creativity and her love of fabrics for inspiration. The products are made of organic fabrics, as she wants her company to make a meaningful environmental statement.

How to Find: Sweet T Baby has limited retail distribution. Most of the sales are done directly through the Web site, or customers may call customer service.

··

TEXAS JEANS® ↑
The company is based in Asheboro, North Carolina.
Telephone: 336-629-3018
Web site: www.texasjeans.com

Texas Jeans® manufactures toddler jeans in sizes 1T–4T and in children's sizes 4–6.

Interesting Fact: According to the company, Texas Jeans are 100% made in the USA. In manufacturing, the company uses only American-made denim and American-made labels, trim, and hardwear. The company moved its production from Texas to North Carolina in 2006.

How to Find: You may order online directly through the Web site. If you don't have a computer or need additional assistance, please call customer service.

. . . .

TONI TIERNEY® CHILDREN'S CLOTHING ✿
903F Irwin Street, San Rafael, CA 94901
Telephone: 415-256-1272
Web site: www.tonitierney.net

Toni Tierney® Children's Clothing handcrafts products for infants and toddlers for ages 3 months, 6 months, 9 months, 1 year, and 18 months. The toddler line is for girls only, sizes 2T, 3T, and 4T.

Interesting Fact: The mission that Toni Tierney has set for her company is not only to have a product line that is made in America but to have her clothes made by stay-at-home moms. Toni wants children to see their moms working so that the children can have a sense that creating with one's hands can be fun. She also wants children to sense that connecting with your spirit through doing creative things can bring joy and spirituality back to work. As much as possible, materials used by Toni Tierney are purchased from American fabric manufacturers.

How to Find: Toni Tierney sells to more than 150 boutiques and also to online stores. If you can't find a store in your area that carries Toni Tierney's designs, please call customer service.

. . . .

TOPNOTCH4KIDS ✿ ✂
1121 11th Street W, Ashlan, WI 54806
Telephone: 800-503-9099
Web site: www.topnotch4kids.com

Topnotch4kids handcrafts infant and children's fleece clothing, baby and toddler hats, mittens, blankets, and kid's purses.

Interesting Fact: Because these products are handcrafted, it is possible to customize the clothing and hats in many different color combinations.

How to Find: You may order through the Web site, or, if you don't have a computer, call customer service for more information about the product line.

TRA LA LA, INC. ✿ ↑

The company is located in the Los Angeles, California, area.
Telephone: 714-532-5328
Web site: www.tralalainc.com

Tra la la™ manufactures clothing for girls from newborns to age 6. All of the clothing is made of 100 percent cotton and uses accents and printed fabrics. The company introduces about eight different collections every season, so it is important to visit the Web site to gain an appreciation for the selection and creativity that goes into the product line. Clothing includes skirts, dresses, outfits, and tees. Please see the Web site to get a better idea of the collections.

Interesting Fact: The founder of Tra la la™ is from France. As a little girl, Anastasia Backstrand dreamed of being a designer and having her own designer label. About 17 years ago, after moving to Southern California, Anastasia finally realized her American Dream.

How to Find: There is a store locator on the Web site. If you don't have a computer or need assistance finding Tra la la clothing, please call customer service.

Mostly for Girls

This part of the listings is devoted to clothing companies that specialize in clothing for girls, covering a wide range of items from underwear to outerwear and from approximately preschool through to 'tweens and beyond. We noticed that different manufacturers call the same article of clothing by different names, so it can get confusing. We strongly recommend that you go to the Web sites to gain an appreciation for the product lines; collections for many companies are constantly changing, and the product lines themselves are quite large.

A.S. TEES ↓

209 Plumbers Road, Columbia, SC 29203
Telephone: 800-717-7751
Web site: www.astees.com

A.S. Tees manufactures tees mainly for girls from school age to preteen, as well as snappies, tees, and bibs for infants and toddlers.

Interesting Fact: Based in South Carolina and founded in 1997, A.S. Tees normally sells in wholesale quantities to stores. However, customers can buy basic shirts through the Web site.

How to Find: Please note that the customer service number is only for large wholesale quantities to the trade. The company is not set up to do transactions over the telephone. However, the company does sell directly to the public through its Web site for less than wholesale quantities.

BABIES 'N BOWS ⊛ ✂

38 Tulsa Drive, Barnegat, NJ 08005
Telephone: 609-660-2396
Web site: www.babiesnbows.com

Babies 'N Bows handscrafts girls' dresses from three months to size 14. It also makes matching doll dresses, petticoats, and hats for all popular brands of 18" dolls. The company can customize.

Interesting Fact: Lori Curtiss founded her company more than 18 years ago. She made a dress for her (then) little girl, and everywhere they went people stopped them and wanted to place orders! One of the line's appeals is that the company makes matching doll dresses in the same high-quality fabrics.

How to Find: You may order through the Web site or call customer service for more information about the product line. The company also does craft shows from Massachusetts to Virginia.

BELLE BAGS ⊛ ✂ ↑

Belle Bags is an online store based in Charlotte, North Carolina.
The company prefers e-mail.
Web site: www.bellebags.com

Belle Bags handcrafts little handbags for girls in many different colors and styles. The company also makes handbags and belts for moms and teens. Belle Bags loves to work with whimsical fabrics. Please note that Belle Bags has the ability to custom-design and monogram.

Interesting Fact: Amy Holzman, founder of Belle Bags, says she gets her fashion inspiration not from New York or Milan fashion shows but in walking down the fabric or trim aisle of fabric stores. She loves to pair fabrics and admits to awakening at 2 A.M. just thinking about fabric combinations.

How to Find: Belle Bags may be ordered directly through the company Web site by clicking on the Shy Siren online store. A number of online stores also carry Belle Bags. Just type in the company name into your favorite search engine.

BINKY COUTURE® ↑ ✂

2463 E. Waterview Place, Chandler, AZ 85249
Telephone: 480-460-0134
Web site: www.binkycouture.com

Binky Couture® handcrafts a high-end clothing collection for girls from infants to age 1. The clothing is made from materials such as supima cotton and French terry that has been hand dyed or batch dyed and then decorated with Swarovski crystals. The products in the collections include hoodies, jackets, tees, dresses, and capris.

Interesting Fact: Binky Couture® is a family-owned and -operated company located in the Phoenix, Arizona, area. In addition to making beautiful clothing, the company also wants to make little girls beautiful inside and out. The company sews inpirational messages into each garment to help nurture a spirit of positive self-image among little girls.

How to Find: The Web site has a store locator for your convenience. There are also several online retailers that sell portions of the collection. If you don't own a computer, please call customer service for the nearest store location.

BOLD MARY ⊛ ✂

591 St. Charles Avenue NE, Atlanta, GA 30308
Telephone: 404-875-2611
Web site: www.boldmary.com

Bold Mary handcrafts girls' skirts, capes, and accessories.

Interesting Fact: The real "Bold Mary" is company founder Augusta McDonald, an actress, artist, and mom and the creative force behind all Bold Mary designs. The New Zealand native moved to Atlanta, Georgia, when her daughter Margaret was a baby.

How to Find: Ordering is typically done through the Web site; however, you may also call customer service to discuss sizing and obtain general information.

CALICO CLOSET

The company is based in the Spokane, Washington, area.
Telephone: 509-948-2529
Web site: www.calicocloset.com

Calico Closet handcrafts clothes for girls sizes 2T–10. Some of the more popular items include halter dresses, birthday and party dresses, tees, and skirts.

Interesting Fact: The founder of Calico Closet dreamed of designing clothing from the time she was a young girl. She would design clothing for her dolls and doodle away at sketches for hours on end. When her own children were born, she designed and made clothing for them that drew the attention of friends, neighbors, and even strangers. When her children were grown, she seized the opportunity to start her own business.

How to Find: The easiest way to find Calico Closet's collection is through its Web site, where you may buy on line. However, there are a growing number of retail locations. See the store locator.

CAT'S PAJAMAS®, THE ⊛ ↑

1285 66th Street, Emeryville, CA 94608
Telephone: 510-655-5554
Web site: www.thecatspjs.com

The Cat's Pajamas® manufactures pajamas, sleep shirts, capri sets, shorts, tank tops, and robes, in sizing appropriate for pre-teens and teens whose bodies have matured. *These pajamas are not sized for girls.*

Interesting Fact: The Cat's Pajamas was founded by two college friends, Lynn and Jenny. They decided very early on that their company would commit itself to the community, and, as a result, the company makes its products in the San Francisco area. The Cat's Pajamas is one of the last pajama manufacturers in America. The company has survived by developing a highly unique niche. It also doesn't hurt that some of the most popular television sitcoms created in the past decade have featured leading women wearing the company's pajamas.

How to Find: Please see the company Web site for its store locator, or you can order directly through the company Web site. Call customer service for assistance in finding the nearest retail outlet.

COTTON CABOODLE®

203 W. Thomas Street, Seattle, WA 98109
Telephone: 206-352-3763
No Web site

Cotton Caboodle® manufactures infant layettes and girls' clothing, including long- and short-sleeved crews, leggings, dresses, yoga pants, bloomers, and many other products.

Interesting Fact: Cotton Caboodle is a woman-founded company established nearly 25 years ago. The company dyes all of its fabrics in its own facility to ensure the quality of its colors as well as to make certain the environmental impact is minimal. It works with close to 40 different colors, with approximately 80 percent of the products made of pure cotton.

How to Find: Please note that the company does not have a Web site. Cotton Caboodle is sold in finer children's boutiques in virtually every major city of the United States, and a limited selection of products is available through online retailers. The public is also invited to shop in the company factory outlet, located in Seattle.

COW TRACK CREATIONS

5730 Nicasio Valley Road, Nicasio, CA 94946
Telephone: 415-662-2321
Web site: www.cowtrack.net

Cow Track Creations handcrafts children's wear, mainly for girls, from size 2 to size 6. Items include dresses and shirts. For babies, the company makes rompers and hats. All of the clothes are one of a kind and are made as the orders are received. The company will customize to your specifications. Limited production.

Interesting Fact: Liz Daniels, the owner of Cow Track Creations, is an organic gardener. Moms may appreciate her organically grown lavender-stuffed pillows.

How to Find: Customers can order directly through the Web site, or you may also call customer service to discuss sizing.

. . . .

IZA-BELLA ⊛ ↓

The company is located in the Atlanta, Georgia, area.
The company prefers e-mail.
Web site: www.iza-bella.com

Iza-bella handcrafts girls' clothing from approximately ages 12 months to 6 years. Products include coordinated tops and bottoms, shirts, tank tops, knit shirts, and dresses.

Interesting Fact: The founder of the company started her business prior to the birth of her daughter, and it just snowballed from that point.

How to Find: Orders may be placed directly through the Web site. Please e-mail the company should you have any questions.

. . . .

KAIYA EVE ™ COUTURE ⊛ ✂

1031 South Broadway, Los Angeles, CA 90015
Telephone: 213-749-3101
Web site: www.kaiyaeve.com

Kaiya Eve ™ Couture handcrafts products for girls, including petticoats and accessories in an array of colors such as rainbow, red, leopard, baby pink, white, turquoise, and black with hot-pink ruffles and choco-late with pink ruffles. The petticoats are machine washable. The company also offers a collection of Kaiya Eve Vintage Couture products. The ages range from toddler to school age.

Interesting Fact: Kaiya Eve ™ Couture is the inspiration of fashion designer Kandi Lightner, a woman who fell in love with vintage petti-coats. In the beginning, Kandi was able to make three little-girl petti-coats from each vintage garment she found in antique shops. The response to her designs was so positive that she was convinced she had the makings of a company. Kaiya Eve is best known for The Original Pettiskirt™, a reflection of the vintage one-of-kind clothing that Kandi is so well known for creating.

How to Find: There is a store locator on the Web site. If you don't have a computer, call customer service for the name of the nearest retail location.

LITTLE MASS ⊛ ↑ O

3435 S. Broadway, Los Angeles, CA 90003
Telephone: 800-977-9086
Web site: www.littlemass.com

Little Mass manufactures an extensive line of sophisticated European-type clothing styled for girls ranging in age from infants to early teen. The combined collection has more than 400 different styles. We recommend that you explore the Web site to get a better idea of the collections.

Interesting Fact: Although the company was founded in 1985 with women's clothing, it was not until 1997 that Little Mass launched its children's line. The clothes are said to offer children the details of European styling combined with a hip, trendy Hollywood style.

How to Find: Little Mass sells only through its many retail outlets. There is a store locator on the Web site. If you don't have a computer, please call the customer service number for the nearest retail outlet.

MALINA ⊛ ✈

3304 Pico Boulevard, Santa Monica, CA 90405
Telephone: 310-396-9782
Web site: www.malinas.com

Malina handcrafts clothing for toddlers and young girls. Please note that certain products in the Malina apparel line are imported. The products made in the United States include all of the cotton clothes, the dresses in the Argyle collection, and the dresses in the "White" collection.

Interesting Fact: A woman-owned company, Malina specializes in casual, comfortable clothing made of fine fabrics for young children.

How to Find: You may purchase Malina Clothing online through the Web site or call customer service for a retail store nearest to your location.

· ·

MATILDA & COMPANY™ ☺

7120 Owensmouth Avenue, Canoga Park, CA 91303
Telephone: 818-887-0070
Web site: www.matildaandcompany.com

Matilda & Company™ handcrafts girls' dresses, separates, gifts, and accessories as well as unique baby clothes. Many of the pieces contain elements of hand embroidery, retro prints, and patchwork. Sizes range from 0 to girls 8/9.

Interesting Fact: Paula Corely founded Matilda & Company™ in 1997. The company specializes in "reworking" clothing and accessories for children by incorporating vintage fabrics into the designs. Each hand-crafted article of clothing is unique and reflects the founder's career background in fashion and an even earlier interest in design that came from working in her grandparents' antique shop.

How to Find: Matilda & Company products may be found in more than 200 children's boutiques across the United States. Please see the Web site for a store locator, or call customer service for the name of the nearest retail outlet.

· ·

MEG DANA & COMPANY ✿

13455 Ventura Boulevard, Sherman Oaks, CA 91423
The company prefers e-mail.
Web site: www.megdana.com

Meg Dana & Company handcrafts a line of apparel for little preschool and school-age girls, including tutus, knits, hats, hair accessories, leg and back warmers, and lounge pants.

Interesting Fact: In 2000, Maggie Dana and her "company," which at that time consisted of her newborn Caylen and three-year-old Daniel, set out to design a collection of clothing and accessories. Maggie was trained as a fashion designer and, at the same time, had always nurtured a love of nature. She wanted to evoke the same feelings with her clothing that flowers have always brought to her sense of color and beauty.

How to Find: Please go to the Web site for a listing of retailers that carry the Meg Dana line. You may also e-mail the company to find the nearest retail locations.

MODEST APPAREL, INC. ✿ ↑
122 Airport Road, Buffalo, MO 65622
Telephone: 866-269-0907
Web site: www.modestapparelusa.com

Modest Apparel, Inc. produces jumpers, skirts, culottes, nightgowns, vests, tops, and undergarments for girls from preschool age to teenage and older.

Interesting Fact: The philosophy behind Modest Apparel is, as its name implies, to manufacture and sell clothing that is much more modest and tasteful than many of the clothes in today's market for girls and young women. After the patterns are cut in the factory, the company utilizes the talents of home sewers within the community to complete the garment. By utilizing home sewers, the company is able to both tightly control quality and support the community.

How to Find: Please order through the company Web site. If you need more information or lack a computer, please call customer service for assistance.

MY VINTAGE BABY® ✿
403 Powerhouse Street, McKinney, TX 75701
Telephone: 972-548-9850
Web site: www.myvintagebaby.com

My Vintage Baby® handcrafts two collections for girls ranging from infants to girls' size 14. The first couture line, Collections by Jessica, reflects a unique, one-of-a-kind look by employing embellishments to create a vintage look. The second line, Leopard Daisy, reflects a different vision, that of a more glitzy, new look. The collections include dresses, skirts, and tops.

Interesting Fact: The company was founded in 2001 by Jessica Wiswall. Jessica had been in the corporate world for many years, but her passion had always been designing. After the birth of her daughter, Jessica began to pursue her dream, making her dining room into a workshop, then moving to her friend (and associate) Lisa's garage. She would take basic children's clothes and add unexpected and fun details. Her vision caught on quickly, The company has grown considerably since that time, with new corporate offices, sales teams, and two showrooms.

How to Find: My Vintage Baby collections are in more than 600 stores nationwide. There is a store locator on the Web site. If you don't have a computer, call customer service for help in finding the nearest retail store.

NEIGE CLOTHING ✿ ✈
The company is located in southern California.
Telephone: 714-558-7751
Web site: www.neigeclothing.com

Neige Clothing manufactures girls' clothing, including dresses, separates, skirts, and dress-up jackets. A few items in the line may be imported; however, almost everything is manufactured in the United States. The size range of the product line goes from 18 months to 'tweens.

Interesting Fact: Adrienne and Cornel, a husband-and-wife management team, founded Neige Clothing in 2003. A graduate of the Parsons School of Design, for many years Adrienne was an assistant designer to Vera Wang. With the Neige line, Adrienne and Cornel have gone about creating a sophisticated and fashionable clothes line that Cornel describes as "timeless." The clothes are designed to be handed down from sister to sister and niece to niece thanks to their durability and nonfaddish nature.

How to Find: Neige is distributed in finer clothing stores and boutiques, as well as through online stores. Customers may also order directly through the Neige Web site.

. . . .

PERI PONCHOS ✿

3436 SE Kelly Street, Portland, OR 97202
Telephone: 503-235-5313
Web site: www.periponchos.com

Peri Ponchos manufactures a wide variety of ponchos for girls in four different sizes.

Interesting Fact: The business started in 2002, shortly after "Peri" hand-sewed a poncho for her little girl. Soon everyone in the neighborhood wanted a poncho.

How to Find: Peri Ponchos are available in several online stores; type "Peri Ponchos" into a search engine. The ponchos are also available at a select number of retailers and directly through the Web site.

. . . .

SPANX® BY SARA BLAKELY® ✿ ↑

3391 Peachtree Road, Atlanta, GA 30326
Telephone: 888-806-7311
Web site: www.spanx.com

Spanx® by Sara Blakely® manufactures body-shaping underwear appropriate for preteen and teen girls and includes slimming apparel, bras and panties, camis, hosiery, tights, and socks.

Interesting Fact: Sara Blakely, the founder of Spanx®, had the courage to develop unique clothing despite many obstacles. Her biggest obtacle was in getting suppliers to believe in her dream. In time, Sara not only launched a very successful manufacturing company but helped to reshape the landscape of fashion in this country. She is an excellent example of the American entrpreneurial spirit. Her story has been told on numerous television shows and in print. It is worth it to go to the Spanx® Web site just to read about her.

How to Find: You may purchase Spanx products through the company Web site, by searching its store locator, or by calling customer care using the toll-free telephone number.

. . . .

SWEET BLOSSOM BOUTIQUE ✿ ✂

P.O. Box 100283, Denver, CO 80250
Telephone: 303-717-8668
Web site: www.sweetblossomboutique.com

Sweet Blossom Boutique handcrafts girls' dresses from size 2T to size 8, as well as fun "tooth fairy" pillows. The company also makes baby blankets. The line is constantly evolving to stay fresh and interesting. The company can customize.

Interesting Fact: Laura Mellberg credits her interest in sewing to the men in her family. When Laura was a child, she was surrounded by sewing machines, as the family business was selling them! Laura likes the idea of having her Web site serve as a platform for other moms to present their handmade products, as well. She is very supportive of women who are staying at home to not only raise families but also to develop home-based manufacturing ventures.

How to Find: Orders may be placed online directly through the Web site. Please e-mail or call with questions about customized items.

Girls' Jewelry and Hair Accessories

There are many companies in America that make jewelry collections for women and men but relatively few American manufacturing companies that design jewelry and hair accessories for little girls; most collections are imported or are very cheap pieces of costume jewelry that are also imported. Please see the complete company listing for jewelry manufacturers and hair accessories in the product index E, under Childrens Products: Jewelry for children and moms and Children's Products: Clothing mainly for girls and girls' hair accessories.

. . . .

LA PETITE FEE™/NSTYLE DESIGNS ❀ ↑ ✂

P.O. Box 7654, Gurnee, IL 60031
Telephone: 866-967-8953
Web site: www.nstyledesigns.com

La Petite Fee™/Nstyle Designs handcrafts a line of jewelry specifically for children under the La Petite Fee™ collection. Items include bracelets, necklaces, and earrings. The high-quality jewelry features sterling silver and breakaway clasps for safety. Each piece is handcrafted in the

USA and made with the help of stay-at-home mothers. The company will custonize.

Interesting Fact: Nancy Gissendaner and her husband, Dan, are the founders of NStyle Designs. As their adult jewelry began to grow in popularity, they received more requests for girls' jewelry. In 2006, they launched the La Petite Fee™ line for girls, which matches the line for moms. They have also introduced the Teen Bling™ jewelry line for girls in middle school and high school.

How to Find: Customers can order online directly through the company Web site, or customers can call the customer service number.

LITTLE GEMS JEWELRY ⊛ ↑
The company is based in the East Bay Area of California.
Telephone: 925-914-2229
Web site: www.littlegemsonline.com

Little Gems Jewelry handcrafts jewelry for girls. According to the company, some of the sterling silver components and some beads may not be made in the United States. However, each piece of jewelry is hand-strung in California. The items in the line include children's necklaces with magnetic clasps to allow for easy dressing. Jewelry contains small pieces and is not suitable for toddlers and preschool children.

Interesting Fact: Karen Blum Boateng, the founder of Little Gems, creates jewelry for new moms. The jewelry for new mothers is called Mothering Rocks, and the crystals are said to bring healing energy for mind, body, and soul. The crystals used are from sustainable sources and are natural and nondyed to ensure that babies who play with mom's necklace will be safe. Mothering Rocks necklaces are made extra-strong to prevent baby's curiosity from breaking the necklaces.

How to Find: Orders may be placed online through the Little Gems Web site.

WEE ONES, INC. ⊛ ↑
33 Cherokee Drive, St. Peters, MO 63376
Telephone: 800-258-9996
Web site: www.weeones.com

115

Wee Ones, Inc. manufactures the following products in the USA: fashion and trend hair accessories, regular hair accessories, pacifier clips, belts, flip-flops, and infant baby caps for toddlers, preschoolers, and older kids. Other products may be imported.

Interesting Fact: Founded in 1973 by the current CEO's mother, Wee Ones™ is one of the leading companies in the nation providing hair accessories for little girls. More than 100 people work out of the St. Peters, Missouri, manufacturing facility to produce hair clips, head-bands, bows, and other accessories.

How to Find: There is a store locator on the Web site, or you may order online. If you don't have a computer or want assistance, call the customer service number.

Mostly for Boys

At the present time, there are relatively few American manufacturing companies that specialize in clothing for boys. However, to judge from the interviews for this book, we anticipate that in the future there will be a growing interest in the manufacture of American-made boys' clothing. The companies we do feature have an excellent selection, and their products range from fun to serious designer clothes. Please refer to the next section in this chapter, "For Boys & Girls," where we list more companies that may meet your needs.

. . . .

CAPITOL CLOTHING CORPORATION ↓
578 NW 27th Street, Miami, FL 33127
Telephone: 800-929-7504
Web site: www.capitolclothingcorp.com

Capitol Clothing Corporation manufactures coordinated two-piece fashion-trend boys outfits in the latest styles and a novelty group line that features unique kids' uniforms such as Safari, Police, and Race Car Driver. The age range of the Capitol Clothing line runs from infant through school age and older.

Interesting Fact: Founded in 1988 by an ex-banker who followed his father's footsteps into the clothing business, Capitol Clothing has been manufacturing unique boys coordinated sets and play uniforms under the brands Little Baron® and Capitol Boys®. The company's original intention was to manufacture overseas, but it was so disappointed with the quality it was getting that it made the commitment to manufacture its entire line in the USA.

How to Find: Orders may be placed through the Web site or by contacting the company through its customer service number.

CITY THREADS™, INC. ⊛
719 S. Los Angeles Street, Los Angeles, CA 90014
Telephone: 213-612-3710
Web site: www.citythreads.com

City Threads™, Inc. manufactures boys' tees, shorts, pants, hoodies, tank tops, and accessories for toddlers to preschool age. The company has just introduced swimwear to its clothing collection.

Interesting Fact: Shayna and her husband started City Threads shortly after the birth of their child. What makes the collection somewhat unusual is that 95 percent of the line is made for boys. They are committed to manufacturing in America as they feel they can better follow the step-by-step progress of each piece and maintain a high degree of control. They described the process as "wanting to touch the fabric many times" until completion.

How to Find: Customers are invited to call or e-mail City Threads for the nearest retail location, or they may order directly from the company through the City Threads Web site.

DIAMOND GUSSET JEANS, INC.
10296 Highway 46, Bon Aqua, TN 37025
Telephone: 888-848-7738
Web site: www.gussetclothing.com

Diamond Gusset Jeans, Inc. manufactures a selection of "husky" boys jeans in sizes 31–37.

Interesting Fact: Established more than 20 years ago, the Diamond Gusset® Brand has a unique gusseted front that is said to give greater comfort.

How to Find: You may order online directly through the Web site or by calling customer service.

....

JOSEPH ABBOUD™ ↑

650 Fifth Avenue, New York, NY 10019
Telephone: 212-586-9140
Web site: www.josephabboud.com

Joseph Abboud™ manufactures the Joseph Abboud boys' line of clothing, which includes suits, sport coats, outerwear, shirts, and ties.

Interesting Fact: Founded in 1987, with offices in New York City and manufacturing facilities in Massachusetts, Joseph Abboud™ is one of the last of the great American men's apparel manufacturers.

How to Find: The Joseph Abboud Web site has a very detailed store locator for the location of stores carrying both the boys' and men's lines.

....

WONDERBOY®, INC. ⚽ ✈

251 Queen Street, Philadelphia, PA 19147
Telephone: 215-462-1177
Web site: www.wonderboyclothing.com

Wonderboy®, **Inc.** produces woven and knit shirts, sweatshirts, and jackets for boys from 6 months to 10 years of age. Pants may be imported.

Interesting Fact: The founder of Wonderboy® is a graphic designer by trade. She is especially interested in the print aspects of the products she creates.

How to Find: Please see the Web site for a very detailed store locator. If you don't have a computer, please call the company for the nearest retail location.

For Boys and Girls

What is interesting about this part of the chapter is that these manufacturers continue to show us that parents can still buy quality American-made clothing products for their children, including jeans, swimwear and outerwear, tees, sweatshirts, and pants. It is good to know that we still have a choice. Many companies are producing in organic as well as nonorganic fabrics, and some companies are happy to customize. Please note that this chapter does not contain companies that make sporting goods. Sporting goods manufacturers are found in Chapter 6, "American-Made Sports and Fitness Equipment."

A WISH COME TRUE ⊛
2522 Pearl Buck Road, Bristol, PA 19007
Telephone: 215-781-2000
Web site: www.awishcometrue.com

A Wish Come True manufactures the "Dress Up" and dancewear products. The collection includes costumes for boys and girls, dresses and tutus for girls, and dancewear for boys, along with totes and accessories.

Interesting Fact: This manufacturer sells its dancewear only through dance studios or online catalogs, but it doesn't sell dancewear directly to the public. However, the "Dress Up" line can be purchased through the Web site.

How to Find: Please do an online search for the dancewear, or contact your local dance studio.

AMERICAN APPAREL® ☺ ↑
747 Warehouse Street, Los Angeles, CA 90021
Telephone: 213-488-0226
Web site: www.americanapparel.net

American Apparel® manufactures an extensive line of products for infants, toddlers, school-age children, and up. Children's products include hoodies, cardigans, tank tops, tees, and pants. Infant products include snappies, fleece pants, tee shirts, and hats. The company manufactures both in organic and nonorganic fabrics.

Interesting Fact: Based in Los Angeles, American Apparel is a publicly traded company. What makes it unique is that it is vertically integrated. Vertical integration means that the manufacturing process, from raw fabric to finished goods, happens in-house.

How to Find: You may order American Apparel® products online directly through its Web site or by calling the customer service number. You can also find its products in American Apparel retail locations around the country.

....

AMERICAN JOE™ AUTHENTIC AMERICAN APPAREL ↓
P.O. Box 942111, Plano, TX 75094
The company prefers e-mail.
Web site: www.americanjoeapparel.com

American Joe™ Authentic American Apparel manufactures casual wear for ages newborn through adult. For boys and girls, the company makes backpacks, tees, sweatshirts, shorts, and jeans. American Joe™ Authentic American Apparel will be introducing organic cotton clothing in 2009.

Interesting Fact: The inspiration for American Joe® came about one day as Nan Moon, the founder of American Joe™, was sorting her son's laundry. She looked at the labels of 15 different tee shirts and was shocked to see that, with the exception of a very old shirt, all the other tee shirts were imported. She decided to see if it was possible to create a company where everything was 100 percent American made. Nan interested her daughter, Dena, in the project, and American Joe Authentic American Apparel was born.

How to Find: Orders may be placed directly through the Web site, or you may call customer service for more complete information.

....

BAHAMA BOB'S APPAREL ✿ ↓
P.O. Box 564, Crossville, TN 38557
Telephone: 865-603-0861
Web site: www.bahamabobsapparel.com

Bahama Bob's Apparel produces Hawaiian-style shirts for boys and girls and baby outfits featuring motorcycles against beach and palm tree designs.

Interesting Fact: The company's story is great fun to read and also typical of the new American manufacturing spirit. Bob and his wife were well known as handcrafters of motorcycle shirts. Not long ago, they went on a vacation to Hawaii and fell head over heels for Hawaiian designs. They began to create unique Hawaiian cycle shirts and sold them at motorcycle rallies, where everyone wanted more. This led to the creation of a new online store, and Bahama Bob's was born!

How to Find: You may order online directly through the Web site. If you don't have a computer or need additional assistance, please call customer service.

BAILEY BOYS, THE, INC.

373 Skylane Road, St. Simons, GA 31522
Telephone: 912-638-3311
Web site: www.baileyboys.com

The Bailey Boys, Inc. produces collections for children from infants size 0 to boys' size 7 and girls' size 10. The clothing may be described as being classically designed, with tried and true designs. The collections break down into Bailey Boys™, Bailey Basics™, and the more upscale Chabre™ product lines. The collections include swimwear, shirts, separates, bloomers, dresses, outerwear, and hats. Baby products include diaper bags, gowns, snappies, hats, and blankets.

Interesting Fact: As a little girl, Diane Bailey spent hours and hours drawing, designing, and creating clothing. As she grew older, and even when in college, Diane would design and sew clothes for herself. After marriage, the young mother found it difficult to find clothes to properly fit her two young boys. She again began designing. In 1987, with a one-room operation and five sewing machines, the company was born. As of this date, Diane's clothing may be found in more than 700 retail stores.

How to Find: The Bailey Boys™ has a store locator on its Web site, or customers may call customer service. If you are in the Saint Simons, Georgia, area, the company invites you to visit its factory store.

BERCOT CHILDREN'S WEAR
2301 Fairfield Avenue, Ft. Wayne, IN 46807
The company prefers e-mail.
Web site: www.bercotchildrenswear.com

Bercot Children's Wear handcrafts two collections of clothes for newborn girls to girls' size 10 and for newborn boys to boys' size 7. For girls, items include dresses, leggings, shirts, and jumpers. For boys, items include shirts and pants, rompers, and hats.

Interesting Fact: Though the company has a French-sounding name, Kristine Bercot describes her Indiana-based design studio as offering a whimsical selection of children's clothing for people who appreciate artful things but who also seek traditional designs based on classic, midwestern needle art skills.

How to Find: You may order online directly through the Web site. If you don't have a computer or need additional assistance, please call customer service.

BITTY BRAILLE ✿ ↑ ★
The company is located in upstate New York.
The company prefers e-mail.
Web site: www.bittybraille.com

Bitty Braille handcrafts tee shirts for infants and toddlers, with names inscribed in braille, along with birthstone charms and braille alphabet tiles.

Interesting Fact: A project taken on by an artist named Julie, Bitty Braille honors those who are sight challenged by creating a unique line of products in braille.

How to find: Orders may be placed directly with the company through its Web site or by calling customer service.

BLACK MOUNTAIN APPAREL™
7031 49th Street, Pinellas Park, FL 33781
Telephone: 727-527-5310
Web site: www.blackmountainapparel.com

Black Mountain Apparel™ manufactures children's fleece jackets and fleece baby jumpers in several exclusive designs and fabrics.

Interesting Fact: Established 17 years ago, Black Mountain Apparel™ is a manufacturer of fleece clothing and accessories.

How to Find: You may order through the Web site, or, if you don't have a computer, call customer service for more information about the product line.

....

BUDDY'S JEANS® ⚙ ↑

306B Franklin Street, New Hebron, MS 39140
Telephone: 877-275-4283
Web site: www.buddysjeans.com

Buddy's Jeans® manufactures jeans in many different colors and styles for boys and girls. The jeans are made of 14-ounce denim and are triple stitched for durability. The denim material used in these products is made in America.

Interesting Fact: Buddy Steverson was in the manufacturing business for 39 years, and, during that time, he sold thousands of his company's jeans all over the world. A cowboy by original vocation, Buddy personally tested the jeans on his ranch. When Buddy decided to retire, he couldn't find family members to take over, and the business was shut down. Jane Little, a lifelong friend of Buddy Steverson, approached the former owner about the possibility of reopening the company. Buddy told her that all that was left were the trademarks and patterns. She decided to take a chance. The company is now producing American-made jeans.

How to Find: Customers may order online directly through the Web site or by calling customer service.

....

CHUCK ROAST, INC. ☺ ↑

P.O. Box 2080, Conway, NH 03818
Telephone: 800-553-1654
Web site: www.chuckroast.com

Chuck Roast, Inc. manufactures outdoor clothing for infants to children's size 14. For infants and toddlers, Chuck Roast makes fleece bunting for babies age 0 to 18 months. The company also makes full zipper jackets, pants, hats, and mittens.

Interesting Fact: Chuck Roast has a deep commitment to the environment. The company is switching all of its apparel production to using post industrial recycled fleece. The process recaptures waste fibers from manufacturing to make new material. The Web site has an interesting section on the environmental benefits of this technology.

How to Find: Customers may order through the Web site, or, if they don't have a computer, they can call customer service for more information about the product line.

COLUMBIA KNIT, INC. ↑
5200 Southeast Haney Drive, Portland, OR 97206
Telephone: 800-889-KNIT
Web site: www.columbiaknit.com

Columbia Knit® manufactures knitwear for toddlers through teens and for both boys and girls. For toddlers, the company offers knit rompers, coveralls, overalls, and microfleece sets. For older children, Columbia Knit® manufactures turtlenecks, mock turtlenecks, knit hats, rugby shirts, and other shirts in different weaves, as well as girls' French terry cotton shirts.

Interesting Fact: The Columbia Knit company has been in business since 1921. The Web site has a kids' sizing chart for your convenience. Please remember that all of the cotton is preshrunk.

How to Find: Although the company has limited retail outlets, you may order online or by calling customer service.

CRIB ROCK® COUTURE ✿ ☺
31129 Via Colinas, Westlake Village, CA 91361
The company prefers e-mail.
Web site: www.cribrockcouture.com

Crib Rock® **Couture** manufactures children's tees, snappies, thermals, raglans, and pants for both boys and girls. Sizes range from 0 to kids' size 14. All Crib Rock clothing is pima or supima cotton and is made entirely in the USA. The brand has recently expanded to include nursery and room décor.

Interesting Fact: In 2004, Crib Rock® founder and CEO Tracy Bobbitt launched Crib Rock with "rock concert tees" that reimagine classic nursery rhyme characters as pop, rock, and hip-hop stars on tour. The line expanded with the nursery rhyme theme and caught the attention of Hollywood. The Crib Rock brand quickly gained popularity with the tots of the Hollywood elite, and children of some of the biggest names have appeared in the tabloids wearing Crib Rock outfits.

How to Find: The Web site has a listing of online retailers, and there is also a brick-and-mortar store locator. Customers may also order directly through the company Web site.

....

FAIRY FINERY™ ❀ ♯
224 Burntside Drive, Golden Valley, MN 55422
Telephone: 888-377-4511
Web site: www.fairyfinery.com

Fairy Finery™ handcrafts imagination play clothing for girls and boys, including capes, hats, dresses, and skirts, as well as accessories. All of the products, including the accessories, are made in Minnesota.

Interesting Fact: Susan Berns, the mother of two grown children and founder of Fairy Finery™, has always been an entrepreneur. Her interest in creating unique "pretend clothes" came after her daughter received an outfit as a present that was poorly made and "inappropriate." Susan created a business that would make quality playclothes that could stand the test of time but also awaken children's imaginations. The products in the collection appeal to children's fantasies and sense of fun. She likes to see the amazement on children's faces when they wear her clothes.

How to Find: Customers may order through the Web site or call for the nearest store location. The studio welcomes visitors in limited numbers. You must call for an appointment.

....

FOCOLOCO ❀ ☺
504 Church Street, North Adams, MA 01247
Telephone: 413-652-1814
Web site: www.focoloco.com

Focoloco produces uniquely designed tees imprinted on American-made organic cotton. Garments are hand dyed locally so that the company can make sure that the process is done responsibly. It even uses 100% recycled, postconsumer paper for all printed materials.

Interesting Fact: Suzy Helme, founder of Focoloco, is an artist and a businesswoman. She started the business thinking it would be an easy way for her to work from home and to take care of her son. To Suzy, her business is a juggling act but one that she deeply loves.

How to Find: You may order online directly through the Web site or by consulting the retail store locator.

GARDEN KIDS™   ↑

The company is located in the Willamette Valley area of Oregon.
Telephone: 714-253-3467
Web site: www.gardenkidsclothing.com

Garden Kids™ manufactures clothing that is sewn by American career seamstresses. The company is known for its high-quality original designs. It makes organic clothing for girls and boys from newborn to 10 years old. However, it also offers pajamas and some shirts and tops for up to age 14. Because of the high demand for organic yarn, the company may import yarn for weaving.

Interesting Fact: The founder of Garden Kids started the company in 1994 by accident. She sewed clothes decorated with garden-themed patches for her children, and everyone stopped her and wanted to know where she had bought the clothes. Garden Kids Clothing is striving to keep its products U.S.-made. Its yarns are knitted and dyed in the traditional textile area of the southeastern United States. It is doing this because it realizes that this is an area that has been hard hit by foreign competition.

How to Find: Garden Kids sales are almost exclusively done through the Web site. There is a small but growing representation of the line in retail and in online stores.

IMAGINATION CREATIONS® ❀

500 Commerce Way W, Jupiter, FL 33458
Telephone: 800-390-9945
Web site: www.imaginationcreationsinc.com

Imagination Creations® produces "enchanted children's" dress-up costumes, accessories, swimwear, dancewear, and other costumes for boys and girls. The age range generally runs from toddler to school age and beyond.

Interesting Fact: A South Florida company, Imagination Creations specializes in costumes, swimwear, and dancewear for children.

How to Find: You may order online through the company Web site, or call customer service for more information.

··

JEN JEN KIDS ⚽ ↓
4174 Sorrento Valley Boulevard, San Diego, CA 92121
Telephone: 858-824-1700
Web site: www.jenjenkids.com

Jen Jen Kids manufactures everyday activewear for girls from age 6 months to 8 years of age. The product line is extensive. For infants, the collection includes bibs and blankets. For girls, Jen Jen Kids offers dresses, tank tops, jackets, pants, skorts, shorts, and purses. The collection also includes shirts for preschool and school-age boys.

Interesting Fact: Founded by two women in 1999, San Diego–based Jen Jen started as a bib and purse manufacturer but quickly expanded its apparel line in 2002 after the very positive reception it received at its first trade show.

How to Find: Jen Jen Kids is widely sold in specialty boutiques across the United States. For the name of the store nearest you, please e-mail or call the customer service number.

··

JOHNSON WOOLEN MILLS® ⚽ ☺ ↑ T
P.O. Box 612, Johnson, VT 05656
Telephone: 877-635-WOOL
Web site: www.johnsonwoolenmills.com

Johnson Woolen Mills® manufactures wool coats, capes, shirts, mittens, and pants in children's sizes 4 through 18 that match the classic clothing for moms and dads.

Interesting Fact: An American manufacturing treasure, Johnson Woolen Mills® has been in existence since 1842, when local farmers would bring their wool to the mill to see it woven into cloth. Now in its fourth generation, the company has survived by making classic rugged woolen outerwear for the entire family, in the same tradition as the clothing it made nearly 20 years before the Civil War.

How to Find: Customers can order directly through the company Web site or can call customer service for a catalog or a nearby store location. Customers are also welcome to visit the company store in Vermont.

KLU™ MOUNTAIN OUTERWEAR ✿ ↑ ✂

3735 Michelle, Idaho Falls, ID 83401
Telephone: 208-524-6180
Web site: www.getaklu.com

Klu™ Mountain Outerwear handcrafts outerwear for children from infants through toddler and in preteen and teen sizes. Products include some of the most amazing hats you've ever seen, along with socks, mittens, buntings, and bonnets. Please note that the company does not keep inventory but makes items when the orders are received. Shipping generally occurs a day after the order is received. Custom orders are accepted.

Interesting Fact: To understand Klu™ Mountain Outerwear, it is important to understand the love that Kevin and Sheila Keefe, the founders of this company, have for the outdoors. Unable to afford a lot of fancy outerwear, the family had no choice but to learn to sew. As they perfected their craft, their designs began to take on a unique style and even humor. They started showing the products at crafts fairs, and soon they were in the outerwear business.

How to Find: Orders for Klu Mountain Outerwear are placed directly through the Web site.

L.C. KING MANUFACTURING ↑

P.O. Box 367, Bristol, TN 37621
Telephone: 800-826-2510
Web site: www.pointerbrand.com

L.C. King Manufacturing manufactures children's jeans, overalls, short-alls, and shorts ranging in children's sizes 2–16.

Interesting Fact: Pointer Brand Everywear® Jeans was started in 1913 and is known for its durable and rugged designs. It is a true American family manufacturing company and has been under continuous family supervision for four generations.

How to Find: Customers may order online directly through the Web site. If you don't have a computer or need additional assistance, please call customer service.

LITTLE CAPERS, INC. ✿

The company is based in the Los Angeles, California, area.
Telephone: 818-785-7887
Web site: www.littlecapers.com

Little Capers, Inc. manufactures long- and short-sleeved tees, along with attachable/detachable capes. The graphics cover a range of Earth-friendly themes. Little Capers™ offers clothing in sizes 2, 4, 6, and 8, for both boys and girls.

Interesting Fact: Little Capers™ was born following the observations of founder Jossamber Shapiro that her young son had become obsessed with being a superhero. He wanted to wear his "towel cape" every-where. While the mom enjoyed the fact that her son was developing a rich fantasy life, she didn't like all of the violence and commercialism that went along with many of the established heroes. She began to pursue concepts that were more positive and less exploitive of young children.

How to Find: There is a store locator on the Web site, or, if a customer prefers, orders may be placed directly through the Web site.

MOUNTAIN SPROUTS® ✿ ☺ ✈

542 Main Street, Grand Junction, CO 81501
Telephone: 866-686-7778
Web site: www.mountainsprouts.com

Mountain Sprouts® manufactures outerwear in a range from 0–24 months and children's sizes 2–8 for both boys and girls. Two main collections are made in the USA: the Sky Series, consisting of light-weight, soft-shell outerwear, and recycled fleece outerwear, which has long been the mainstay of the company. Please note that the Web site indicates which products were made in the USA. Other products are imported.

Interesting Fact: In 2000, in Grand Junction, Colorado, sisters Jen, Julie, and Penny Rieke started a manufacturing company that chose to specialize in children's outerwear.

How to Find: Mountain Sprouts has a store locator on its Web site, or you may purchase online directly through the company Web site. Customers are encouraged to call customer service for assistance.

MOUSEWORKS, THE ☺ ↑
4646 Buddy's Place Lane, Earlysville, VA 22936
Telephone: 434-973-6032
Web site: www.themouseworks.com

The Mouseworks handcrafts baby and toddler hats from fleece and also makes fleece hats for adults. The company can customize. Limited production.

Interesting Fact: The Mouseworks uses scraps of fleece left over by the big companies in order to make their unique hats and clothes for children. While the fabric used is new, it has all been "saved" from being discarded. Ryan Williamson, the owner of the company, has a strong commitment to the environment. He is most proud of the fact that his company produced only one garbage bag of production trash during the past year.

How to Find: You may order through the Web site, or, if you don't have a computer, call customer service for more information about the product line.

MY GREEN CLOSET ✿ ☺
640 Windemere Curve, Plymouth, MN 55441
Telephone: 612-396-9025
Web site: www.mygreencloset.com

My Green Closet produces kidswear made of organic fabrics for toddlers through school age, sizing 2T to children's size 6. The clothing selection includes girls' tops, bottoms, and dresses and boys' tops and bottoms.

Interesting Fact: The founders of the company were confused about where they should go with their careers. The couple always bought organic foods for health purposes, and the foods led to an interest in organic farming, which ultimately led to a curiosity about organic fabrics and green manufacturing. They started to design clothes made from organic fabric. They use local labor to produce their clothes so that the products don't have to be shipped long distances in containers.

How to Find: Customers may order online directly through the Web site or can call the customer service number.

NEWBERRY KNITTING ✿
1420 Curry Road, Schenectady, NY 12306
Telephone: 518-355-1630
Web site: www.newberryknitting.com

Newberry Knitting manufactures leg warmers, mittens, and gloves for children from toddlers to teens.

Interesting Fact: Started in 1946, Newberry Knitting is one of the few glove manufacturers still producing products in the United States.

How to Find: You may order through the Web site, or, if you don't have a computer, call customer service for more information about the product line.

ORIGINAL FLAP HAPPY®, THE ✿ O
2330 Michigan Avenue, Santa Monica, CA 90404
Telephone: 310-453-3527
Web site: www.flaphappy.com

The Original Flap Happy® manufactures hats, swimwear, tees, pants, shorts, dresses, and skirts.

Interesting Fact: The Original Flap Happy® is a southern California–based company specializing in children's clothes. Sizes range from infant size 0 to size 14. The company gets its name from its sun hats that are made with flaps.

How to Find: Flap Happy does not sell directly to the public; its sales are made to retailers. If you can't find a retail store in your area, please call the company for assistance.

....

PATSY AIKEN DESIGNS ✿ ✈
4812 Hargrove Road, Raleigh, NC 27616
Telephone: 919-872-8789
Web site: www.chezami.com

Patsy Aiken Designs manufactures children's wear in an extensive home-party line, from infant size 0 to children's size 16. For girls, the company makes swimwear, dresses, tops, skirts, tees, pants, and accessories. For boys, the collections include swimwear, tees, shorts, two-piece outfits, and hats. Some knits are imported, but most of the product line is made in North Carolina.

Interesting Fact: Founded in 1979, Patsy Aiken started her business by selling her designs to boutiques in Coronado, California, when her husband, Joel, was stationed there while in the navy. Friends and neighbors helped her sew, and her children served as models and quality testers. All of this activity took place in a small room over the Aikens' garage. Two years later, her husband joined the fledgling company.

How to Find: The company's children's products are sold through home parties, or you may purchase the clothing directly through the Web site. Please contact the company if you need more information.

....

POLKA DOT MARKET ✿ ↑ ✂
The company is based in Nashville, Tennessee.
Telephone: 615-537-2623
Web site: www.polka-dot-market.com

Polka Dot Market manufactures "Big Initial" tee shirts for boys and girls, as well as girls' dresses, skirts, and tutus. The company also makes aprons for boys and girls and totes for moms. Everything in the boutique line is sewn in Nashville. The company can customize large orders.

Interesting Fact: Sally is in love with polka dots! She established her company in 2004, just after she had her second baby. Polka Dot Market's products are designed to have a bright, preppy, and simple look.

How to Find: You may purchase Polka Dot Market clothing directly through the Web site or by calling the customer service number.

- -

ROBIN'S HOODS™ BY NATURE & DESIGN ✿ ✂ ↑

41 Barrows Lane, Eden Mills, VT 05653
Telephone: 802-279-0137
Web site: www.robinshoods.com

Robin's Hoods™ by Nature & Design handcrafts unique children's hats constructed of felt. The sizes range from about 3 months to teenagers. Nature & Design also makes hats for women. The company can customize. Limited production.

Interesting Fact: Robin LaMonda had been designing and crafting felt hats since she discovered the art as a teenager. Later in life, she was motivated to rediscover her hat-making passion thanks to her twin boys, who would not keep a knit hat on their heads even on a subzero, windy Vermont winter day.

How to Find: The best way to order Robin's Hoods™ felt hats is through the Web site. In 2009, the company will be expanding its retail distribution. Please see the store locator on the Web site.

- -

ROUND BELLY CLOTHING ✿ ☺ ✈

5250 24th Street SW, Pine River, MN 56474
Telephone: 218-851-2133
Web site: www.roundbelly.com

Round Belly Clothing produces children's clothing made of organic cotton. Size range is from children's size 2 to size 12. Girls' clothing includes dresses and skirts, and boys' clothing includes pants and shorts. For babies, the company makes snappies, separates, dresses, bibs, hats, diapers, bedding, and blanket bags. All products are made in the USA except the organic knit sweaters. The sweaters are imported from Germany.

Interesting Fact: The company started by producing maternity clothes, largely inspired by the founder's pregnancy. However, a great deal changed when the founder learned that her son was diagnosed with autism. The family radically changed their fast-food diet and became involved with organics. Hence, the Round Belly line for little kids, called Eco-sprouts, carries only clothing made from organic fabric.

How to Find: Customers may purchase Round Belly Clothing directly through the Web site. There is limited retail distribution. Please call customer service if you need assistance.

· ·

ROUND HOUSE™ MANUFACTURING CO.   T
1 American Way, Shawnee, OK 74804
Telephone: 405-273-0510
Web site: www.round-house.com

Round House Manufacturing Co. manufacturers Round House™ bib overalls for toddlers and school-age and older children, both boys and girls. Styles include Classic denim, Stonewashed, Engineer, Camouflage, and Carpenter variations.

Interesting Fact: Shawnee, Oklahoma, was well established as a major railroad center by 1902. The Rock Island Railroad and the Choctaw Railroad had both established roundhouses in the region. In 1903, the Shawnee Garment Manufacturing Company was established, and, as a result, more than 100 employees started making denim bib overalls for the Choctaw Railroad workers. By 1910, Round House had moved to larger facilities; it did so again in 1995. The company is Oklahoma's oldest continuously running manufacturer, and we have designated it an American manufacturing treasure.

How to Find: The Round House™ Web site has a store locator, or you may order online or, if you prefer, call the customer service number for assistance.

· ·

SASSY SCRUBS®   ❀ ✂
1 Keuka Business Park, Penn Yan, NY 14527
The company prefers e-mail.
Web site: www.sassyscrubs.com

Sassy Scrubs® produces a wide variety of colorful and fun scrubs for kids ranging from size 2T through sizes 8–10. In addition to scrubs, the company also makes aprons and men's ties in fabrics that can match the scrubs worn around the office. The company can customize.

Interesting Fact: Karen Bradley, the founder of Sassy Scrubs®, once worked in the nursing agency field. She saw that the scrubs worn in most hospital and nursing home settings were dull, boring, and perhaps a bit formidable. The company enables professionals to design the scrubs. Spurred on by customers and by her own children, Karen decided to make scrubs for kids for play, and they were a big hit. The company is committed to international relief and actively supports orphanages in China.

How to Find: Customers normally purchase scrubs through the Sassy Scrubs Web site. However, there is no stock inventory of children's scrubs, and each set must be custom designed.

SOS FROM TEXAS ☺ ↑

Box 767, Samnorwood, TX 79077
Telephone: 800-245-2339
Web site: www.sosfromtexas.com

SOS from Texas manufactures the following items for boys and girls from cotton grown in the company's fields: short- and long-sleeved tees, baby snappies, baby blankets, and baby bibs. Children's sizes range from 0 to sizes 14–16. For teens, the company makes sweatshirts and other items.

Interesting Fact: SOS from Texas, which stands for "Save Our Soil," not only specializes in making products from organic cotton but also grows its own cotton. The Oldham family has raised cotton in the same fields for more than a century. The company prides itself on using crop rotation methods to keep the soil rich and never adds pesticides in order to welcome beneficial insects to the land. It is one of the few remaining American companies making apparel from cotton grown in its own fields.

How to Find: You may order directly from the company through its Web site or by calling the customer service number for assistance.

. . . .

STERLINGWEAR OF BOSTON™, INC. ↑ o

175 McClellan Highway, E. Boston, MA 02128
Telephone: 617-567-6465
Web site: www.sterlingwear.com

Sterlingwear of Boston™, Inc. manufactures navy peacoats for children in five "civilian" colors, including oxford gray, burgundy, red, camel, and blue, in addition to the classic navy blue. Sizes run from school-age through teenage for both girls and boys.

Interesting Fact: Now in its third generation, Sterlingwear of Boston™ has been providing outerwear and dress uniforms for the different branches of the military since 1968 and peacoats for the U.S. Navy since 1982. The company has taken the expertise required by government standards and created a commercial line of peacoats. For children, the company has launched a collection called the Navigator™.

How to Find: To find and buy a Sterlingwear of Boston™ pea coat, type the name "Sterlingwear of Boston" into a search engine and view online retailers. For more information, please call customer service.

. . . .

TUTTI BOWLING WEAR ↑

850 S. Broadway, Los Angeles, CA 90014
Telephone: 800-777-4284
Web site: www.2t2t.com

Tutti Bowling Wear manufactures children's and youth bowling shirts and leisure shirts, as well as shirts sized for teens and adults.

Interesting Fact: Tutti Bowling Wear was established in 1984 as a manufacturer of bowling shirts and leisure shirts in retro colors and designs. These shirts are just plain fun. Your child certainly doesn't have to be a bowler to wear one!

How to Find: Customers may order directly through the Web site or by calling customer service.

. . . .

U.S. WINGS® ⊛ ✈

16424 Norton Road, Stow, OH 44224
Telephone: 800-650-0659
Web site: www.uswings.com

U.S. Wings® manufactures and distributes kids leather "A-2" jackets and kid-size navy peacoats.

Interesting Fact: Established in 1986, U.S. Wings® is the largest supplier of leather military flight jackets in the United States. Some of the items in its product line are imported, but the made-in-the-USA selections are well marked.

How to Find: You may order through the Web site, or, if you don't have a computer, call customer service. Specify that you're interested in products made in the United States. Representatives will direct you to the products.

Children's and Infants' Footwear and Socks

It is difficult to say that the American shoe and hosiery industries have reinvented themselves and that business is booming. However, there are manufacturers that have found ways to specialize and to effectively compete against cheaply made imports in certain niche markets. The products in this and in many other sections of this book are very competitively priced. American consumers have been convinced that imports are cheap and that American-made products are significantly more expensive. This is not always the case, as can be demonstrated by the footwear that is listed in this part of the chapter. Please note that athletic socks may be found in Chapter 6, "American-Made Sports and Fitness Equipment."

....

HOY SHOE COMPANY, INC. ⊛ ↓ ✈

4970 Kemper Avenue, St. Louis, MO 63139
Telephone: 314-772-0900
Web site: www.saltwater-sandals.com

Hoy Shoe Company, Inc. manufactures Sun-San® children's sandals in 10 different styles and many different colors. Depending on the model, shoe sizes are designed for infants (0–8), children (9–12), and youth (13–3). Other products are imported.

Interesting Fact: Founded in 1944, the Hoy Shoe Company's CEO is Margery B. Hoy. Located in St. Louis, the company is one of the very few American manufacturers that use leather in the manufacture of their sandals. According to the company, the insoles are made of split leather, and the uppers are leather, as well. The soles are made of hard or soft rubber and are "boat approved."

How to Find: There are numerous online retailers that carry the Hoy Shoe. Customers may also order directly from the Web site. Please call customer service if you need assistance.

....

OKABASHI BRANDS, INC. ☺ ↑
P.O. Box 1508, Buford, GA 30515
Telephone: 800-443-6573
Web site: www.okabashi.com

Okabashi Brands, Inc. manufactures kid-size flip-flops and Euro-sport-type sandals in bright colors. Okabashi recycles a percentage of its waste plastic from manufacturing directly back into the new shoes.

Interesting Fact: The company's name suggests that its products are made in Asia. However, they are manufactured in Georgia. The company name refers to the foot reflexology system that has its roots in the Far East.

How to Find: Okabashi orders may be made directly through the Web site or by calling customer service.

....

PIPER SANDALS™ ✂ ↑
The company is based in San Antonio, Texas.
Telephone: 800-441-2259
Web site: www.pipersandals.com

Piper Sandals™ handcrafts sandals for children. It makes two basic styles that come in six different colors. As these sandals are custom made, each pair of sandals is inscribed with the name of the child (or any other inscription you would like). The company also makes sandals for teenagers and adults, both women and men.

Interesting Fact: Established by Dave Piper in 1971, the Piper Sandal Company is a delightful throw-back to an era where handcrafted shoes were as valued as the men and women who made them. Based in San Antonio, Texas, the Piper Sandal Company fashions custom sandals from your tracings of your child's feet. According to the company, many of the tools it uses today are the same types of tools that were used during the industrial revolution.

How to Find: Orders for Piper Sandals™ may be placed directly though the Web site for stock items, or you may call customer service for assistance.

....

PRINCIPLE PLASTICS/SLOGGERS® ❀

1136 W. 135th Street, Gardena, CA 90247
Telephone: 877-750-4437
Web site: www.sloggers.com

Principle Plastics/Sloggers® manufactures garden footwear for school-age and older categories. Sloggers® come in many different styles and colors.

Interesting Fact: Shortly after World War II, when surplus natural rubber was plentiful, the founder of Sloggers® had the innovative idea of taking rubber parts and gaskets and turning the parts into footwear. His first successful product was a rubber boot. His attention then turned to the emerging plastics industry, and the boot product soon gave way to a plastic shoe covering for leather shoes called "Drizzlies." Drizzlies gained huge nationwide popularity. In fact, Principle Plastics hired one of the first major celebrity spokespeople after World War II, the singer Doris Day! Drizzlies did well for many years, until men and women started to change their taste in shoes. Responding again to shifts in fashion, the 1980s saw the company switch its production to garden clogs.

How to Find: Sloggers® are sold throughout the United States at major department stores and hardware chains, as well as in garden centers and independent stores. You can also order directly through the Web site.

....

WHEELHOUSE DESIGNS® ❀

221 Main Street, Hyde Park, VT 05655
Telephone: 800-252-4245
Web site: www.wheelhousedesigns.com

Wheelhouse Designs, Inc. is a manufacturer of socks mainly for girls and women. Sizes start at 4–6. The socks come in numerous and fun designs. The most popular socks include those with horses and all of the dog breeds. Other designs include birds, butterflies, flowers, "cow spots," and cats.

Interesting Fact: Gail Wheel had no intention of going into the sock business. She had built a fairly successful business representing tee shirts and resisted a manufacturer that wanted her to work with its sock line. After insisting that she at least give it a try, the manufacturer convinced Gail to open her box of sock samples and start to sell them. Almost immediately, she had the idea of putting fun designs on the socks for specialty sales. This time it was the manufacturer that said "No!" Not to be deterred, Gail decided to start her own sock company, and she now sells her socks in specialty stores throughout the United States.

How to Find: The best way to order Wheelhouse Designs socks is through the Web site. Please call customer service if you need assistance.

WIGWAM MILL, INC. ↑ ✿
3402 Crocker Avenue, Sheboygan, WI 53082
Telephone: 920-457-5551
Web site: www.wigwam.com

Wigwam Mill, Inc. manufactures socks for youth, from toddler up. Styles are available for hiking, athletics, snowsports, and general outdoor activities. Wigwam also offers a selection of knit hats for a wide range of weather conditions. Adult sizing for both women and men may be found on the Web site, as well.

Interesting Fact: An American manufacturing treasure, Wigwam Mill was founded at the beginning of the twentieth century as the Sheboygan Knitting Company. It had a fire in 1904 and emerged from the ashes as the Hand-Knit Hosiery Company. In 1957, the company again renamed itself, this time Wigwam Mill. Wigwam® is now in its fourth generation of continuous family ownership. The company makes socks for outdoor activities, including sports and work, as well as for people with special health needs.

How to Find: The Wigwam Mills Web site has a store locator that is linked with the guide to the various sock styles. The socks are distributed throughout the United States.

CHAPTER 5

American-Made Children's Furniture

I was introduced to the world of tools by my friend Mike's father, who was also named Mike. However, back then it would have been unthinkable to call a friend's father by his first name. "Mr. D" always seemed old to me and always stern. Part of his distance, I am sure, was a result of his poor sense of hearing. I was told that Mr. D. had had rheumatic heart disease as a child. His irregular heart and hearing loss kept him from the military.

Neither Mr. D. nor his wife, Alice, had it easy growing up. First-generation Russian-American, they had to scrape and save everything they could before, during, and after the Great Depression. They were constantly reminded by *their* parents that no matter how rotten things seemed, it was nothing compared to what it had been like in Russia.

Mr. and Mrs. D. taught their children frugality but also about frugality's partner, self-reliance. Mr. D. built his own home, a beautiful brick home with white trim. When he finished the home, he built a brick garage big enough for two cars, with ample room for a full-size workshop. Such a feat takes not only a lot of skill but also many tools.

Mr. D. owned any kind of tool you could imagine. This is no nostalgic exaggeration; there were tools everywhere. There were tools for working with wood, metal, and cement; electric tools; automotive tools; pneumatic tools; hand tools; and antique tools. This listing does not include the garden tools and mowers, which were staggering in their bounty, as well, nor does it include the air compressors, pneumatic gadgets, battery testers, and anything else that could be used to fix combustion engines. Mr. and Mrs. D. shopped at garage sales and estate sales long before they were fashionable. Mrs. D. bought *anything*. Mr. D. bought tools.

Mike and his father amazed me by the reverence with which they treated all these tools. Everything was stored, sorted, shelved, labeled, sharpened, cleaned, or oiled after use. In fact, Mr. D. could build or fix just about anything with these tools. If he couldn't fix something, he broke it down and carefully saved the parts. The same was true with wood. Wood wasn't thrown away; it was revered, and neatly stacked. Mike knew the names of all kinds of wood and how they would take stains. Did I mention all the stains and brushes?

However magical the workshop garage and the home filled with restored furniture might have been, the unfinished basement was a monument to anything electrical—a Thomas Edison–type basement!

There were dozens of radios, televisions, fans, tape recorders, old *wire* recorders, and any meter, tester, tool, and part to fix them. In fact, Mr. D. developed a side business fixing electrical things for friends and neighbors, but what was his main business?

In today's ego-filled parlance, Mr. D. might be called something fancy, like "Senior Scientific Research Associate." In his day, he was a technician. What the scientists at his factory conceived, Mr. D. built. Mike told me that during the war years his father had achieved a top security clearance, the highest security clearance given to civilians. Mr. D. helped to build the gyroscope. He probably knew more about gyroscopes than almost anyone else. He helped develop systems to guide aircraft on their missions. Without the work of technicians such as my friend's father, I shudder to think of what would have happened to our nation.

Lately, I have begun to think about "technicians." What happens to a country that doesn't value its woodworkers, cabinetmakers, metalworkers, moldmakers, and technicians? What happens when a nation outsources all of its Mr. Ds?

My friend Mike would go on to become a shop teacher, and, in time, he would renovate a home for his new wife. Mike taught thousands of students in his career, and undoubtedly some became technicians. They will be good at their craft, as they follow a direct lineage from a tinkerer with an irregular heartbeat who helped America win a war.

This section is devoted to American manufacturing companies that make furniture and children's room furnishings with their hands.

American-Made Children's Furniture

American craftsmen have given rise to many rich traditions when it comes to building furniture and producing room decorations. From the very beginning of our nation, American furniture makers experimented with shaping, molding, carving, and casting. We developed a unique, American feel for fine woodworking and the art of transforming iron. Much later on, we worked with wood composites, plywood, and plastics with the same creative energy.

Much has changed in furniture manufacturing, but, at the center of it all, American makers of children's furniture focus now, as they have always done, on quality and safety. While we have lost many of our once-proud children's furniture manufacturers to the imports, it is heartwarming to find companies that have never left our shores and even more wonderful to see new companies that feel that Americans still want American-made children's furniture.

Let's take a look at those American manufacturers that proudly make furniture and room accessories for your child.

* Outdoor Furniture (includes furniture made from recycled plastic, plastic/wood composites, and wood)

* Indoor Furniture (includes children's furniture for any room of the house for toddlers through teens)

* Children's Carpeting (includes playroom and bedroom carpeting)

☆
Made Here, Baby!

❈ Educational and Play Furniture (includes furniture for the home, classroom, or daycare center, role-play furniture such as wooden play kitchens or puppet show stages)

Outdoor Furniture

The outdoor furniture companies are at the forefront of designing products that are made of either recycled plastics or use wood that has been responsibly harvested and then replanted. Please see the product index E under Children's Products: Outdoor furniture for all companies that make outdoor furniture.

....

ALLAGASH WOOD PRODUCTS, INC. ☺ ✂ ↑
133 Allagash Road, Allagash, ME 04774
Telephone: 866-727-3033
Web site: www.allagashwoodproducts.com

Allagash Wood Products, Inc. manufactures picnic tables for children in four sizes, plus a hexagonal table, children's Adirondack chairs, settees, rockers, and block sets. All products are made from northern white pine. Allagash Wood Products can customize.

Interesting Fact: Allagash Wood Products stands apart from other outdoor furniture manufacturers in that it actually handles all aspects of the business, from cutting and drying the wood from its own forests to making its own shipping boxes. Any trees that are taken from its land are responsibly replanted.

How to Find: Customers can order directly from the Web site. A down-loadable form is provided if you wish to fax in an order. Customers are welcome to call the company for more information.

....

AMERICAN RECYCLED PLASTIC, INC. ☺ ↑
1500 Main Street, Palm Bay, FL 32905
Telephone: 888-674-1525
Web site: www.itsrecycled.com

American Recycled Plastic, Inc. manufactures a children's-size picnic and play table from recycled plastic that is available in many colors. The company also makes recycled plastic bicycle racks in 4', 6', and 8' lengths in different colors to match garage décor, as well as storage bins for any room in the house. Children's rocking chairs made of recycled plastic are also available; however, these are usually made in multiple quantities for schools. The company also produces outdoor furniture for adults.

Interesting Fact: The founder of American Recycled Plastic started the business more than 20 years ago, long before the green movement became fashionable. The process takes milk containers, grinds them up into flakes, adds color, and produces plastic lumber. Each product the company makes represents hundreds of plastic containers that would have otherwise gone into the South Florida landfills.

How to Find: The best way to order American Recycled Plastics products is by calling customer service. Representatives will be happy to assist you.

. . . .

CONVERSION PRODUCTS, INC. ✿ ✂
P.O. Box 981, Biddeford, ME 04005
Telephone: 888-236-2212
Web site: www.conversionproducts.com

Conversion Products, Inc. manufactures outdoor furniture from recycled plastic. For children, the company is introducing a junior-size Adirondack chair and a child-size side table. It also makes planters from recycled plastic that can create perfect first-garden containers for young children. Conversion Products has the ability to customize.

Interesting Fact: A husband-and-wife management team runs the day-to-day operations of Conversion Products. The furniture is entirely made from recycled milk containers.

How to Find: Orders may be placed directly through the Conversion Products Web site, or you may call customer service for assistance.

. . . .

LOLL DESIGNS ☺ ↑
1325 N. 59th Avenue W, Duluth, MN 55807
Telephone: 877-740-3387
Web site: www.lolldesigns.com

Loll Designs manufactures furniture from recycled materials. For children, the company makes a three-slat chair, as well as an "H-back" chair, along with cubby benches and foot stools. Loll Designs also makes a full line of adult-size products for outdoor and indoor use.

Interesting Fact: Unlike companies that manufacture outdoor furniture in classic Adirondack styles, Loll designs takes a modern approach. The furniture is made from either HDPE (high-density polyethylene) or a wood fiber composite. Many of the pieces in the product line have the look and feel of much more expensive furniture and can work as indoor children's-room furniture. Whether for outdoor or indoor purposes, the furniture requires virtually no maintainence.

How to Find: The best way to buy Loll Designs chairs is directly through the company Web site.

Indoor Furniture

In conducting interviews with the companies that make up this part of the chapter, we were surprised by the number of American manufacturers that still make upholstered furniture for children, in addition to those companies that are producing wooden furniture. We use the word "surprising" because many people assume that American manufacturers can no longer compete against furniture companies that have resorted to shipping cheap imports. However, there is a growing wave of American manufacturers that have learned how to manufacture more efficiently and to control their inventories.

In addition, as fuel and shipping costs have continued to rise, the expense of bringing in container-load quantities of furniture from countries such as China has been steadily climbing. It is often cheaper to ship within the United States directly from an American factory to the customer than it is to load the furniture into a container in some foreign land, ship it thousands of miles into an American warehouse, and then send it on to the customer or retailer.

When we combine better manufacturing efficiencies with cheaper shipping, we find that American manufacturers can better compete against imported products.

Prices for American-made furniture range from heirloom-quality pricing to very affordable, depending on your specific needs and budget. All of these companies are very pleased to answer your questions, and some of the companies can customize. Please go to the product index E, and look under the following headings for a listing of all the furniture makers found in this book: Children's Products: Indoor furniture, room decorations, mattresses, and bedding; Children's Products: Outdoor furniture; and Children's Products: Educational and play furniture.

BEAN BAG CITY ⊛ ↑
1480 W. Spring Valley-Painterville Rd., Spring Valley, OH 45370
Telephone: 800-800-6050
Web site: www.beanbag.com

Bean Bag City manufactures bean bag chairs in youth and teen sizes, as well as chairs for adults. The youth chairs are appropriate for kids up to 4' 6" tall, while the teen chairs are good for kids up to 5' 2".

Interesting Fact: Founded in 1975, Ohio-based Bean Bag City was started in order to give its workers something to do in the off season, as the company originally focused its business on boat covers. The bean bags are made in four different sizes, and parents can choose from more than 70 different colors. The company offers materials to refill the chairs if, over time, the filling loses its "energy."

How to Find: Customers may order directly through the Web site. Please call customer service for assistance. If you are in the Dayton area, you are invited to visit the factory store.

BEAN PRODUCTS, INC. ☺ ↑
1500 S. Western Avenue, Chicago, IL 60608
Telephone: 800-726-8365
Web site: www.beanproducts.com

Bean Products™ manufactures small bean bag chairs for children and child-size cube ottomans. The bean bag chairs are available in several different fabrics, including sustainable fabrics such as hemp.

Interesting Fact: Bean Products™ invented the body pillow, which is especially comfortable for pregnant women. The company also makes a wide range of yoga mats and pillows for meditation, sleep, and comfort. Many of the products in its line are made of organic and/or sustainable fabrics.

How to Find: Customers may order directly through the Bean Products Web site, or they can call customer service for information.

....

BERG FURNITURE ↓ ↑

The company is located in the Barrington, New Jersey, area.
The company prefers e-mail.
Web site: www.bergfurniture.com

Berg Furniture manufactures children's furniture for all age groups. For infants, the company makes cribs and dressers. Furniture for older children includes beds, dressers armoires, desks, and bookcases.

Interesting Fact: Berg Furniture has undergone an odyssey across the continents. The original intention of the company was to manufacture overseas. After being disappointed by the quality of the furniture it was importing, the company made the courageous decision to manufacture all of its products in America in its own factory. It feels that in order to achieve the level of quality it desires, it must manufacture in the United States.

How to Find: There is a store locator on the Berg Furniture Web site. Customers may also e-mail customer service to find the retail location nearest their home.

....

BERNHAUS FURNITURE ✂ ↑

1331 US Highway 27N, Berne, IN 46711
Telephone: 888-589-7083
Web site: www.bernhausfurniture.com

Bernhaus Furniture handcrafts children's rockers, high chairs, and wrap-around chairs. The company can customize on request.

Interesting Fact: Located in Amish country, Bernhaus Furniture was established in 2003 in order to produce high-quality, handcrafted furniture at affordable prices. The company does not charge for delivery within 75 miles of the factory.

How to Find: Please call the toll-free customer service number to place an order.

. . . .

BRIGHTON PAVILION®/JANE KELTNER COLLECTIONS ✿ ↑

94 Cumberland Street, Memphis, TN 38112
Telephone: 800-487-8033
Web site: www.paintedfurniture.com

Brighton Pavilion®/Jane Keltner Collections handcrafts changing tables, cribs, highchairs, table and chair sets, toy chests, armoires, kid-size bookcases, nursery chests, rockers, and rocking benches. Parents can order any item in the adult line in a kid-size version.

Interesting Fact: The heirloom-quality, handpainted furniture in the Brighton Pavilion®/Jane Keltner Collection is crafted on what is termed "full case construction." For example, instead of resting on thin strips of wood, drawers rest on solid hardwood. The company was founded by a woman artist about 18 years ago. In 1999, the company was sold to a woman-led management team. The philosophy of the company is that in order to survive in America, a manufacturer must have the highest level of customer service and make products that can match the quality of any manufactured anywhere in the world.

How to Find: Brighton Pavilion strongly believes in customer service. It welcomes inquiries about where to find or buy any piece of furniture in the collection.

. . . .

CELERY FURNITURE ☺

428 E. Mendenhall Street, Bozeman, MT 59715
Telephone: 406-582-8988
Web site: www.celeryfurniture.com

Celery Furniture manufactures armoires and storage units, rockers, shelving, and kid-size desks. The product line is constantly changing and growing. Celery Furniture builds its furniture using bamboo or with formaldehyde-free, medium-density fiberboard. Adhesives are nontoxic.

Made Here, Baby!

Interesting Fact: Dan Harding, the founder of Celery Furniture, grew up in his parents' antique store, where he not only was influenced by Early American, Mission, Shaker, Mid-Century Modern, and other styles but also absorbed the concepts of sustainability, reuse, and recycling. He enjoyed how his parents would use the antiques in their home before putting them up for sale. Dan's love of design led him to architecture school, and this enabled him to develop many theories as to what furniture should represent. He embraces the idea that if something is designed well, it is timeless; it can have the elements of the old and familiar but at the same time be fresh and new.

How to Find: There is a store locator on the Web site, with listings for brick-and-mortar and online retailers. Customers can buy directly through the Web site, as well, or, if more information is needed, call customer service.

COOL SOFA ↑ ✂
3687 Harbor Boulevard, Costa Mesa, CA 82626
Telephone: 877-235-6797
Web site: www.coolsofa.com

Cool Sofa manufactures sofas, chairs, and loveseats in wild colors and prints. Every piece in the collection can be customized.

Interesting Fact: Cool Sofa has been around since 1975 and specializes in sofas, loveseats, and chairs that are made to order and are factory direct to the customer. To give an idea of their customization abilities, Cool Sofa actually made furniture to order for a tree house! It routinely works from pictures or descriptions submitted by customers.

How to Find: Customers may order directly through the Web site or call customer service for assistance. Cool Sofas does not have retail stores.

ECO TOTS ™ ☺
P.O. Box 20533, Indianapolis, IN 46220
Telephone: 317-257-7450
Web site: www.ecotots.com

Eco Tots ™ manufactures eco-friendly, easy-to-assemble tables, shelves, seats, and desks that are perfect for children's rooms. Scale is appropriate for preschool and school-age children. The furniture comes in many different colors and styles to coordinate with room décor.

Interesting Fact: The Eco Tots™ furniture line is certified by the Forest Stewardship Council as made from sustainably harvested wood. The wood is formaldehyde-free and is available in many eco-friendly finishes. The product selection is noted for its people-friendly assembly, as the pieces simply snap together. There will be no late nights as mom and dad look for little parts!

How to Find: There is a store locator on the Web site and a listing of online retailers that carry Eco Tots products.

JUST KIDS STUFF

Just Kids Stuff is located in the Windsor, Colorado, area.
Telephone: 970-568-0080
Web site: www.justkidsstuff.com

Just Kids Stuff manufactures toddler/preschool beds for children between the ages of 18 months and approximately 3 years. The beds are designed in many unusual shapes, such as pirate ships, princess carriages, bulldozers, race cars, and firetrucks. The company also makes toy chests in several different styles.

Interesting Fact: Just Kids Stuff started its life nearly 30 years ago. It is a company that began with a dream, then watched the dream go away and then come back to life. Along the way, the company tried to manufacture overseas and became so disenchanted with the quality of the goods that came out of the Far East that it brought manufacturing back to the United States. The products are now made in a woodworking shop in the Midwest under the founder's constant supervision.

How to Find: There are numerous online retailers that carry the product line. Type "Just Kids Stuff" into a search engine to locate the names of stores near you. Customers may also order directly through the company Web site.

KIDS & PETS FURNITURE ✿

The company is located in the Park City, Utah, area.
Telephone: 800-825-2178
Web site: www.kidsandpetsfurniture.com

Kids & Pets Furniture manufactures kid-size, upholstered toddler chairs, rocking chairs, and upscale bedding. The company will be introducing a line of chaise lounges in 2009. The chairs are only 20 inches in height, but they aren't toys; they are solid-wood framed and upholstered and come in chic colors that can match any room's color scheme.

Interesting Fact: Melanie Desautels had originally intended to import her upholstered chairs. However, she wasn't satisfied with the quality of any item presented to her, and she started production in the United States. As the name of the company implies, it makes several items for pets, as well.

How to Find: You may purchase Kids & Pets Furniture directly through the company Web site, or call customer service if you need more information.

KIDSCHAIRS™ ✂

1364 London Bridge Road, Virginia Beach, VA 23453
Telephone: 757-301-7464
Web site: www.kidschairs.com

KidsChairs™ handcrafts chairs, loveseats, ottomans, recliners, and toyboxes. The recliners are appropriate for children ages 4–9, while the chairs and sofas are built for children to age 10. The company can customize.

Interesting Fact: KidsChairs is a husband-and-wife-owned manufacturer based in Virginia. As parents, the owners feel a special commitment to quality. For example, the company is proud of the fact that the frames are all made of solid pine and the fabric is cotton. Of interest is the scale of these pieces; though kid-size, the furniture is as sturdy as full-size adult furniture.

How to Find: Orders may be placed directly through the Web site or by calling customer service.

LILIPAD STUDIO ❊ ☺ ✂

400 S. Main Street, Hailey, ID 83333
Telephone: 208-788-7500
Web site: www.lilipadstudio.com

Lilipad Studio produces heirloom-quality, handcrafted, handpainted furniture for toddlers to school-age children. Items include tables, chairs, footstools, and stepstools. Limited production.

Interesting Fact: This woman-founded studio specializes in brightly painted, whimsical furniture for toddlers and preschool children. Talented artisans from the surrounding Sun Valley community contribute their creative energies to the production of this unique product line.

How to Find: A boutique company, Lilipad studio has limited distribution in retail and online retailers. You may call customer service for additional information. The company plans to allow shopping through its Web site in the future.

....

LITTLE COLORADO™, INC. ❀ ✂

The company is based in the Golden, Colorado, area.
Telephone: 303-964-3212
Web site: www.littlecolorado.com

Little Colorado™, Inc. manufactures an extensive collection of children's products, including bedroom furniture, chairs, table and chair sets, stools, personalized children's gifts, role-play furniture such as play kitchens and doll cradles, shelves, bookcases, play tables, potty chairs, and toy chests. Outdoor furniture includes picnic tables and Adirondack chairs. Because of the size of the product line, it is recommended that parents research the Little Colorado™ Web site. The company can customize.

Interesting Fact: Founded in 1987, Little Colorado™, Inc. is a family-run business that manufactures handcrafted, solid-wood children's furniture. The company is widely known for its leadership in child safety issues, and it is committed to American manufacturing. The company employs 35 full-time craftspeople and, due to rapid growth, is now in its third location.

How to Find: Little Colorado makes its products available through online stores, catalogs, and small and large retail store chains. If you don't have a computer, please call customer service.

....

LITTLE RIVER WINDSORS ↑ ✕ T

245 Little River Road, Berwick, ME 03901
Telephone: 207-698-7951
Web site: www.littleriverwindsors.com

Little River Windsors handcrafts Windsor chairs for toddlers and older children in a youth chair and a kids' chair model. The company also makes adult-size furniture and miscellaneous pieces for homes with Early American décor. Limited production.

Interesting Fact: Fred Freeman Chellis owns this company, which can trace its woodworking craftsmanship back to the beginning of the nineteenth century. He is the sixth generation of fine woodworkers in his family, practicing a near-dying art in this age of computer-generated products. Mr. Chellis specializes in handcrafting Windsor chairs that are heirloom quality and that will get passed on to future generations in your family.

How to Find: Please contact Little River Windsors by e-mail or telephone.

....

MISSION TIME DESIGNS ✿ ✕ ↑

8067 Road W, Liberty Center, OH 43532
Telephone: 419-533-3317
Web site: www.missiontimedesigns.com

Mission Time Designs handcrafts several Mission oak pieces to children's scale. These pieces include kid-size dining tables and chairs, toy boxes, benches with cubbies for storage, children's desks, kid-size "bar stools," and ministorage units. The company makes a full line of products for adults. Limited production.

Interesting Fact: Based in Ohio, Mission Time Designs produces handcrafted furniture in the Mission style. The furniture is made of solid oak in three workshops that are located in Ohio and Michigan. Connie, the founder of Mission Time Design, has had a passion for wood since childhood. She built her own home and many of the pieces of Mission-style furniture in the home.

How to Find: Customers may order directly through the Web site. Please call customer service for assistance.

OAK DESIGNS, INC. ✿

9050 S. Willow Street, Manchester, NH 03103
Telephone: 603-669-9280
Web site: www.oakdesigns.com

Oak Designs, Inc. specializes in juvenile furniture, including bunkbeds, canopy beds, beds with storage units, beds with bookcase headboards, bookcases, dressers, and storage units.

Interesting Fact: Oak Designs is a family-owned and -operated furniture manufacturer. All of the furniture is made to order in accordance with your choice of style and wood. The company builds furniture in oak, cherry, and birch.

How to Find: At this time, Oak Designs distributes only to the northeastern United States; however, it is expanding. The company sells only to retail stores. Contact Oak Designs to find a vendor.

ROEBUCK STUDIO ✿   ↓ ✂

521 W. Middle Street, Chelsea, MI 48118
Telephone: 734-478-3349
Web site: www.roebuckstudio.com

Roebuck Studio handcrafts children's furniture such as tables, chairs, and rockers. The designs are as whimsical and clever as they are functional. In 2009, the company will be introducing mobility toys such as bunny scooters and unique toy boxes.

Interesting Fact: Barret and Katherine Roebuck are designers and woodworkers who have a passion for whimsical yet functional children's furniture, along with a commitment to sustainable materials and recycling. Products are built from either recycled wood or locally sourced woods such as birch. The couple strongly supports American-made products and believes in supporting the local economy whenever possible

How to Find: Please contact Roebuck Studio directly through the Web site if you have an interest in its products. A limited number of retail outlets and online retailers carry the company's products.

••

VAUGHAN-BASSETT® ☺

East Oldtown, Galax, VA 24333
Telephone: 276-236-6161
Web site: www.vaughan-bassett.com

Vaughan-Bassett® manufactures the Cottage Collection of furniture with youth sizing. The furniture elements include beds and bunkbeds, chests, commodes, computer desks, dressers, nightstands, and mirrors. Collections may be ordered in six different finishes.

Interesting Fact: Founded in 1919, Vaughan-Bassett manufactures more than 95 percent of its furniture in the United States, in its manufacturing plants in Virginia and North Carolina. The company has grown to be the largest manufacturer of adult bedroom furniture in the United States. Vaughan-Bassett has a strong environmental commitment. The company's One-for-One® program plants tree seedlings for each tree taken in manufacturing.

How to Find: When a customer enters her zip code, a sales representative e-mails information on the nearest retail location. The company prides itself on highly personalized customer service.

••

VENTURE HORIZON™ O

1129 Maricopa Highway, Ojai, CA 93023
Telephone: 805-640-7300
Web site: www.venturehorizon.com

Venture Horizon™ manufactures bookcase and storage systems for children's rooms.

Interesting Fact: Established in 1985, Venture Horizon specializes in ready-to-assemble (RTA) furniture. It manufactures storage products for nearly every room in the house, including the kitchen. For children, Venture Horizon makes colorful bookcases and storage units.

How to Find: This Web site is strictly for the use of wholesale customers. To find the nearest distributor, please do an Internet search for "Venture Horizon children's bookcase."

VERMONT TUBBS, INC. ↑ T

One Tubbs Avenue, Brandon, VT 05733
Telephone: 802-247-3414
Web site: www.vermonttubbs.com

Vermont Tubbs, Inc. handcrafts a large selection of American-made youth bedroom furniture made of solid ash or birch. Items include bunk-, storage, and twin beds, nightstands, dressers, chests, bookcases, and storage units. Each piece is bench-built by a single craftsperson. All pieces are signed and dated by the craftsperson who made them. The furniture is made with water-based glues, and the paint is free from lead and other metallics.

Interesting Fact: An American manufacturing treasure, the company was founded in 1840 by William F. Tubbs. Mr. Tubbs started the company in order to produce hardwood snowshoes and skis out of ash wood. To this day, the company uses its expertise in bending wood to make some of its bedroom furniture, employing the same technology that it once used in making skis. Vermont Tubbs has a strong commitment to green manufacturing; it purchases locally sourced materials and uses sustainable forestry methods.

How to Find: Vermont Tubbs has a store locator on its Web site. If you can't find a retail store in your area or if you don't have a computer, please call the customer service number for assistance.

WHIMSY WOODS CHILDRENS FURNITURE ✂

P.O. Box 730, Eureka Springs, AR 72632
Telephone: 479-253-7797
Web site: www.khjwhimwoods.net

Whimsy Woods Childrens Furniture handcrafts toy boxes and toy chests, chairs, tables, stepstools, bedroom furniture, desks, rocking chairs, role-play toys, outdoor furniture, and storage units. The company can customize.

Interesting Fact: Whimsey Woods specializes in handpainted children's furniture and toys. Its wooden furniture is made for it by local craftspeople or by other American manufacturers. The pieces are hand-painted in the company's Ozark mountain studio. No two pieces are ever exactly alike, which is part of their charm.

How to Find: Customers may order through the company Web site. If you don't have a computer, please call the customer service number.

••

WILD ZOO, INC. ™

61568 American Lane, Bend, OR 97702
Telephone: 888-543-8588
Web site: www.wildzoo.com

Wild Zoo, Inc. ™ manufactures computer desks for toddlers through preschool, grade school, and older, including buddy desks so that children can work together. The company also makes shelves, play tables, and printer stands.

Interesting Fact: Wild Zoo addresses the fact that younger and younger children are using computers. The company has created a line of computer desks with dimensions suitable for children from ages 2 and up, with separate product lines for grade school and older. The furniture is shipped "knocked down," but it is ready and easy to assemble. Several finishes are available.

How to Find: Orders may be placed through the Web site. For additional information, please use the customer service number.

••

YOUNG AMERICA®BY STANLEY FURNITURE, INC. ↑ ✈

1641 Fairystone Park Hwy., Stanleytown, VA 24168
Telephone: 276-627-2540
Web site: www.youngamerica.com

Young America®by Stanley Furniture, Inc. includes children's furniture for infants, preschool, 'tweens, and teens. The infant product line include cribs, toddler "conversion" beds, and a full line of bedroom furniture. According to the company, about 70 percent of all Young America® products are made in the USA.

Interesting Fact: The Young America® line by Stanley Furniture is predominantly bedroom furniture, ranging in pieces for infants through teens.

How to Find: The Young America brand by Stanley Furniture sells its products through a network of independent retailers. There is a store locator on the Web site. Please call customer service for more information on the Young America® brand product line.

Kid's Carpeting

Carpets may be used for play or decoration, and both types are featured in this chapter. The play carpeting may be used in play areas, either outdoors or indoors, and often features educational themes to help teach children everything from the alphabet to geography to zoo animals. Decorative area carpeting is available in a wide variety of shapes and colors, with companies having the ability to customize to match your décor. American carpet manufacturers are making a very strong commitment to green manufacturing and recycling.

CARPETS FOR KIDS® O
115 E. 9th Avenue, Portland, OR 97214
Telephone: 503-232-1203
Web site: www.carpetsforkids.com

Carpets for Kids® manufactures theme-based carpets that not only are fun but also allow children to learn as they are playing. Some of the learning themes include alphabets, numbers, bilingual and faith-based themes, geography, and layouts such as town or city maps, ponds, and barnyard life.

Interesting Fact: Founded in 1991, Carpets for Kids® is one of the industry leaders in providing educational carpeting for children.

How to Find: Carpets for Kids does not sell directly to the public; however, the Web site has a listing of educational product distributors.

You can also do an Internet search by typing "Carpets for Kids" into a search engine.

....

COLONIAL BRAIDED RUG COMPANY

3414 W. Stage Coach Trail, Shelby, NC 28150
Telephone: 800-676-6922
Web site: www.braided.com

Colonial Braided Rug Company handcrafts braided rugs in numerous colors and sizes to coordinate with your child's room bedding. The company has a selection for any room in the house.

Interesting Fact: Founded in 1946, Colonial Braided Rugs use residential carpet yarn throughout each of its rugs. The rugs are composed of 100% carpet yarn. Carpet yarn is as durable as wool, and it is colorfast and low maintenance. The yarn is partially composed of recycled fibers, so there are environmental benefits, as well. The rugs are completely machine washable, and the larger ones can be cleaned like a regular carpet.

How to Find: Colonial Braided Rugs does not sell directly to the public. However, if you e-mail the company, it will give you the name of a dealer close to your location. If you need assistance, call the toll-free number.

....

FLAGSHIP CARPETS

1546 Progress Road, Ellijay, GA 30540
Telephone: 800-848-4055
Web site: www.educationalrugs.com

Flagship Carpets manufactures carpets for children in several categories, including educational, daydream, animals, and neon rugs.

Interesting Fact: Flagship Carpets has been serving the education industry for more than 40 years and is the only educational carpet company that is a start-to-finish manufacturer. The company has an in-house recycling program, stemming from the fact that its rugs are 100 percent recyclable.

How to Find: The Web site has a "Where to Buy" section. If you need further assistance, please call the customer service number.

....

JOY CARPETS™
104 W. Forest Road, Ft. Ogelthorpe, GA 30742
Telephone: 800-645-2787
Web site: www.joycarpets.com

Joy Carpets™ manufactures carpeting for children as well as for adults. The children's carpeting is available in many styles and themes and is intended to educate as well as to decorate.

Interesting Fact: Established in 1973, Joy Carpeting is a pioneer in the field of recreational carpeting. As the company has grown, it has made a strong commitment to recycling programs and to green manufacturing. It monitors its suppliers, uses recycled packaging, strongly endorses reuse and donation of older carpets to charitable organizations, and does whatever is possible to reduce waste.

How to Find: Like many of the carpet companies, Joy Carpets sells to retailers and not to the public. If you can't find these carpets at your local retailer, please call the customer service number for assistance.

....

KATHY'S BRAIDED RUGS
25541 Military Road, Cascade, MD 21719
Telephone: 301-241-3243
Web site: www.kathysbraidedrugs.com

Kathy's Braided Rugs handcrafts braided rugs in numerous colors and styles, all of which are either machine washable or can be easily cleaned by steam.

Interesting Fact: A woman-founded and -owned company, this Maryland-based manufacturer has the ability to customize braided rugs in several different colors. If you are decorating a child's room, the company can work with you to create a unique color combination if you can't find a stock color you like. In additional to carpeting for children or adults, it also makes a unique "dog bone"-shaped rug, perfect for your dog's food and water bowls!

How to Find: Customers can order directly from the Web site. An order form is provided for those who wish to fax orders into the company. Please call the company for more information.

．．

RUG FACTORY STORE

560 Mineral Springs Avenue, Pawtucket, RI 02862
Telephone: 401-724-6840
Web site: www.rugfactorystore.com

Rug Factory Store produces several carpet collections specifically made for children's rooms. Carpets come in stripes, solids, and patterns and in numerous styles and shapes. Rug Factory Store has the ability to customize rugs to match almost any decorating scheme. Customers may also order rugs made of bamboo yarn or natural fibers.

Interesting Fact: Rug Factory Store is the consumer sales branch of Rhode Island–based Colonial Mills.

How to Find: Rug Factory Store may be accessed online, or customers may call customer service for assistance.

Educational and Play Furniture

Furniture may be used strictly for function, such as a bed, or it may be used to educate and to teach children how to play together. The companies featured in this part of the book make a wide variety of furniture for arts and crafts, child's play, coordination skills, and storage. This is furniture capable of being used in home settings, daycare centers. or schools.

．．

CHILDREN'S FACTORY, THE ✈ ⊙

245 W. Essex Avenue, St. Louis, MO 63122
Telephone: 877-726-1696
Web site: www.childrensfactory.com

The Children's Factory manufactures soft play products such as climbers, play centers, and ride-ons. It also makes soft block sets and climbing equipment. All of the soft play toys and climbing equipment are made in the USA. Other items offered may be imported.

Interesting Fact: This St. Louis–based company is a leader in what is known as "soft play" toys. As the name implies, these products are safe for toddlers and children of preschool age. These products promote exercise, socialization, coordination, and dexterity. In cases where there is a fabric rather than a vinyl covering, the materials have been made to resist spills and are easy to clean.

How to Find: The Children's Factory does not sell directly to the public; however, if you call or e-mail the company, it will direct you to the distributor nearest your location.

JONTI-CRAFT®, INC. ❀ ☺ O
171 Highway 68, Wabasso, MN 56293
Telephone: 800-543-4149
Web site: www.jonti-craft.com

Jonti-Craft®, Inc. manufactures art easels, block sets, computer stations, balancing toys, wooden play kitchens, puppet show stages, kid-size castles, kid-size play furniture, and role-play furniture. The company has recently launched a green line of products called Sprouts®.

Interesting Fact: Jonti-Craft's husband-and-wife management team, originally from Wabasso, Minnesota, scraped together every penny they had to buy Jonti-Craft from the original owner. They moved away from Wabasso and set up a home near the factory. Soon after they purchased the company, the factory burned to the ground. The owners lacked sufficient insurance to rebuild. The father of the newly wed wife went to the people of the town of Wabasso and asked his friends and neighbors for help. Wabasso is a small town with friendly people. The father asked the townspeople to do something that seems to be out of a Jimmy Stewart movie; he asked the townsfolk to move what was left of the Jonti-Craft factory back to Wabasso. The townspeople got together, arranged a truck caravan, and drove two hours to the burned-down factory and back in order to move the remaining machinery to their town. The young couple started the company again with just three employees in a garage. They now have 150 employees and will remain in the small town of Wabasso for as long as there is a company.

How to Find: Jonti-Craft distributes its products through educational distributors. Please call or e-mail the company for the distributor nearest your location.

....

STEFFY WOOD PRODUCTS, INC. ↑

701 W. Mill Street, Angola, IN 46703
Telephone: 800-656-8586
Web site: www.steffywood.com

Steffy Wood Products manufactures furniture for toddlers and preschool children, including puppet theaters, exercise equipment, role-play furniture such as vanities, bookcases, and storage systems. For infants, the company makes changing tables and storage shelving for baby products such as diapers.

Interesting Fact: The founder of Steffy Wood Products and several of his co-workers were laid off from another furniture company as that company was in the process of going out of business. He had a strong belief that if he could put together a core of talented workers and find the right focus, he could be a success in the children's furniture niche. In 1999, Steffy Wood Products was started with three employees. The business expanded rapidly and had to move because it had outgrown its space. In 2009, Steffy will need yet an even larger factory and will add to its workforce of 30 employees.

How to Find: The company has a listing of distributors who will sell directly to customers, or customers can call Steffy customer service for more detailed information on the product line.

....

TRAIN TABLES ONLINE, INC.

The company is located in the Westfield, Indiana, area.
The company prefers e-mail.
Web site: www.traintablesonline.com

Train Tables Online, Inc. manufactures activity tables and train tables for children. Tables are available in four different hardwoods with a choice of stains and finishes. In 2009, the company will sell finished wood tabletops so that the train tables can be easily converted into coffee tables or end tables to enable multiple uses.

Interesting Fact: Train Tables Online was inspired by an industrial designer and woodworking devotee searching for a children's activity table that could be both decorative and functional. The result was a 100 percent solid hardwood table made of maple, red oak, poplar, or cherry. The company decided on solid wood as an alternative to cheaper pressed wood, as pressed wood may generate fumes from its glue that may bother children with allergies.

How to Find: You may order through the Web site or call customer service.

- -

WEE-BOOS, LLC ✂

P.O. Box 451, Crescent, OK 73028
Telephone: 888-449-2667
Web site: www.wee-boos.com

Wee-Boos, LLC manufactures storage chests in the shapes of footballs, basketballs, golfballs, baseballs, and soccer balls. For large orders, such as schools and alumni associations, the company has the ability to customize any of these storage units to match school colors.

Interesting Fact: The founders of Wee-Boos® were originally in the retail toy business and had worked their way up to three stores. In 2005, realizing that, due to competition, their share in the market was declining, they decided to launch their own manufacturing company. They decided upon making better toy storage rather than better toys. The Wee-Boos® toy storage chests are large enough to hold about 12 basketballs and are perfect for storing all of those toys left on the floor.

How to Find: Customers can order directly from the Web site. An order form is provided that can also be sent in by fax. If customers need assistance, they can call the customer service number.

- -

WHITNEY BROTHERS EDUCATIONAL TOYS ↓ O T

93 Railroad Street, Keene, NH 03431
Telephone: 800-225-5381
Web site: www.whitneybros.com

Whitney Brothers Educational Toys manufactures role-play toys for preschool and school-age children. These toys include wooden refrigerators, stoves, and kitchen islands, playhouse furniture such as rockers, reading benches, and playhouse "cubes." For infants, the company makes cribs, highchairs, and changing cabinets.

Interesting Fact: An American manufacturing treasure, Whitney Brothers Educational Toys and Furniture was established in 1904. It uses classic woodworking techniques to make children's play and classroom furniture.

How to Find: Whitney Brothers sells its products to educational products distributors, not to the general public. Please e-mail the company for the nearest distributor in your area.

··

WOOD DESIGNS ☺ ○
P.O. Box 1308, Monroe, NC 28111
Telephone: 800-247-8465
Web site: www.wooddesigns.org

Wood Designs makes play kitchen "appliances" such as wood refrigerators, stoves, sinks, and kitchen islands, sand and water tables, hard maple block sets, and puppet show stages. The company also manufacturers storage units, as well as a full selection of literacy products.

Interesting Fact: Based in North Carolina, Wood Designs specializes in early learning furniture. It is proud of its strong focus on child safety. This is evidenced by its Tip Me Not™ storage unit products, which have been designed to have low centers of gravity to make them tip resistant, and Healthy Kids™ furniture, which is a wood-based line of formaldehyde-free products.

How to Find: Wood Products does not sell directly to the public. However, its products are widely available in teacher's stores, on the Internet, and in catalogs devoted to teacher's supplies.

CHAPTER 6

American-Made Sports and Fitness Equipment

In May 2005, the U.S. Department of Health and Human Services issued an important white paper on childhood obesity. The report presented some shocking evidence. The number of American adolescents who were overweight had tripled from 1980 to 2002. About 16 percent of children were considered obese. Even more troubling was the fact that the obese children, as a group, had gotten heavier. Several factors were blamed for this trend, from poor diet to food advertising. However, in terms of leading causes, physical inactivity was seen as one of the biggest problems.

We can blame television, computers, school systems, video games, and even ourselves, but all the blame in the world won't get kids off of the couch. What can we do to motivate our children to exercise? Whenever an issue as important as this one comes to the surface, there are all kinds of experts offering their opinions. Often, it seems as if these experts are the same people who give us advice on heartburn, sunscreen, or screen doors, for that matter.

For the chapter on American-made sports and fitness equipment, we thought it would be interesting if we called upon our own experts. These aren't fellows in white lab coats with stethoscopes or talking heads in designer suits but coaches and fitness experts who are considered to be among the very best in the United States.

Our experts are women who either are moms or work with

young athletes nearly every day of the year, or both. This was a rare opportunity for us to ask questions of great athletes and coaches who are at the front lines of sports and fitness in America and to get a more personal look at what world-class coaches and athletes believe.

Our experts included Jennifer Arndt, currently Assistant Swimming Coach at the University of Tennessee. Prior to coaching, she had an outstanding career at the University of Michigan, where she swam for four years for the Wolverines, helping the squad bring home Big Ten championships in 1997, 1998, and 2001. She was team co-captain in 1999–2000. Jennifer was an Olympic Trials Qualifier and an All-American. She earned Michigan's Academic Achievement Award and was honored by the Big Ten in 1997, 1998, and 2001.

Another of our experts, L. Shell Dailey, is currently a Women's National Basketball Association (WNBA) Regional Scout, as well as the Women's Basketball Coordinator at the IMG Academies in Bradenton, Florida. Shell has been an Assistant Coach and Head Coach at the collegiate level and an Assistant Coach and Interim Head Coach at the professional level for the WNBA Silver Stars. She played her collegiate basketball at the University of Texas, where she was a team captain.

Alicia McConnell, another of our experts, is Director of Athlete Services and Programs for the U.S. Olympic Committee (USOC) in Colorado Springs, Colorado. Alicia is considered to be one of the greatest squash players to have ever played the game and was the #1 ranked women's player representing the United States from 1981–1988; she was also ranked #14 in the world in 1988. She also represented the United States in squash at the Pan American Games in 1995 and was a member of the U.S. Women's Lacrosse Team in 1984–1985.

We spoke with our three experts about sports and children.

Made Here, Baby!: Shell, we'll start with you as the mother of a four-year-old. How did you get your son off to an early start to enjoy exercise?

Shell Dailey: Eric has been pretty lucky because he's grown up around professional basketball players. They roll him around like a little ball, they get down on the floor and tickle him, and they just love him. What surprised me, though, is how much he observes them and copies them. When they jump rope, he wants to jump rope. When they do drills, he wants to do drills.

Made Here, Baby!: Jennifer, did it start early for you?

Jennifer Arndt: Well, let me answer it this way. My grandmother waterskied until the age of 75, and she was responsible for getting my mom in the pool. She and my grandfather are now 82. They lift weights with a personal trainer in their garage. My mom won the YMCA Nationals in 1969 in swimming and then swam for the University of Wisconsin before there was an official women's team. My mom is 58. In her free time she competes in triathlons and practices yoga. In growing up, we made exercise a family activity.

Made Here, Baby!: Alicia, is your experience similar?

Alicia McConnell: I also grew up in an active family. We went on ski trips, to the beach, hiked, and we did it together. It's helpful if the parents are active. I didn't grow up in the country, either; we lived in the city, so all of us tended to walk wherever we went. Most kids in the neighborhood walked, played stickball, stoopball, skateboarded, and rode bikes.

Made Here, Baby!: So it seems that exercise role models are important.

Shell: Children today need role models, and they're not getting them. In this age of video games, children often entertain themselves for hours at a time, and I don't think that's good.

Alicia: It is helpful if the family does something together, even if it's to walk around the block. If both parents are inactive and heavy, it's going to be tough. The kids might become inactive and heavy. I recently heard about a new program where children are given physical education homework. The kids go home, and in order to complete the assignment, they have to get a parent or guardian to exercise with them.

Shell: If no other children are around, Eric, my husband, and I will just go to the park and play. We roll down hills together or kick a soccer ball or just have fun. We must play with Eric as though we are four years old. I just let him have fun.

Jennifer: The women in my family are mothers who value fitness and have passed it along to their children and grandchildren. On our vacations, we played in the water or did yoga together. When we traveled, sitting in the airport was not an option. We walked.

Made Here, Baby!: Suppose the parents *are* fairly active but they can't get their children to get off the couch?

Alicia: I also believe in a reward model. Again, it often comes down to the parents, but I realize the environment plays a role as well. If your kid wants to play video games, that's fine, but offer that if they want to play for another half hour, they have to play basketball for a half hour first. Or try this: walk up to your kid and say, "I bet I can beat you at basketball," and then go out and play. If your child loves the competition of video games, they might take the competition into other areas.

Made Here, Baby!: We know that kids are concerned with body image. Do you think that part of the problem might be that kids are bombarded with all of these images of athletes with their perfect bodies and they think, *hey I can never look like that, what's the use?*

Alicia: Yes, there are naturally great athletes, but most aren't born that way. The difference between a child who's an athlete for life and one who isn't is a really fine line. Of course, one size doesn't fit all. A major problem is that parents have to recognize that different children have different body types. Although there are exceptions, chances are that a shorter, heavier, stocky child won't feel comfortable playing basketball or volleyball with tall, thin kids. However, the shorter and stockier kids might do better at sports such as judo or weightlifting. I think the choice of sports offered to kids in our schools is very limiting. We focus so much on football, baseball, and basketball, but wouldn't it be nice if other sports were offered?

Jennifer: I am certain there is some truth to the statement that some kids will give up because they don't see themselves as athletes, but I have seen all shapes and sizes do well if they are determined to do well. I wish there was a way to remove the word "failure" from our vocabulary. In my opinion, it's simply not a good word! There is always something you can learn, try, and do differently. If swimming isn't your thing, try dancing!

Shell: I am 6'3" and my husband is 6'7" so chances are my son will be taller than either of us. However, that doesn't mean we will push him into playing basketball. Eric can pick whatever sport he wants. His hero is Tiger Woods. So I don't care if he winds up liking tennis, swimming, or golf *as long as it's what he wants to do.*

Made Here, Baby!: So if my child doesn't want to play basketball or baseball, I should be encouraging them to try something completely new.

Alicia: I think there are only three things a parent should encourage in a young child: motor skill development such as gymnastics, athletics such as running, jumping, and throwing, and swimming. These exercises can be most anything. For example, if a child likes to juggle, jump rope, or play hopscotch, it really is about just getting them moving, and eventually that can lead into learning other sports.

Made Here, Baby!: Let's talk a little about pressure. Do you think sometimes there's too much pressure put on some children by some parents to be perfect at athletics? Do kids go back to sitting on the couch because they feel the pressure?

Shell: My opinion of organized sports may surprise people. Most kids won't be professional athletes, and they don't need the pressure from their parents. We don't all have the bodies of professional athletes. There is a whole creative side to play. Let your kids make up games. Parents also need to consider if they want their kids to play organized sports because the kids want it or because they want it. I don't care if my child plays organized sports or not.

Alicia: I also think that some parents must lighten up. Most of our athletic programs have become so structured that many children stop enjoying sports. It is important that children are encouraged to play sports for themselves, not just because their parents want them to excel.

Jennifer: I think too much pressure can be put on children to do well. We even see it in some of our college women on a regular basis. Pressure can come from many sources so there is not one person or group to blame. I am happy that the swimming world sees the value in developing women more slowly so that their swimming careers can be a lifetime. It seems like it's a trend to move a child from cheerleading camp to a swimming camp to tennis lessons and just to keep moving them around. I think even that can feel like pressure. Let's just play!

Made Here, Baby!: So you're saying that the world doesn't come to an end if a child wants to just go out to a skate park or ride her bicycle for an hour or two, rather than playing soccer?

Alicia: I just think there's a sport for everybody. I would love to see every child play and have fun. The earlier a child learns to be active, the better. Sports can transform a child. Don't wait. Help your child find something they love.

Shell: And I just want to see a smile on my child's face. Children are innocent. We can poison that innocence with too much pressure.

The experts agreed that children should be encouraged, not pressured, to enjoy physical fitness and not to be afraid to try new things. In this chapter, parents will get the chance to "visit" with many different American manufacturers that make sports and fitness products.

These products can help your child move. As the experts stated, there is no single right exercise or sport to fit all children. Whether she or he decides to try soccer, kayaking, swimming, baseball, skateboarding, or zipping around the streets on a scooter, there are American manufacturers to meet your needs.

In this chapter, we have also included several American manufacturers of athletic uniforms. Any type of uniform your child, league, or school might desire for almost any sport can be purchased from the companies listed on these pages either directly or through your local sporting goods dealer.

American-Made Sports and Fitness Equipment

A walk down the aisles of most major sporting goods retail stores would convince many Americans that our country has ceased to manufacture sports and fitness equipment for children. Nothing could be further from the truth. Many American manufacturers of sports and fitness equipment are still hanging in there, still fighting a courageous battle against formidable opponents.

American manufacturers believe that any differences in price between their products and the imports are more than outweighed by superior quality and an absolute dedication to customer service. Virtually every company listed in this chapter welcomes your e-mail questions or telephone calls. Each wants the chance to fight for your business.

- ❅ Sports and Fitness Clothing (includes clothing for all sports)
- ❅ Fitness Equipment (circuit training equipment specifically made for children)
- ❅ Sporting Goods (includes a broad range of items from soccer goals to baseball bats to jump ropes)
- ❅ Anything on Wheels (includes skateboards, bicycles, roller skates, scooters, and many other products)
- ❅ Water Sports (includes canoes, kayaks, and water exercise equipment)
- ❅ Winter Sports (includes snowshoes, ice skates, sleds, and snowboards)
- ❅ Hiking, Traveling, or Going to School (includes backpacks)

Sports and Fitness Clothing

One of the great surprises in the sports and fitness area is the large number of American manufacturers that still make clothing for just about any sport that is played. What is even more interesting is that sports apparel is the domain not just of large corporate operations but also of smaller companies, including women-owned companies. It is not always possible to buy sports apparel directly from the manufacturer; however, there are ways to buy their products either from local sporting goods stores or through an online store.

● ●

ADAMS USA, INC.   ↑ ✈
610 S. Jefferson Avenue, Cookeville, TN 38501
Telephone: 800-251-6857
Web site: www.adamsusa.com

Adams USA® manufactures football and batting helmets, chin straps, compression shorts, and sliding shorts for older boys and girls, 'tweens and up, and moisture-wicking material called Adams Wear for both older boys and girls, 'tweens and up. Other products are imported.

Interesting Fact: Based in Tennessee, Adams USA® has been in business for about 58 years. The company manufactures and/or distributes equipment for nearly every sport.

How to Find: There is a store locator on the Web site, or customers can type Adams USA into a search engine to locate online stores.

....

AERO TECH DESIGNS, INC. ✿ ↑ ¤

1132 4th Avenue, Corapolis, PA 15108
Telephone: 412-262-3255
Web site: www.aerotechdesigns.com

Aero Tech Designs, Inc. manufactures children's cycling shorts and jerseys in teen and, of course, all adult sizing.

Interesting Fact: Cathy Schnaubelt Rogers was always an avid cyclist, so it is not surprising that she might have pursued her dream to do something with cycling. Her dream led her to creating a cycling shorts and jerseys company in Pennsylvania. We think that's a good thing; she now employs many people and helps them realize their dreams. Aero Tech Designs provided the cycling uniforms for the 1982 U.S. Olympic cycling team when it competed in Barcelona.

How to Find: Customers may order directly through the Web site, call customer service, or visit the company store, in Corapolis, Pennsylvania.

....

COOL CLOTHING, USA ✿

6016 Carnegie Street, San Diego, CA 92122
Telephone: 760-401-7100
Web site: www.coolclothingusa.com

Cool Clothing, USA produces long- and short-sleeved shirts and shorts that have moisture-wicking properties. The clothing is made of Cool-Max® material and is great for 'tweens and teens who are athletes or like to hike, camp, or work out. The material used in the shirts is very elastic, so the smaller men's sizes, for example, can easily fit a growing teenager. The company does not specifically make children's-size clothing; however, given the elasticity of the material, preteens and teens may be able to wear the athletic shorts in addition to the tees.

Interesting Fact: Cool Clothing, USA was founded by husband-and-wife team Craig and Johana. Craig is an Operation Iraqi Freedom veteran who field-tested the CoolMax® material in Iraq, while Johanna is a marathon runner. They both know the value of clothing that rapidly wicks away moisture. When they started their company, they sought to use the material for civilian clothing.

How to Find: You may order directly from the company through the Web site, or call customer service if you have any questions.

DODGER™ INDUSTRIES ✿ O

1709 15th Avenue, Eldora, IA 50627
Telephone: 800-247-7879
Web site: www.dodgerindustries.com

Dodger™ Industries manufactures team uniforms and shorts in the USA for track and field, volleyball, soccer, basketball, softball, and lacrosse, along with practice clothing. The sizing starts from a youth small, which is the equivalent of children's size 6, and goes up to teens.

Interesting Fact: Dodger Industries is headquartered in Eldora, Iowa, with manufacturing, decoration, warehousing, and distribution in Fayetteville and Clinton, North Carolina. The company has been in business for more than 50 years.

How to Find: Dodger Industries sells to sporting goods dealers and not direct to customers. If a customer will e-mail the company, a representative will tell them the nearest retail location, or parents and coaches can call customer service for assistance.

EAGLE USA, INC. ↑ O

375 E. Third Street, Wendell, NC 27591
The company prefers e-mail.
Web site: www.eagleusaonline.com

Eagle USA™ manufactures sporting apparel for boys and girls, women and men. Sports apparel includes clothing for baseball, softball, football, soccer, basketball, field hockey, lacrosse, volleyball, and tennis. The company also manufactures compression clothes, sweat clothes, and other apparel. Youth sizes range from children's size 6/8 through to teens.

Interesting Fact: Eagle USA™, another of the great American sports apparel companies, is headquartered in North Carolina.

How to Find: Eagle USA has a retail locator on its Web site that will direct customers to the nearest location. Please note that the online ordering section on the Eagle USA Web site is for dealers only.

. . . .

PRIETO SPORTS ↑

9536 East Gidley Street, Temple City, CA 91780
Telephone: 800-551-8411
Web site: www.zeeni.com

Prieto Sports manufactures sports uniforms primarily for teams, as there is a minimum quantity for orders.

Interesting Fact: For 18 years, this family-owned American company has specialized in making sports uniforms for baseball, basketball, soccer, softball, and volleyball. Clothing is available for both boys and girls, with sizing starting with children approximately 40–50 pounds in weight.

How to Find: Customers may order through the Web site. Coaches or leagues wishing to customize uniforms are asked to call customer service. The Web site has a sizing chart for your convenience.

. . . .

RACE READY® ⊛ ↑

P.O. Box 251065, Glendale, CA 91225
Telephone: 800-537-6868
Web site: www.raceready.com

Race Ready® makes running clothes cut for both male and female long-distance runners. The clothing is not appropriate for young children; however, if your teenage athlete is seeking American-made running apparel, Race Ready has many different items that may be suitable.

Interesting Fact: The founder and the co-founder of Race Ready® are both marathon runners.

How to Find: There is a store locator on the Web site for your convenience, or customers may order directly through the Web site. If you don't have a computer or need further assistance, call customer service.

SOARK® RUNNING APPAREL ✿ ↑

401 E. High Street, Baldwin City, KS 66006
Telephone: 785-594-6431
Web site: www.soark.com

Soark® Running Apparel manufactures running shorts and tops for school-age children, teenagers, and older teens. According to the company, by the time the child is around 14 years of age, he or she is ready to transition from kid's sizing to x-small or small adult sizes.

Interesting Fact: Established in 1986, Soark® specializes in clothing for runners. Soark's founders began in the business at the very start of the running movement. They were designers for some of the world's largest running apparel companies before launching their own company.

How to Find: You may order online through the Soark Web site or by calling customer service.

TRENWAY TEXTILES ↑ ○

P.O. Box 2180, Johnson City, TN 37605
Telephone: 800-251-7504
Web site: www.trenwaytextiles.com

Trenway Textiles manufactures socks in youth, preteen, teen, and adult sizes.

Interesting Fact: Founded in 1977 by Harlen Booth, Trenway Textiles remains an American manufacturer of athletic socks for nearly every major sport. Offerings include athletic socks for baseball, softball, cheerleading, football, hockey, soccer, and leisure wear.

How to Find: Trenway Textiles does not sell to individual customers but sells only in quantities to retail stores. Please ask for Trenway socks, or special-order them through your local retailer. However, if you are a coach or athletic director, you may call Trenway Textiles for assistance.

Fitness Equipment

There is a debate among trainers as to whether weightlifting is good or bad for children in terms of long-term fitness and muscular development. An alternative to weight training is circuit training, where children and preteens can build muscular strength with a controlled motion that is much safer than free weights. The two companies in this part of the chapter have excellent reputations and can give expert advice. The equipment pieces can be purchased individually for a home gym or as an entire circuit for a school setting. Please see the product listings in the index for all companies making fitness equipment.

∙∙

AMERICAN MADE FITNESS EQUIPMENT, LLC® ↑
275 West Reynolds Street, Pontotoc, MS 38863
Telephone: 800-489-7191
Web site: www.americanmadefitnessequipment.com

American Made Fitness Equipment, LLC® manufactures hydraulic circuit training equipment specifically for children, from older grammar-school-age through 'tweens. The selection includes eight different machines. The entire system is appropriate for schools, and single pieces are good for home gyms.

Interesting Fact: The company has a strong commitment not only to building its products in America with American steel but also to improving the health of Americans. It makes separate lines of products for men, women, and children. Adult circuit training equipment is not meant for young athletes; one size does not fit all. The company wants kids to have fun while exercising and to gain positive rewards from fitness.

How to Find: Please contact American Made Fitness Equipment for professional advice and information on purchasing its hydraulic circuit training equipment.

LEGEND FITNESS®

140 Richardson Way, Maynardville, TN 37807
Telephone: 866-7-Legend
Web site: www.legendfitness.com

Legend Fitness® manufactures eight separate pieces of circuit training equipment for kids for in-home gyms and school settings. This is serious equipment and should never be misused. The equipment is most appropriate for older grammar-school-age kids through 'tweens and beyond.

Interesting Fact: Based in Tennessee, Legend Fitness®, was founded in 1977. The company manufactures strength training, circuit training, and weight-lifting equipment. It makes products for men, women, and children. The kids' circuit training system is designed to work muscle groups and maintain cardiovascular fitness and, at the same time, be appropriate for developing bodies.

How to Find: Call the customer service number for details and pricing. The company has dealers throughout the United States.

Sporting Goods

The products in this listing cover a wide range of equipment for baseball, basketball, gymnastics, hockey, softball, team handball, and conditioning. All of these companies welcome your telephone calls or e-mails with questions on their equipment. Several of these companies also have the ability to customize to better meet the needs of your young athlete or the requirements of your athletic program or league.

BARNSTABLE BAT, INC. ☺ ↓ ✂

40 Pleasant Pines Avenue, Centerville, MA 02632
Telephone: 888-549-8046
Web site: www.barnstablebat.com

Barnstable Bat, Inc. manufactures a complete selection of baseball bats for children ages 8–12, with larger sizes for teens and adults. While the company supplies bats to the Major Leagues, they also supply bats to Little Leaguers. Barnstable Bat also makes a very popular baby keepsake gift item called the baby birth bat. The baby birth bat is a 26 bat engraved with the baby's name, birth weight, date of birth, and other information. The company uses sustainably harvested birch, ash, and maple in the production of its bats. The company can customize.

Interesting Fact: Established in 1992 and based near Cape Cod, Massachusetts, Barnstable Bat® is an integral part of the more than 100-year tradition of baseball in New England. In fact, the Cape Cod Baseball League is considered the premier league for college players who are seriously considering tryouts for the major leagues. Many of the greatest superstars in major league baseball passed through the Cape Cod League, including Frank Thomas, Nomar Garciaparra, and Albert Belle. Barnstable Bat® supplies bats to the Cape Cod Baseball League.

How to Find: Order directly through the Web site, or call the customer service number for more information on any of the products. The company also has a retail store in Centerville, Massachusetts.

. . . .

FOLD-A-GOAL® ↑ ⚽

4856 W. Jefferson Boulevard, Los Angeles, CA 90016
Telephone: 800-542-4625
Web site: www.fold-a-goal.com

Fold-a-Goal® manufactures a wide selection of soccer goals for team practice or individual skills practice. The soccer goals are 100 percent American-made. The company also makes practice goals and goals for team handball, as well as a complete line of goal accessories. Other soccer products on the Web site may be imported.

Interesting Fact: Fold-a-Goal makes soccer goals in many different styles, from regulation size down to pop-up soccer goals.

How to Find: Individuals, coaches, or leagues may order equipment directly through the Web site. A catalog is available on request, or you can call customer service for additional information.

HEARTLAND SPORTS MANUFACTURING ↑

14655 Edgewood Road, Rogers, MN 55374
Telephone: 800-634-7350
Web site: www.supersteelgoals.com

Heartland Sports Manufacturing manufactures a complete line of goals for hockey, soccer, and lacrosse. The company has just introduced a baseball rebounder, which enables a young baseball or softball player to work on fielding grounders and pop-ups, or to improve pitching skills. For hockey players, the company manufactures a balance beam to improve puck handling and shooting, as well as off-ice shooting platforms.

Interesting Fact: Heartland Sports Manufacturing was established in 1982. Its rebounder equipment allows children to practice skills at home or with friends and obviously encourages exercise.

How to Find: Customers may order directly through the Web site, or they can call the customer service number for more complete information on any of the products.

JUMP ROPE STORE®, THE ↑ ✂

P.O. Box 11507, Portland, OR 97211
Telephone: 888-456-7802
Web site: www.jumpropestore.com

The Jump Rope Store® manufactures the original Olympic Jump Rope, which is in wide usage throughout the United States by athletes at all levels of ability and by kids just having fun and keeping fit at home or school. The jump ropes are available in 18 different colors and five sizes, depending upon the size and the needs of the child.

Interesting Fact: For more than 35 years, The Jump Rope Store® has manufactured the Olympic Jump Rope in custom colors and sizes in Portland, Oregon. The company has committed itself to manufacturing in the United States because it wants to be in charge of the quality of its products. The jump rope is the original segmented jump rope that is used in schools, health clubs, and training facilities across the nation. The company has the ability to customize colors for athletic teams, schools, alumni associations, and camps.

How to Find: Customers may order the jump ropes through the company Web site. If you are in Portland, you are welcome to stop by the store at 3059 NW Yeon Avenue, or call the store at 503-226-4221 should you have a question about appropriate-size jump ropes for a child.

· ·

LOUISVILLE SLUGGER® ✈ T
800 W. Main Street, Louisville, KY 40202
Telephone: 800-282-2287
Web site: www.slugger.com

Louisville Slugger® manufactures hardwood baseball bats in a wide variety of weights, sizes, and styles. The aluminum and composite bats are imported.

Interesting Fact: In 2009, Louisville Slugger® will be celebrating its 125th anniversary. Louisville Slugger is an American manufacturing treasure. There is probably no other brand that has been associated with any sport as closely as this company has been with the sport of baseball. From the littlest of ballplayers right through to Major Leaguers, Louisville Slugger has been part of nearly every baseball player's experience. Louisville Slugger is now in its fifth generation of continuous family management. The founder, a carpenter from Germany, was watching his first baseball game and saw how the bats kept cracking. He knew he could do better and did!

How to Find: The Louisville Slugger Company has established a network of dealers and online stores. To find the nearest sporting goods store, go to the store locator on the Web site or type Louisville Sugger into a search engine.

· ·

MYLEC, INC.®
155 Mill Circle, Winchester Springs, MA 01477
Telephone: 978-297-0089
Web site: www.mylec.com

Mylec, Inc.® manufactures goals, sticks, balls, goalie pads, and other equipment for street hockey and ice hockey. Mylec also makes goals for youth soccer and decking for roller sports.

Interesting Fact: Raymond W. Leclerc, the founder of Mylec, may be credited with the idea of playing hockey off the ice. In 1971, he created the first goals and equipment and street hockey was born. Today street hockey is played throughout the United States on sneakers or roller blades. Mylec, Inc.® products are widely used for the sport.

How to Find: The company's products are sold through major sports retailers and independent sporting goods stores. Please do an online search for hockey shops that specialize in street hockey.

NEEDAK® SOFT BOUNCE™ REBOUNDERS

120 W. Douglas Street, O'Neill, NE 68763
Telephone: 800-232-5762
Web site: www.needakrebounders.com

Needak® Soft Bounce™ Rebounders manufactures exercise rebounders or mini-trampolines. Like any other piece of exercise equipment, the rebounder can be used for healthy exercise, but it can be improperly used. To address this concern, the company has produced DVDs for children and their parents to learn the proper way to exercise. If supervised, children as young as toddlers can enjoy rebounding.

Interesting Fact: Rebounders, or mini-trampolines, were introduced as a form of exercise in the 1970s. Unfortunately, as the craze took off, the quality of mass-produced, often imported pieces declined. Robert Sanders started selling rebounders in the mid-1980s, and he was so dissatisfied with the quality of the imported products he was representing that he decided to establish his own manufacturing company, in O'Neill, Nebraska. The Needak® Soft Bounce™ Rebounder is the result of his efforts.

How to Find: Customers may order directly through the Web site, or call the customer service number for more complete information on any of the products.

TC SPORTS, INC.

7251 Ford Highway, Tecumseh, MI 49286
Telephone: 800-523-1498
Web site: www.tc-sports.com

TC Sports, Inc. manufactures a full line of sports accessories—the equipment that supports play, improves training, and increases safety. Sports included are gymnastics, baseball, basketball, soccer, football, and strength training. The company makes equipment such as goals, padding, kicking cages, beginner's balance beams, chin bars, basketball goals, and nets. This equipment is appropriate for school-age and older kids.

Interesting Fact: Founded in 1964, Michigan-based TC Sports specializes in equipment for virtually every sport your daughter or son practices.

How to Find: TC Sports has a store locator for your convenience. If you can't find a particular product, please contact the company for assistance.

WIFFLE BALL, THE, INC.
275 Bridgeport Avenue, Shelton, CT 06484
Telephone: 203-924-4643
Web site: www.wiffle.com

The Wiffle Ball, Inc. manufactures the Wiffle® Ball in junior, baseball, and softball sizes, Wiffle® plastic bats in two different sizes, Wiffle® plastic golf balls, and Wiffle® flying saucers and scalers.

Interesting Fact: The first Wiffle® ball was produced in 1953 and is now in its third generation. The Wiffle® ball's design came from the inspiration of the grandfather of the company's current owners. The company's founder was watching his son and his son's friend play a made-up stickball game featuring a plastic golfball and a broom handle. The golfball had perforations, and no matter how hard it was pitched or hit, it couldn't cause any damage. The grandfather knew a thing or two about pitching, as he had been a semipro baseball player. After a great deal of testing, he came up with a design that had eight long perforations.

How to Find: Wiffle® products are widely distributed throughout the United States and are available at most sporting goods stores and children's product retailers.

Anything on Wheels

American children have always been fascinated with finding unique ways to move, from soapbox racers to skateboards to roller blades. Not only do these activities promote fitness; they also give children a certain sense of freedom and are just plain fun.

....

BEER CITY™ SKATEBOARDS

P.O. Box 26035, Milwaukee, WI 53226
Telephone: 414-672-9948
Web site: www.beercity.com

Beer City™ Skateboards manufactures a wide selection of skateboard decks, from microsized decks for young children to 9 wide for adults. Beer City Skateboards also sells mounting hardware.

Interesting Fact: Established in 1994, Beer City™ Skateboards decided to launch its brand in response to the low-quality products that were being imported. The company is proud of the fact that it manufactures in the USA and also that its founders were skaters themselves and understand the products from personal experience. The skateboard decks are constructed from hard rock maple that is found in Wisconsin. The company is among the few skateboard manufacturers left in Wisconsin. Incidentally, the company name refers to the founder, Mike Beer, and not to the beverage!

How to Find: There are many skateboard shops that carry the Beer City Skateboards brand, or customers can buy a deck directly through the Web site.

....

BIKE FRIDAY® ✂ ↑

3364 W. 11th Avenue, Eugene, OR 97402
Telephone: 800-777-0258
Web site: www.bikefriday.com

Bike Friday® manufactures customized folding bicycles, with sizing to fit kids preteen and up. For younger children, parents may wish to consider tandem bikes or even triple bikes as an alternative to an expensive customized bike. The company can customize.

185

Interesting Fact: According to the company, the Bike Friday® bicycle got its name from Robinson Crusoe's trusty companion, Friday. Just as Friday went everywhere with Robinson Crusoe, the Bike Friday has the ability to fold up and go most everywhere, including on an airplane or train or in the closed trunk of a car. There are several models, from moderately priced to expensive, depending upon the needs of the user. The company also sells pre-owned models and offers tandem bikes and customized bikes for those with special needs, as well.

How to Find: For ordering, especially for children, please call the customer service number to better understand proper fitting.

· ·

COHORT® SKATEBOARDS

732 Park Lane, Corona, CA 92879
Telephone: 951-279-5129
Web site: www.cohortusa.com

Cohort® Skateboards manufactures skateboards appropriate for older grammar-school-age children, 'tweens, and older teens.

Interesting Fact: California-based Cohort® Skateboards is a manufacturer of decks, complete decks, skateboards with wheels, accessories, and protective gear. Everything is made in the USA. The company's vision is to satisfy the needs of the skateboard purist and, therefore, it is dedicated to American-made quality.

How to Find: Customers can order through the Web site or e-mail the company for further information.

· ·

MASON CORPORATION ↑ ★

8114 Isabella Lane, Brentwood, TN 37027
Telephone: 800-821-4141
Web site: www.masoncorporation.com

Mason Corporation manufactures several models of self-propelled riding scooters such as The Original Flying Turtle® and The Roller Racer®, which not only are fun but also build strength and cardiovascular endurance. The riding toys are recommended for children between the ages of 3 and 12. The highly unique scooter design was developed by a retired aircraft engineer.

Interesting Fact: Founded in 1981, the Mason Corporation makes many different types of products. For children, it is best known for its self-propelled riding vehicles that move by having children swing the handlebars from side to side. There is a model of the self-propelled vehicles, designed by a physical therapist, for children with special needs. While the riding toys might be considered purely toys, we are placing them in this section because they also help to develop fitness in young children.

How to Find: The Mason Web site has an independent dealer locator for your convenience. If customers can't locate a dealer near to their location, they can call customer service for assistance.

ORIGINAL BIG WHEEL®, THE/J. LLOYD INTERNATIONAL

The company is based in Cedar Rapids, Iowa.
Telephone: 319-365-5842
Web site: www.originalbigwheel.com

The Original Big Wheel®/J. Lloyd International manufactures the Big Wheel® and the girls' version, the Princess®. The products have been redesigned to comply with the latest safety standards and are appropriate for preschool children and older kids.

Interesting Fact: Is The Original Big Wheel® a toy, or does it encourage physical fitness at an early age? An argument can be made for either side. The Big Wheel® traces its origins to the 1960s, when it was introduced by Louis Marx Toys at the 1969 New York Toy Fair. Through the 1980s, the Big Wheel® became one of the most recognizable brands in America. Unfortunately, by 2001, the company was forced to go out of business. The good news is that the Big Wheel® has been revived after being purchased by J. Lloyd International. The Big Wheel rides again.

How to Find: Hot Wheels® and Princess® are available in mass retail and specialty store outlets throughout the United States and through online stores. Parts may be ordered from the company through the Web site.

SACRIFICE SKATEBOARDS

2948 Rubidoux Boulevard, Riverside, CA 92509
Telephone: 408-626-7600
Web site: www.sacrificeskateboards.com

Sacrifice Skateboards manufactures skateboard decks and also sells accessories.

Interesting Fact: Established in 1999, California-based Sacrifice Skateboards is another of the independent deck manufacturers that is competing against imported skateboard products.

How to Find: The best way to find Sacrifice Skateboards is to go to your local skateboard shop. The company also allows customers to order through its Web site.

SKATE ONE CORPORATION

30 S. Patera Lane, Santa Barbara, CA 93119
Telephone: 800-288-7528
Web site: www.powellskateboards.com

Skate One Corporation manufactures team and pro rider decks, along with skateboard accessories.

Interesting Fact: Powell Skateboards was founded in 1976 by George Powell. He has continued to make his skateboards for more than 30 years.

How to Find: The best way to purchase Powell Skateboards is from a local skate shop.

SKATELUGE ™

P.O. Box 716, Westborough, MA 01581
Telephone: 508-366-4091
Web site: www.skateluge.com

Skateluge ™ manufactures the Skate Luge, Street Luge, and Buttboard for older children through teens. The company strongly recommends that skaters use protective equipment and follow safe courses.

Interesting Fact: The history of the Skate Luge™ goes back to the early 1970s, when the company's founder and his two brothers started to experiment with ways to ride down hills with the help of gravity. After many trials, they designed a product that provided stability and control. The company's products are entirely made in the USA.

How to Find: You can order through the Web site, call customer service, or e-mail the company for further information.

··

XOOTR LLC
2001 Rosanne Avenue, Scranton, PA 18509
Telephone: 800-816-2724
Web site: www.xootr.com

Xootr LLC manufactures scooters in many different styles and price ranges generally for school-age children and older kids. Other products are imported.

Interesting Fact: According to the company, when it first designed the Xooter® Scooter, it expected that its prime customer would be college students. As it turns out, older people love the scooter as much as middle school and younger students. The Xooter® is easily carried, is very quick, and can maneuver much better than the old-time scooter models. The Xooter Scooter is manufactured in the USA and, depending on the model, may be made of all domestically sourced parts or domestic and imported parts.

How to Find: Xooter Scooters may be purchased directly through the Web site, or you can call or email customer service to see if there is a dealer in your area.

Water Sports

Whether you like to swim, canoe, or kayak, American manufacturers make excellent products for you or your child to use as you enjoy water sports. All of the companies listed in this part of the book have a strong orientation toward customer service. The kayak and canoe companies, especially, understand that your child's needs will considerably vary depending upon his or her size, experience, and the water conditions. They may work with you directly or suggest a retailer in your area.

· ·

AQUA JOGGER® ↑
4660 Main Street, Springfield, OR 97478
Telephone: 800-922-9544
Web site: www.aquajogger.com

Aqua Jogger® manufactures the Aqua Jogger® Junior buoyancy belts, as well as the Tri-Fit® rhythmic breathing educational materials.

Interesting Fact: Established in 1987, Aqua Jogger® is addressing the needs of those who appreciate the cardio and low-impact advantages of exercising in water. Many athletes, young and old, do aqua aerobics to supplement their other exerise programs. The company started about 20 years ago. Interestingly, the technology was initially developed to treat injured long-distance runners at the University of Oregon.

How to Find: Customers can order directly through the Web site or by e-mail, or they can call the company for further information.

· ·

JACKSON KAYAK ↑
325 Iris Drive, Sparta, TN 38583
Telephone: 931-738-2628
Web site: www.jacksonkayak.com

Jackson Kayak manufactures kayaks specifically intended for children. The kayaks come in five different series, with 10 different models, for children ranging from 30 pounds to 150 pounds. Jackson Kayaks is one of the few kayak companies, and perhaps the only one, in the United States with such an extensive collection of products that it can accommodate children of all ages and ability levels.

Interesting Fact: Jackson Kayaks manufactures the Fun 1®, along with several other kayak models that are specifically designed for children. When the company was founded in 2004, the very first product off of the assembly line was a child's kayak.

How to Find: There is a store locator on the Jackson Kayak Web site. If you are unable to find a dealer close to you, please contact the company for assistance.

KŌKATAT WATERSPORTS WEAR ↑

5350 Ericson Way, Arcata, CA 95221
Telephone: 800-225-9749
Web site: www.kokatat.com

Kokatat Watersports Wear manufactures paddling suits, jackets, and pants for kids approximately middle-school age and up. The company also makes sizes suitable for teens and adults, both men and women.

Interesting Fact: Established in 1971, Kokatat has been based in Arcata, California, since that date, employing residents from the community. Its mission is to make watersports gear for paddling, sailing, and other watersports. Many of the company's employees are active outdoors people and especially like kayaking.

How to Find: Please refer to the company Web site for a detailed store locator list. You may also call customer service to find the store nearest your location.

MOHAWK CANOES ↑

The company is based in Fort Smith, Arkansas.
Telephone: 877-226-6329
Web site: www.mohawkcanoes.com

Mohawk Canoes manufactures the Solo 13® and Solo 14® canoes for children. The canoes are lighter and more maneuverable than larger canoes.

Interesting Fact: Mohawk Canoes was founded more than 40 years ago and is still a family-owned and -operated business. The company prides itself on the durability of its products, and many of its canoes have been in continuous use for decades.

How to Find: Orders may be placed directly through the Mohawk Canoe Web site. However, because the company is so focused on customer service, it encourages you to call first to ask about the best canoe for you or your child.

OLD TOWN® CANOES AND KAYAKS T
P.O. Box 548, Old Town, ME 04468
Telephone: 800-343-1555

Old Town® Canoes and Kayaks handcrafts a selection of canoes for recreation, trips, expeditions, and sporting purposes. The canoes are available in the classic wood construction or are made of other materials, such as fiberglass, polyethylene, or advanced composites. Some models are smaller and very stable and are more suitable for children. Old Town® Kayaks are also available in many different styles depending upon the family needs. The Dirigo 140 and Dirigo Tandem Plus models are made for family recreation and have removable child seats so that your child can be in front of you as you paddle. There are also smaller, stable models better suited for older children and teens. It is highly recommended that if you wish to purchase an Old Town canoe or kayak for your child you visit with your local Old Town dealer for professional advice.

Interesting Fact: An American manufacturing treasure, Old Town® is still located in the same town as when it opened its doors, around 1898. Generations of Maine craftsmen from the same families have passed down their canoe- and kayak-making art from father to son.

How to Find: The Web site has a dealer locator for your convenience. If you don't have a computer, please call the customer service number for assistance.

WENONAH CANOE, INC. ↑
P.O. Box 2476, Winona, MN 55987
Telephone: 507-454-5430
Web site: www.wenonah.com

Wenonah Canoe manufactures canoes and kayaks for children as part of its overall product line. The company recommends the Fisherman 14″ and the Aurora 16″ as they are small, stable, and maneuverable and provide a secure platform for outdoor enjoyment. Wenonah has a separate brand, called Current Designs, with its own Web site: www.cdkayak.com. A selection of kayaks may be found on that site. The company recommends the Raven model for use by children, but several other models are also appropriate, depending upon the child's abilities. Wenonah also manufactures stabilizer floats that can attach to the canoe to make it virtually impossible for the canoe to flip. The starting age for children to use canoes and kayaks is 9 to 11 years. The company stresses the importance of having adult supervision for children who are learning to canoe or kayak, as well as the proper safety equipment.

How to Find: Wenonah Canoes and Current Designs Kayaks are available in sporting goods stores and specialty outdoor sports stores. If you are unable to locate the model you want or want to ask questions about the products, please e-mail or call customer care.

Winter Sports

These companies in this part of the chapter specialize in manufacturing products to help your child enjoy exercising all through the winter months and to appreciate the beauty of nature. The list includes manufacturers of snowshoes, sleds, ice skates, and snowboards. With snowshoes and ice skates especially, different models are made for different purposes; for example, a child who enjoys snowshoe racing would use a different shoe than a child who does wilderness hikes.

Please feel free to contact any of these companies should you have questions in regard to proper size and fit, terrain, and nearest retail locations.

. . . .

CRESCENT MOON™ SNOWSHOES   ⊛   ☺   ↑
1199 Crestmoor, Boulder, CO 80303
Telephone: 800-587-7655
Web site: www.crescentmoonsnowshoes.com.

Crescent Moon™ **Snowshoes** manufactures several models of snowshoes. For children up to 80 pounds, it offers a kid's shoe. The Silver 13 model is good for older children and young adults. There is an enhanced version of the Silver 13 that has a higher level of performance for teens and for women.

Interesting Fact: Jake Thamm and his wife are active outdoors people who especially love to ski and snowshoe. Dissatisfied with the snowshoes and the bindings made available to them, they decided to start their own snowshoe company in 1996. Crescent Moon™ has embarked on a major program to make its operations as green as possible. To that end, it no longer uses PVC in its products and essentially recycles all of the materials left over from manufacturing.

How to Find: The company sells through a network of retailers. Please see the store locator on the Web site or the listing of online stores that also carry the product. If you need assistance, call customer service.

. . . .

HAVLICK SNOWSHOE

2513 State Highway 30, Mayfield, NY 12117
Telephone: 800-867-7463
Web site: www.havlicksnowshoe.com

Havlick Snowshoe manufactures snowshoes for children from as young as 10 years of age through teens. Generally speaking, children starting at 70 pounds in weight are able to comfortably wear the company's snowshoes. The company recommends the 22" Havlick Sprinter, 25" Tracker, and 25" Adirondack models. New for 2009 will be a 21" racing model.

Interesting Fact: The husband-and-wife founders of Havlick Snowshoes started their business as a hobby in the mid-1960s but did not get truly serious about expanding their operations until the mid-1980s. The company's areas of expertise include snowshoes for racing, heavy duty hiking, and recreational use.

How to Find: Havlick Snowshoes may be purchased directly through the Web site, or customers may call customer service for the name of the nearest retail outlet. The company has a factory store located in upstate New York.

. . . .

MAD RIVER ROCKET™ SLED COMPANY, INC. ⊛ ☺ ↑

2 Brook Road, Warren, VT 05674
Telephone: 802-496-9882
Web site: www.madriverrocket.com

Mad River Rocket™ **Sled Company, Inc.** manufactures sleds made of recycled plastic that are appropriate for older children and teens.

Interesting Fact: The Mad River Rocket™ sled was created by an architect in 1984. It is a unique sled that combines sledding with downhill skiing. According to the company, it was the older kids who really started to explore the downhill limits of these highly maneuverable sleds.

How to Find: There is a detailed store locator on the Web site, as well as online retailers. If you prefer, order directly through the Web site, or contact the company for more information.

MOUNTAIN BOY SLEDWORKS

1070 Greene Street, Silverton, CO 81433
Telephone: 800-989-5077
Web site: www.mountainboysleds.com

Mountain Boy Sledworks handcrafts fine wooden sleds for children and their parents, in self-propelled pull and push models. The products the company makes in America include the Elegant Flyer and the Royal Flyer, which are classic wooden sleds, the Bambino Deluxe and the Superior classic pull sleds, and the classic wooden kicksleds. Other products in the line are imported. Custom engraving is available on the wooden sleds that are made in the USA.

Interesting Fact: The company has a strong commitment to sustainable forestry, recycling, and green manufacturing techniques.

How to Find: There is a detailed store locator list on the Web site, or you may contact the company directly and order through the company Web site.

REDFEATHER SNOWSHOES®

2700 Commerce Street, LaCrosse, WI 54603
Telephone: 800-525-0081
Web site: www.redfeather.com

Redfeather Snowshoes® manufactures two serious snowshoe models for elementary and middle-school children, as well as the Snowpaw design for preschoolers' outdoor fun.

☆
Made Here, Baby!

Interesting Fact: Redfeather Snowshoes® was founded in 1988 by a snow-bound triathlete with the idea of designing a better snowshoe that would allow racers to train during the snowy Colorado winter months. Redfeather has committed itself to creating unique bindings that reduce fatigue. In the area of children's products, Redfeather wants to make the snowshoe experience fun for children. For example, it recently introduced the Snowpaw shoe, which leaves animal tracks.

How to Find: There are three ways to buy Redfeather snowshoes: through the company Web site, by accessing the store locator, or by finding an online retailer.

. . . .

RIEDELL® SHOES, INC. ✿ ↑ ✈
122 Cannon River Avenue, Red Wing, MN 55066
Telephone: 651-388-8251
Web site: www.riedellskates.com

Riedell® Shoes, Inc. manufactures the following items in the United States: ice skate model 121 (Blue Ribbon beginner skate) and higher, including intermediate and advanced skates; roller skate artistic boot model 121 and higher; and speed boots 122 and higher. Other models may be imported.

Interesting Fact: In 1945, Paul Riedell saw an opportunity to turn his love of roller skating into a business. He started Riedell Shoes, in Red Wing, Minnesota. Throughout the years, he and his wife, Soph, manufactured only top-quality, handcrafted skating boots and built a reputation for supplying the world's best skates with exceptional fit and comfort. The company is now in its third generation of Riedell family members.

How to Find: The Riedell® Web site has a dealer locator for your convenience. If you can't locate a retail store near to your location, please call customer service.

. . . .

SINED SNOWBOARDS
P.O. Box 7399, Breckenridge, CO 80424
Telephone: 970-389-5223
Web site: www.sinedsnowboards.com

Sined Snowboards manufactures snowboards in various sizes and performance characteristics.

Interesting Fact: Headquartered in Colorado, Sined Snowboards manufactures its snowboards in California. The boards contains an aspen core (aspen is one of the predominant trees found in the mountains of the western United States).

How to Find: The Sined Snowboards Web site has a store locator, as well as a directory of online stores. You are also welcome to call customer service for assistance.

Hiking, Traveling, or Going to School

At some point, it's hard to say when exactly, kids started carrying their books in backpacks. At that point, the backpack was transformed from something that was used on hikes to an essential piece of back-to-school equipment. In addition to the companies listed here, please refer to the product index E under Children's Products: Backpacks for hiking, travel, or going to school.

BATTLE LAKE OUTDOORS, INC.
203 Main Street West, Clarissa, MN 56440
Telephone: 800-243-0465
Web site: www.battlelakeoutdoors.com

Battle Lake Outdoors™ manufactures a large selection of packs and bags ranging from backpacks and fanny packs to duffel bags, travel bags, and specialty bags for sports such as hockey. For children through teens, Battle Lake Outdoors™ makes several models of backpacks. The company recommends the Rainbow Pack or the Standard Day Pack for school use. For smaller children, there are smaller fanny packs and the Monarch pouch.

Interesting Fact: Battle Lake Outdoors is a family-owned and -operated business that was founded in 1988.

How to Find: The best way to purchase Battle Lake Outdoors products is directly through the company's Web site. Call customer service if you require additional assistance.

DRIFTER BAGS

5423 Pearl Road, Parma, OH 44129
Telephone: 800-547-7274
Web site: www.drifterbag.com

Drifter Bags manufactures a selection of backpacks, fanny packs, and daypacks suitable for school-age children, 'tweens, and older teens, depending on the model. The company has the capability to monogram or to customize.

Interesting Fact: Founded in 1977, Drifter Sport and Travel Bags, Inc. began as a parachute rigging business. As the company expanded its operations, it wanted to create travel products that were as reliable as its parachutes.

How to Find: Orders may be placed through the Web site or by calling the customer service number.

HUGGAGE

Huggage is an online company based in North Carolina.
Telephone: 919-403-7095
Web site: www.huggage.com

Huggage manufactures a plastic overnight case for children ages 3 and up.

Interesting Fact: Huggage manufactures a kid-size suitcase for overnight trips or for carrying school supplies, art projects, or just about anything. The suitcase comes with a strap for ease of carrying and comes in either red or blue.

How to Find: You may order directly from the Web site or call customer service.

CHAPTER 7

American-Made
Toys and Games

It's no mystery that 2007 was a pretty miserable year for most of the toy industry. Of the 473 total product recalls that year,[1] the U.S. Consumer Products Safety Commission (CPSC) had recalled 61 toys involving more than 25 million product units.[2]

Unfortunately, there was no magic line separating 2008 from 2007. The recalls came in with the ringing of the New Year. According to Consumers Union,[3] in just the first four months of 2008, 5.9 million toys were recalled. Many of these toys—in fact, hundreds of thousands of these toys—violated lead paint standards. Many more toys posed serious choking hazards or had major design flaws, and who knows what the inspectors will find next?

In addition to the safety issues, there was also the matter of value. By "value," we don't just mean the cost of a toy, though some toys have become pretty expensive, but whether the toy will have meaning to our children. It seems as though many toys have simply lost their *value*. Who hasn't seen a situation where a really expensive toy in a fancy package that a child practically screamed for was

---

1. www.ConsumerUnion.org, May 15, 2008.

2. News from the Consumer Products Safety Commission, Release #08-086, available online at www.cpsc.gov.

3. Consumers Union Report, May 15, 2008, "Still Not Safe: New Recalls Underline Need for Strong Hazardous Product Legistlation," www.consumersunion.org.

quickly ignored for a silly little gift that was given almost as an afterthought?

In 2007 and again in 2008, we often saw the perfect storm, where an expensive toy was also dangerous or where it had little value, except to the companies profiting from them.

All of these issues led us to ask an important question: When we walk down the aisle of our favorite toy store and we see what we think is a great toy, how do we really know that it's a great toy? That leads to other questions: How do we know it's a safe toy? How do we know our children won't toss it aside right after the wrapping comes off? We don't always know the answers to those questions, but the Oppenheims usually do.

Except for Santa Claus, the Fairy Godmother, and Geppetto the Toymaker (Pinocchio's dad), there are probably no two people in America as knowledgeable about toys as the mother-and-daughter team of Joanne and Stephanie Oppenheim.

The Oppenheims are regular contributors on the subject of toys and educational products to NBC's *Today Show*. Joanne is one of our nation's most trusted authorities on child development and education. She has written more than 50 books for and about children, not to mention 14 annual editions of the Oppenheim Toy Portfolio. Stephanie is also a child development expert, as well as an attorney and a co-founder of the Oppenheim Toy Portfolio, www.toyportfolio.com.

What makes the Oppenheim Toy Portfolio unique is that these experts, who also happen to be moms, don't accept fees from toy companies to test their products. They are impartial, and their standards are high. The Oppenheims use a panel of real-life testers, young and old, from every walk of life, to put toys, games, and educational materials through their paces. They ask tough questions about safety issues and demand straight answers. They also question each toy's value.

To the Oppenheims, fun-looking toys are serious business. However, that doesn't mean that Joanne and Stephanie are beyond poking a little fun at themselves or remembering back to their own childhood toy experiences.

For this chapter, we thought we would ask Joanne and Stephanie to reminisce about the toys they loved as children. Then we asked Joanne and Stephanie, as toy experts, to take a step back from themselves and to consider why they think they liked those toys.

Made Here, Baby!: Joanne, we will first start with you. Please think back to your own childhood, way before you ever thought you would be doing this kind of work. What were the toys you loved?

Joanne Oppenheim: As a young child, all my favorite toys had wheels. There was a kiddy car, tricycle, doll carriage, roller skates, and even a wagon. We used the wagon to take bottles back to the store for refunds that we could spend for ice cream cones.

I also loved my dolls and my doll house—especially the doll house, because my dad used a giant battery to make a doorbell that rang. He was trying to teach me about electric circuits, I am sure. There was also a light he rigged up in the little dollhouse that always came undone. For me, the doll house was all about the stories I made up. Pretend play was central. I remember my older brother's collection of soldiers [this was during World War II]. He conducted war games while I played the stereotypical games that girls played in the late 1930's and early 1940's. We did, however, play together building Tinkertoy® windmills [Tinkertoy is a registered trademark of Hasbro], and making a library from our book collection using handmade cards and checkout slips.

I liked playing Chinese checkers. Maybe I liked Chinese checkers because of the colors of the marbles or the sound of them dropping on the tin tray. But, most of all, it seemed to be a game I was good at playing. Being the youngest of six cousins, it was hard for me to compete with all the others. For some reason, maybe it was because they let me win, I liked this game!

Made Here, Baby!: Stephanie, what toys do you remember?

Stephanie Oppenheim: Ironically, given what I do now for a living, I didn't play with too many specific toys as a kid. Given my mother's background in education and child development, we were given lots of open-ended play materials such as blocks, art supplies, and big empty appliance boxes for making our own pretend settings.

I wasn't big on stuffed animals or dolls. Much to the disappointment of my mother, as I am the youngest of three and the only girl, I really didn't play with the beautiful dollhouse my parents brought home. In fact, if a potential play date was going to involve stuffed animals or dolls, I would pass in favor of more active whole-body play opportunities.

If I had to single out one particular toy, it would be the spectacular oversized, ride-on Steiff pony I got for my fourth birthday. It was a sad day when I had to admit I didn't fit it anymore!

Made Here, Baby!: Joanne, we are fascinated with your love of toys with wheels. Please step back from your childhood now, and explore why you think this was so.

Joanne Oppenheim: Looking back, I realize that the wheeled toys were also about pretend and being big enough to do what the older kids could do. But, I'd say that the pretend pieces were central.

Making up stories was something I did with props or daydreaming in the back of the car on long trips. Being able to entertain oneself, to have the free time to daydream, seems to be a lost art for today's kids, who are inundated with images on screens of every kind. Even the toys they play with have premade stories that rob play of one of its essentials—the creativity of making one's own cast of good guys and bad. Just as we had more time to play without adult supervision, we were free to make up our own games. We would say, *Wanna play war, or store, or school, or whatever?* Too many toys we see today dictate the play, and, in my opinion, they limit the richness of play. We call them bossy toys that tell kids what to do or leave kids with little more to do than push a button. When that happens, the fundamental values of play are lost.

Made Here, Baby!: Stephanie, please step back from your childhood, as well.

Stephanie Oppenheim: I wish I could say that I determined my own play interests from the start, but the truth is that my older brothers played a huge role in determining what toys were cool and engaging. They made fun of the one Barbie® [Barbie® is a registered trademark of Mattel®, Inc.] doll I received. She was quickly banished even though she had on amazing white go-go boots!

As with most younger siblings, I wanted in on the action, so I was much more involved with their projects. This meant that I was an excellent assistant when we were trying to run Hot Wheels® [Hot Wheels® is a registered trademark of Mattel®, Inc.] tracks throughout the house.

I was also thrilled to be included when we made our homemade tents that took up the entire room. I also spent a great deal of time outside in our bottomless sandbox, digging up my brothers' lost treasures. The treasures were an assortment of toys, and, much to my mother's chagrin, a fair number of good teaspoons. My brothers also told me that if I kept digging, I would get to China just like on Looney Tunes® [Looney Tunes® is a registered trademark of Warner Brothers]. In my own defense, I was much younger, and I idolized both of my brothers. In terms of active play, my blue banana seat Schwinn® bicycle [Schwinn® is a registered trademark of Schwinn, Inc.] was my pride and joy. The day I was given permission to ride down the hill on my own meant that I was truly one of the big kids.

As a professional toy reviewer, I find that the toys that are more open ended are still the products that score consistently well with our testers.

Our big cardboard blocks could be a throne, a rocket, a road, or whatever we wanted them to be on any given day. The appliance box we were given as children could be a castle one day and store the next day. The sandbox was the site of many great epic battles and adventures or just a great place to flood with a garden hose! Most of the toys I enjoyed were really just great props for our imagination. It's comforting to me that these are still the types of toys that test best year after year.

While there is certainly room for novelty in toyland, we've found that most kids want to be at the center of their play experience. One of our testers, a six-year-old, left a talking doll at her friend's house. When the mother offered to go back and get the doll, the six-year-old said she had left the doll on purpose because the doll talked too much! Another seven-year-old tester was offended by talking action heroes; the tester said, "I have my own adventures!"

The message from both Joanne and Stephanie seems to be all about adventure: let's let our children have their adventures, but let's let them create and play with toys that are safe and give real value.

☆
Made Here, Baby!

We were struck by the fact that two of our nation's leading toy experts fondly remembered simple activities filled with fantasy: digging clear down to China, for example, or riding to the store in a toy wagon. After all of these years, isn't it nice to know that Jo-anne still remembers the sounds of marbles plopping onto a game board and that Stephanie can feel the wind blowing through her hair as she rushes down a hill on her bicycle? What happens when we allow children to lose out on these very simple pleasures?

Fortunately, the American manufacturers of toys, puzzles, and games detailed in this chapter are proud to make products that can provide children with years of safe adventures.

Now, we're not saying that all toys from one country are unsafe, while all toys from another country are dangerous. That would be a cruel and untrue thing to say. What we are saying is that parents, grandparents, aunts, and uncles have many more choices than we might think.

The toy companies listed in this chapter and throughout this book have been making children's products for a pretty long time. They are very good at what they do. They understand things like choking hazards and the importance of using baby-safe paints and finishes. It is not enough for something to look like a toy; it must be safe as a toy. If you are shopping at a holiday fair or a flea market, don't be afraid to ask questions! Homemade toys might look great, and maybe they are great, but be wary. Reputable companies, even the very tiniest of our American toy companies, will happily answer your questions.

We started by saying that 2007 was a pretty miserable year for most of the toy industry. However, something very nice did happen for the toy industry in 2007 and again in 2008. America began to discover or, maybe, to rediscover that America still has toy, game, and puzzle manufacturers! "Where were you all these years?" people seemed to ask.

The companies were almost like little beacons for parents. During all of the hoopla, hand wringing, and the public apologies from the multinational companies, American manufacturers and crafts-people, quietly working away in wood, fabric, and plastic, were still producing magnificent products. In fact, many American manufacturers gleefully admitted that during the worst of it, their phones were ringing off the hook. The phones are still ringing.

What a concept! Americans buying American!

American-Made Toys and Games

In this chapter, we get to meet new friends and old. Here we can find the classic toys and games of our grandparents and even great-grandparents, along with some of today's most innovative and award-winning games and puzzles.

- ❊ American Classic Toys (includes American handcrafted wood toys)

- ❊ Let's Build This Together (American model making and doll-houses)

- ❊ Puzzles and Games for All Ages (includes building sets)

- ❊ Fantastic American Plastic Toys (the world of plastic toys)

- ❊ Arts and Crafts

- ❊ Everything Plush and Cuddly

- ❊ Just Plain Fun (includes kazoos, garden gnomes, and flying saucers)

- ❊ Outdoor Play (includes swing sets and sandboxes)

American Classic Toys

It is not too difficult to think of many of the toys in this listing as works of art, rather than as toys. The wooden toys, especially, made by American craftspeople of native hardwoods, are hand rubbed or painted and take us back to a time and place many of us thought had been forgotten. The craftsmanship of some of the pieces make it tempting to buy them as living room decorations. Not surprisingly, toymakers such as Horace Sanders of Sanders Handcrafted

Toys or the Buchmann family of Buchmann's Toymaker Shop would prefer that the toys be given to children. What keeps these toymakers going? It is children's laughter, of course!

This part of the chapter also offers us many surprises, toys we thought had been lost, such as traditional children's wagons, balsa wood airplanes, metal tricycles with inflatable tires, gnome houses, the Slinky®, and rocking horses. It is comforting to know that our classic toys haven't left us.

ANIMALS AND ARKS
4487 Rabbit Run Road, Trumansburg, NY 14886
Telephone: 866-291-2882
Web site: www.wildapples.com

Animals and Arks handcrafts toys for toddlers through preschool and makes keepsake items for the entire family. The toy line includes toddler push and pull toys in various animal shapes, wooden puzzles, and theme and habitat toys. In terms of themes, the company makes a Noah's Ark complete with animals, classic Nativity sets in three different sizes, and toy sets using other biblical subjects such as Jonah and the Whale. Habitat toys include a doghouse with little dogs, Kitten Caboodle cat with kittens, and even a dinosaur habitat.

Interesting Fact: The head toymaker, Gunther Keil, emigrated from Germany more than 35 years ago. He lives on 55 acres of land, where he raises sheep, keeps bees, and utilizes the wood from the trees grown on his land. Virtually all of the wood used is recycled or reclaimed from the trees in the area.

How to Find: Orders may be placed through the Web site or by contacting the company through the customer service number.

BEKA, INC. ↑
542 Selby Avenue, St. Paul, MN 55102
Telephone: 888-999-2352
Web site: www.bekainc.com

Beka, Inc. manufactures classic block sets and block wagons, children-size tables, storage carts, easels, creative play theaters, bean bag toss games, and art supplies. The company still produces looms and weaving and knitting accessories for older children and adults.

Interesting Fact: Established in 1973, Beka started as a manufacturer of weaving looms made out of hard maple and sold its products primarily to yarn stores. In the 1980s, Beka, Inc. changed its focus to wooden toys and larger creative play products that were also made of American hardwoods.

How to Find: Beka, Inc. welcomes consumers to buy directly through its Web site. Many independent toy stores carry the company's products, as do catalog companies and online retailers. Customers can type Beka into a search engine to find several online retailers.

BERLIN FLYER WAGONS ⌑
Holmes County Road 120, Berlin, OH 44610
Telephone: 330-893-3281
Web site: www.berlin-flyer.com

Berlin Wagons manufactures traditional children's red wagons constructed of wood and metal. The wagons are available in different styles and sizes.

Interesting Fact: Founded more than 30 years ago and located in Amish Country in Ohio, Berlin Flyer Express Wagons prefers to sell its production to a select number of online Web sites and stores, rather than to sell through its own Web site. The wagons feature a no-tip design that is especially valued by parents. These are classic, very well-constructed products that were almost thought to have been lost. The company also manufactures cedar chests and closets.

How to Find: The Web site has a store locator for your convenience. The company also invites the public to stop by its factory when in the area.

BUCHMANN'S TOYMAKER SHOP ⊛
111 Spruce Tree Lane, Syracuse, NY 13219
Telephone: 315-488-6741
Web site: www. buchmannstoymakershop.com

Buchmann's Toymaker Shop handcrafts dollhouse furniture, dollhouses, classic wooden toys such as a Noah's Ark, giraffe and stacking clown ring-toss games, pull toys, hobby horses, rocking horses, and circus wagons with little wooden animals.

Interesting Fact: The Buchmanns were first inspired to start a toy company as the result of the heirloom dollhouse furniture that had been handed down in their family for four generations, originating in their native Bavaria. They founded their company in 1976 because they wanted to pass along the simple joys of old-fashioned childhood. What child wouldn't want to have the Buchmanns for relatives? Mr. Buchmann handcrafts the toys, and Mrs. Buchmann paints them, using classic Bavarian patterns and colors. All the toys and furniture are copywritten and signed and dated by the Buchmanns. The line of doll furniture and wooden toys, with their Bavarian folk-art motif, has been purchased by Hollywood celebrities and may be seen in toy shops around the world.

How to Find: Customers may order through the Web site, or they can call customer service for more information.

· ·

CHICKORY WOOD PRODUCTS
11027 N. Industrial Drive, Mequon, WI 53092
Telephone: 262-242-4410
Web site: www.chickorywoodproducts.com

Chickory Wood Products handcrafts a large assortment of wooden trains; trucks, such as firetrucks, steam rollers, and school buses; airplanes, such as helicopters, jumbo jets, and biplanes; toy guns of all different kinds; and boats, such as car ferries, naval vessels, and speed boats. The company also makes bread boards and customized children's stepstools.

Interesting Fact: Chickory Wood Products was started by a single father of two children. The story almost sounds like a fairy tale, except for the fact that it is real. The family was deeply in debt, and it was approaching Christmas time. The father owned a machine shop and did the only thing that made sense: He ripped apart a broken wooden pallet and turned the wood into a beautiful toy. He took a chance and entered a craft fair with his toys and won first place in the toy competition. The business was launched for real at that point.

How to Find: To order, please contact the company through its Web site or call customer service.

....

CUBBY HOLE TOYS ✿ ✈

98 Oregon Avenue, West Dundee, IL 60118
Telephone: 800-848-0291
Web site: www.cubbyholetoys.com

Cubby Hole Toys manufactures personalized puzzle stools, alphabet stepstools, name puzzles, inlaid board games, coat racks, and interlocking name puzzles. Other products may be imported. Made in USA items are clearly marked.

Interesting Fact: Founded more than 30 years ago, this family-owned business came about after a father made a toy for his son, and things just seemed to grow after that point. Cubby Hole Toys specializes in personalized wooden products for children.

How to Find: Cubby Hole Toys are widely available on retail Web sites devoted to children's products, or inquiries may be placed directly with the company.

....

D AND ME WOOD TOYS ✿ ↑

119 Heritage Drive, Stevensville, MT 59870
Telephone: 866-326-3638
Web site: www.dandme.com

D and Me Wood Toys handcrafts wooden trucks and cars, such as Montana logging trucks, mini-car carriers, dump trucks, farm tractors, and ABC block trucks, train sets, classic pull toys such as the Klickity Klacker and Flip Flop, doll furniture, and full-size wooden toy boxes. For older children, the company makes a Tic-Tac-Toe game.

Interesting Fact: In addition to a beautiful selection of wooden toys, the company also sells handmade quilts.

How to Find: Orders may be placed through the Web site or by contacting the company through its customer service number.

209

. . . .

DON EDWARDS WOODEN TOY WORKS

The company is located in DeRuyter, New York.
Telephone: 877-485-8697
Web site: www.donedwardstoyworks.com

Don Edwards Wooden Toy Works handcrafts wooden trucks, boats, doll cradles, toddler-size rockers, and games made from furniture-grade white pine. Some of the items in the product line include giant trucks, grinning-clown ring-toss games, monster-size pickup trucks, marble games, and doll cradles. The company also makes a giant biplane toy, large enough for a child to sit on, and a toddler rocker. All products are finished with nontoxic, water-based treatments.

Interesting Fact: Don Edwards was a broadcaster for 30 years and then taught broadcasting at Syracuse University before starting his wooden-toy company. While the leap from academia to toymaking might seem unexpected, Don always loved woodworking. Starting at age 7, he worked with his grandpa, a master woodworker from Germany. The young boy apprenticed with his grandfather for many years. Don's factory is housed in a renovated dairy barn in upstate New York.

How to Find: Orders may be placed through the Web site or by contacting the company through its customer service number.

. . . .

DOODLETOWN ™ TOYS, INC. ⚽

P.O. Box 814, Big Lake, MN 55309
Telephone: 763-263-5123
Web site: www.doodletowntoys.com

Doodletown ™ Toys, Inc. handcrafts wooden toys for toddlers through school age. Toys include personalized name trains, where cars of the train spell out the child's name; block sets; doodles, which are small trucks and cars perfect for kid-size fingers; pull toys such as Gertie Grasshopper; clocky puzzles; larger trucks and trains; sword and shield sets; and bags of blocks or bags of small cars and trucks.

Interesting Fact: Founded in 1972, the motto of Doodletown Toys® is "Little Toys for Little Hands™." The company concentrates on making products that are child-safe but especially focuses on toys that appeal to children and not just to parents.

How to Find: Orders may be placed through the Web site or by contacting the company through their customer service number.

....

EZ 2 LOVE® ✿
EZ 2 Love is located in the Bellwood, Pennsylvania, area.
Telephone: 814-742-7407
Web site: www.ez2love.com

EZ 2 Love® handcrafts a complete line of classic wooden toys, including trains, planes, cars, pull toys, and push toys, as well as a toddler tool kit in which the tools themselves are made of wood. In addition to the beautifully crafted toys, EZ 2 Love also makes baby rattles, rocking horses, and a unique old-fashioned wooden pull sleigh, which is appropriate for children up to 3 years of age and certainly can be handed down from one generation to the next.

Interesting Fact: Darryl has been a toymaker for more than 30 years, following in the tradition of his grandfather, who was a cabinetmaker. Prior to working at his business on a full-time basis, he was a vocational education instructor.

How to Find: Please contact the company through the Web site or by calling customer service. The company also does numerous craft shows throughout Pennsylvania.

....

GREEN MOUNTAIN BLOCKS ☺ ↑
P.O. Box 146, Danville, VT 05828
Telephone: 888-329-4673
Web site: www.greenmountainblocks.com

Green Mountain Blocks manufactures wooden building blocks in all shapes and in kits of various sizes. These kits run from the simplest of shapes to an architect kit and a superkit that allows for a great deal of creativity and design. The games include a ring-toss game, and, for older children, the company makes the board game Mancala, which is a game that goes back to ancient Africa. The company uses locally grown and sustainably harvested hardwood lumber, and all products use 100 percent natural materials.

Interesting Fact: In 1996, the company's founder had two motivations for starting his toy company: he has seven children, and he also needed a new hobby! Since that time, he has sold block sets to thousands of customers throughout the United States.

How to Find: The company sells exclusively through the Web site.

....

PAUL K. GUILLOW, INC. ⊛ ↑
40 New Salem Street, Wakefield, MA 01880
Telephone: 781-245-4738
Web site: www.guillow.com

Paul K. Guillow, Inc. manufactures classic balsa wood glider planes (with and without propellors) in nearly 20 different styles, authentic scale Word War I and World War II balsa wood airplane model kits, plastic and foam airplanes, and model building supplies. The line is appropriate for children from preschool and up, depending upon the product. Because they contain small parts, the kits are not appropriate for young children.

Interesting Fact: Paul K. Guillow was a World War I navy aviator, and he founded his company because of his love of flying and his feeling that Americans might have an interest in model airplanes based on World War I aircraft. In 1927, after the flight of Charles Lindbergh, Guillow's business took off. When Mr. Guillow passed away in 1951, his wife, Gertrude, took over the company as both president and treasurer. She grew and diversified the company until 1980, when she turned over the company to her management team.

How to Find: Please go to the Web site to find a store locator. You may also order the toys and models online. Call customer service for further assistance.

....

HEARTWOOD ARTS ↑ ✂
8999 Soda Bay Road, Kelseyville, CA 95451
Telephone: 707-277-0130
Web site: www.heartwoodarts.com

Heartwood Arts handcrafts wooden gnomes, gnome houses, blocks, bridges and castles, miniature wooden cups, plates, and saucers, and large wooden play clips to enable children to build play forts and caves. There is a picture of a child-size gnome play house on the Web site. The gnome play houses are works of art and are built by special request.

Interesting Fact: William Bluhm has been designing, sculpting, and carving products from wood since he was 11 years of age. He is now in his sixties. Mr. Bluhm has a deep love and respect for the woods of northern California, and his designs reflect the shapes, colors, and feel of the woods. Prior to starting Heartwood Arts in 1980, he worked with troubled children as a counselor. He was very influenced by the Waldorf philosophies of imaginative play and, as a result, his toys bring to life imagination and fun.

How to Find: Mr. Bluhm often prefers to speak directly to customers when they place their orders. He likes to get to know people. Customers can download a form from the Web site and fax the order into the company.

HIS IDEA CRAFTS
1790 Market Street, Dayton, TN 37321
Telephone: 423-570-0783
Web site: www.allhishorses.com

His Idea Crafts handcrafts rocking horses in a wide selection of styles. The prices vary depending upon the size of the rocking horse, the decoration, and, of course, the type of wood that is specified. Customers may choose products made of pine, maple, oak, walnut, or cherry. Two sizes are available: for children up to 5 years of age, and a larger size for children to 8. Please note that these are heirloom quality and can be thought of as wonderful toys or as room decoration or both.

Interesting Fact: The seed of a business idea was nurtured in John Sprankell in 1986 when he decided to make a wooden rocking horse for his daughter. It was not until 1995, when he was 56 years of age, that he launched the company. John credits his faith for giving him the motivation to try something new after 33 years in the corporate world. Working side by side, John and his wife have sold their rocking horses in all 50 states and have shipped them to 17 countries.

How to Find: Orders may also be placed by calling customer service or directly through the Web site.

HOLGATE TOYS® T

P.O. Box 528, Bradford, PA 16701
Telephone: 814-368-4454
Web site: www.holgatetoy.com

Holgate Toys® manufactures several different wooden toy product lines, with each line consisting of many items. The main product lines include Classic Toys, Mr. Rogers' Neighborhood® Toys, Personalized Toys, and Limited Edition Toys. The Classic Toys include block wagons, the Rocky Color Cone, Slate & Chalk, wooden trucks, cars and trains, the Hickory Dickory Dock Clock, and lacing toys. Mr. Rogers' Neighborhood® includes trolleys and walking puppets. Personalized Toys include stepstools and stepchairs that can be customized with your child's name. Limited Edition toys are wonderful reproductions of toys going back to the 1930s and further. It is certainly worth your time to review all of the company's offerings on its Web site. The age range of Holgate Toys begins with toddlers and runs through school age.

Interesting Fact: Holgate Toys® is arguably the granddaddy, or grand-mommy, for that matter, of all of the toymakers in America and is clearly a national manufacturing treasure. Holgate Toys® was established in 1789, the same year George Washington took his first oath of office and the U.S. Constitution was signed. It is a testament to the quality of Holgate's product line that it has remained in business for more than 220 years. If your parents, grandparents, or even great grandparents were born in this country, it is safe to say that they would recognize Holgate Toys.

How to Find: There are several ways to order Holgate Toys: through the company Web site, through Internet toystores, or by visiting your local specialty toy shop.

JOHN MICHAEL LINCK–TOYMAKER ☺

2550 Van Hise Avenue, Madison, WI 53705
Telephone: 608-231-2808
Web site: www.woodentoys.com

John Michael Linck–Toymaker handcrafts wooden train sets, where each train car may contain up to 10 different varieties of wood; block wagons with blocks; classic lawnmower clacker toys; riding wooden airplanes made from red oak, cherry, or walnut that roll on tire casters; a riding crane, also on tire casters; doll beds; and children's treasure chests.

Interesting Fact: After being trained as a cabinet maker in Germany, Mr. Linck's grandfather sailed to America in 1867 to begin a career in woodworking. Mr. Linck represents the third generation of fine woodworkers in his family. The toys are as much pieces of art as items to be played with, and, indeed, some people simply like to collect them. However, they are as durable as they are attractive. John uses sustainably harvested wood in all of his toys, sourced from a third-generation Wisconsin woodcutting family that selects all of the wood used in production.

How to Find: Orders may be placed through the Web site or by contacting the company through its customer service number.

KNOCKABOUT TOYS ☺ ↑
P.O. Box 208, Searsmont, ME 04973
Telephone: 207-975-1452
Web site: www.knockabouttoys.com

Knockabout Toys makes wooden trucks for children as part of its Little Rigs line. These include cargo trucks, steam rollers, delivery trucks, firetrucks, and pickup trucks. The toys are made from pine, maple, and birch. Two other lines comprise the Knockabout Toys product line: the Big Rigs and Executive Rigs. The Big Rigs are larger trucks, such as 18-wheelers, logging trucks, and tankers, and measure more than two feet in length. The Executive Rigs are not meant to be toys but are for display. They are true-to-scale, crafted models, with many moving parts and several types of wood. The Executive Rigs are heirloom quality and are a high-end product. They are beautiful in their design and in the way in which the wood is honored.

Interesting Fact: Jim Jefferson, the owner of Knockabout Toys, tries to build his products using scrap or recycled wood products whenever possible.

How to Find: To order, please contact the company through its Web site.

....

LAURI® TOYS ⊛

51 Magnetic Avenue, Smethport, PA 16749
Telephone: 800-451-0520
Web site: www.lauritoys.com

Lauri® Toys manufactures a large selection of learning toys for toddler, preschool, and school-age children. These products include alphabet and pre-reading games, handpuppet craft kits, peel and stick craft kits, Dot-2-Dot Lacing™ activity kits, Lauri Crepe Rubber Puzzles, seasonal and model-making kits, and Lauri Manipulatives, which offers a large selection of dexterity and developmental games.

Interesting Fact: Lauri® Toys was founded by a retired school teacher in 1961 who wanted to create better teaching aids for toddlers, preschool, and school-age children. She knew she wanted to create a new puzzle but didn't know how to manufacture the pieces. She realized the crepe rubber used in her husband's shoe repair business would be perfect, and so her first product was born. The puzzle concept that Lauri made would go on to become an award-winning classic that has won international recognition.

How to Find: Lauri® Toys are widely available in retail stores throughout the United States and through many online stores. Please go to the Lauri Toys Web site or call customer service.

....

LEHMAN'S, INC. ⊛ ↑ ✈

One Lehman Circle, Kidron, OH 44636
Telephone: 888-438-5346
Web site: www.lehmans.com

Lehman's, Inc. manufactures children's toys and quilts sourced from Amish craftspeople. Products include toy trains, marble toys, wooden tops and yo-yos, and sock monkeys. Some of the products on the Web site are imported. Lehman's will indicate the Made in USA items.

Interesting Fact: Founded in 1955 by Jay Lehman and now supported by the expert marketing direction of Glenda Lehman Ervin and other family members, the company was originally formed to assist the local Amish communities by finding them lanterns and other products to help them maintain their self-sufficiency. Soon the customer base expanded, and it was not long before almost everyone who needed emergency light or power sources came to Lehman's for these products. Then an interesting thing happened. Americans seeking better-made products from another era began asking Lehman's where they could find Amish quilts and toys, and before long the people that Lehman's were supplying also became their vendors! If you are in the vicinity of Kidron, Ohio, it is worth your while to stop in at Lehman's. The retail space comprises 30,000 square feet and is large enough to accommodate four pre–Civil War buildings in addition to the impressive selection of products. Lehman's carries many products that most Americans believe to be long gone.

How to Find: Orders may be placed directly through the Web site or by calling customer service.

LINDENWOOD, INC. ↑
P.O. Box 1355, Grand Rapids, MI 49501
Telephone: 616-248-4453
Web site: www.unclegoose.com

Lindenwood, Inc. manufactures classic alphabet blocks, foreign-language blocks, and specialty blocks for adults. Blocks are made out of basswood with beveled edges and using nontoxic inks.

Interesting Fact: Lindenwood, Inc. makes Uncle Goose™ Alphabet Blocks. In addition to English, blocks also come in Danish, Dutch, French, German, Greek, Hebrew, Italian, Norwegian, Polish, Russian, Spanish, Swedish, Braille, and Sign. Uncle Goose™ has recently introduced blocks for teens and adults featuring Sudoku and hieroglyphics.

How to Find: Please refer to the retail store locator on the Web site or purchase through the company online. Call customer service for assistance.

MAPLE LANDMARK OF VERMONT, INC. ✿ ↑ ↓ ¤
1297 Exchange Street, Middlebury, VT 05753
Telephone: 800-421-4223
Web site: www.maplelandmark.net

Maple Landmark of Vermont, Inc. manufactures an extensive selection of wooden toys for children. The age range generally runs from infants to age 8. For infants, there are 11 different types of wooden rattles. For toddlers to preschool, there are classic pull and push toys; alphabet and number blocks; hobby horses; name trains of many different types; engines and cabooses, along with annual collector engines; cars, trucks, farm, zoo, and circus animals on wheels; wooden train tracks along with bridges and buildings; yo-yos and wooden whistles; games for older children, including Chinese checkers, checkers, Tic Tac Toe, several types of cribbage; and Mancala games. Room decorations include personalized coat racks and knob racks.

Interesting Fact: Maple Landmark Woodcraft® is a family-owned and-operated business with an intense loyalty to American manufacturing. Three generations of family members, along with 30 dedicated crafts-people, design and manufacture wooden toys. Under the banner of Maple Landmark Woodcraft® products are the Name Trains Wooden Railway System® and the Montgomery Schoolhouse® products, along with many other fine products. Because of the size of the line as well as the ways products can be personalized, it is worth your time to explore the Web site.

How to Find: The company has an extensive dealer network. Please go to the Web site to use the store locator. You may also order through the Web site, or call customer service if you need assistance.

....

OLD FASHIONED BLOCKS
70 New River Road, Manville, RI 02838
Telephone: 800-962-6785
Web site: www.oldfashionedblocks.com

Old Fashioned Blocks handcrafts many different kinds of wooden toys for toddlers to school-age children. The items include blocks and block wagons, ABC blocks in classic lettering, wooden castle blocks, push lawnmowers, rocking horses, lambs, lions, and tabletop skittles games. Dollhouse furniture includes armoires, doll cradles, beds, highchairs, and ironing boards.

Interesting Fact: All of the toys sold by Old Fashioned Blocks are manu-factured in its Rhode Island workshop. The blocks and many other wooden toys are made from hard maple. The company states that over the past 15 years it has supplied blocks to more than 10,000 classrooms.

How to Find: To order, please contact the company through the Web site or call customer service.

··

POOF-SLINKY, INC. ✤ ↑ ✈

45400 Helm Street, Plymouth, MI 48170
Telephone: 800-329-toys
Web site: www.poof-slinky.com

Poof-Slinky, Inc. manufactures classic toys and games. The American-manufactured products include the Original Metal Slinky® and plastic versions of the Slinky®, Poof® foam sports balls including the soccer-ball, basketball, football, and the power spiral football, Slinky® pom-poms, and Slinky® spin-wheels. Other products are imported.

Interesting Fact: The Original Metal Slinky® was discovered by accident. In 1943, a young naval engineer was designing cushioning devices utilizing springs, and one of the springs fell off the workbench and started to walk down books stacked next to the workbench. He brought it home to his wife for her opinion, and the two of them decided to start a company!

How to Find: Poof-Slinky, Inc. products are sold throughout the United States at all major toy chains and specialty shops. Customers may also order through the Web site.

··

POPPYWOOD TOYS ☺

225 Rogue River Parkway, Talent, OR 97540
Telephone: 541-512-9447
Web site: www.poppywood.com

Poppywood Toys manufactures dollhouse furniture including doll high-chairs, large and small doll cradles, wooden toy barns with barn animals, gnome homes, and wooden cars.

Interesting Fact: As a toymaker, Poppywood Toys wants children to have fun with their products, but, at the same time, the company feels a strong sense of environmental responsibility. Whenever possible, the company uses recycled wood for its toymaking operations.

How to Find: To order, please contact the company through its Web site or call customer service.

. . . .

POPULAR POPLAR TOYS ⚽

HC 60 Box 194, New Martinsville, WV 26155
Telephone: 304-455-2495
Web site: www.popularpoplartoys.com

Popular Poplar Toys handcrafts toys from poplar wood and accents the poplar with other West Virginia hardwoods such as black walnut, cherry, and oak. The toys include large, medium, and small train sets; circus trains and individual train cars; classic marble toys; large, medium, and small wheeled vehicles such as dump trucks, tractors, firetrucks, graders, tankers, and bulldozers; airplanes and helicopters; sternwheeler boats; classic wooden games; craft toys such as lap looms; and animal jigsaw puzzles.

Interesting Fact: In business as American toymakers, Charles and Shirley Smith of New Martinsville have been creating wooden toys, puzzles, and games for more than 25 years. Charles was once a construction worker and used his time in the winter, when the work was slow, to hone his woodworking skills. Shirley was a schoolteacher but gave up that occupation to work full time with her husband.

How to Find: Orders may be placed directly through the Web site or by calling customer service.

. . . .

ROCKIN' CHOPPERS ✂

The company is located in the Lake Lure, North Carolina, area.
Telephone: 828-625-8560
Web site: www.rockinchoppers.com

Rockin' Choppers handcrafts rocking chairs in the shape of a motorcycle. This may indeed be one of the most unusual children's rocking toys you've ever seen. The chairs are made using poplar dowels (no screws, nails, or metal fasteners are used) to avoid any injury to children, and the main wood used is a Baltic birch. The seats are covered in real leather. All of the finishes used are nontoxic. This is a limited-production item, and no two are ever exactly alike.

Interesting Fact: About 6 years ago, Louis, the owner of Rockin' Choppers, was looking for an interesting present for his nephew's first birthday. Unable to find anything he liked that could be store bought, he started playing around with bits and pieces of wood he had in the basement. He was particularly fascinated with a couple of large dowels that were sticking out of a box and reminded him of a motorcycle tailpipe. One wooden piece led to another, and, before he knew it, he had created the very first Rockin' Chopper, a motorcycle rocking chair!

How to Find: If you have an interest in a Rockin' Chopper, it is probably best to call the company. These are heirloom-type products, custom-made, and require time to make.

SANDERS HANDCRAFTED TOYS

The company is located in the Alexandria, Louisiana, area.
Telephone: 318-445-5443
Web site: www.sanderstoys.com

Sanders Handcrafted Toys handcrafts a selection of wooden toys for toddlers through school-age kids. All toys are made from select hardwoods, including eastern maple, ash, and black walnut; then they are rubbed with nontoxic mineral oil. The toys include wooden cars and trucks, such as cranes, car carriers, and tow trucks; wooden train sets such as freight trains and zoo trains; crayon holders; pull and push toys; and bookends. Not shown on the Web site is a children's glider horse made upon request.

Interesting Fact: Horace Sanders is a retired engineer who loved working with wood so much that he bought a wooden toy company. The story Mr. Sanders tells is that he used to buy the company's toys for his nieces and nephews. One day Horace casually told the owner that if he ever wanted to retire and sell the company he should let him know. Not long after, he did receive a phone call, and Horace found himself in the toy business. Due to several back surgeries, he must work from a wheelchair. He works in pain but considers the woodworking to be therapeutic for his back, and the fact that he likes to make children happy with his toys nourishes his spirit, as well.

How to Find: Orders may be placed directly through the Sanders Handcrafted Toys Web site. Call customer service if you don't have a computer.

....

SEASON'S NATURAL TOYS® ❀ ✈ ✂

The company is located in the Brevard County, Florida, area.
Telephone: 888-WEE-HAUS
Web site: www.seasonsnaturaltoys.com

Season's Natural Toys® handcrafts fantasy wooden toys in vibrant,
nontoxic colors. These Made in USA toys include the Original Treehouse, which is an heirloom, handmade house about two feet in height;
wooden toy furniture, such as a treehouse kitchen; Wee Houses, such
as the Toadstool House, Acorn House, Fairy Cottage, and Witch House;
Wee doll families; wooden forest trees; and play silks. Please note that
some of the pieces are small, and, per the company, they are not recommended for children under 3 years of age. Some products are imported.
Made in USA products are clearly marked.

Interesting Fact: An illustration of the new face of American manufacturing, this woman-owned company was purchased from the original
woman founder. Season's Natural Toys has dedicated itself to creating
products that spark imagination and creativity in young children with
enchanting, natural Waldorf toys.

How to Find: Orders may be placed through the Web site or by
contacting the company through its customer service number.

....

SMART MONKEY TOYS

P.O. Box 1371, Wisconsin Rapids, WI 54495
Telephone: 866-387-5610
Web site: www.smartmonkeytoys.com

Smart Monkey Toys manufactures large blocks for role play and
smaller blocks for improving language skills.

Interesting Fact: Smart Monkey Toys are large and small blocks made
from specially constructed cardboard. The blocks are intended to
develop role-playing skills for toddlers and preschool children, while
the smaller blocks, or Little Reader block sets, are intended to improve
reading and grammatical skills. Each set of 18 reader block sets contain
noun blocks, adjective blocks, verb blocks, and pronoun and preposi-
tion blocks.

How to Find: Orders may be placed directly through the Web site or by calling customer service.

. . . .

UNDER THE GREEN ROOF ✿

8835 Nicol Hill Road, Cottondale, AL 35453
Telephone: 205-553-7660
Web site: www.underthegreenroof.com

Under the Green Roof handcrafts classic wooden toys and decorations. The products include wooden letter children's name room decorations; wooden animals on wheels, both handpainted and handstained and finished in animal shapes such as horses, zebras, turtles, and elephants; handpainted dinosaurs on wheels; personalized children's name puzzles; classic American sock monkeys and Jumping Jacks; wooden tray puzzles, wall clocks, and bookends; circus trains; and trays.

Interesting Fact: Based in Alabama, Under the Green Roof draws upon the talents of local craftspeople for its unique selection of toys and games. Many of the toys are classic, such as the Sock Monkeys, which goes back to the 1920s.

How to Find: Orders may be placed directly through the Web site or by calling customer service.

. . . .

VALLEY ROAD WOODWORKS ○

The company is located in the Quarryville, Pennsylvania, area.
Telephone: 800-311-6333
Web site: www.durabletoys.com

Valley Road Woodworks is a company based in Amish country that handcrafts wagons and tricycles in its welding and woodworking shop. The Valley Road Speeder Amish Wood Wagons come in several different styles, colors, and tire combinations. These are true wood and metal wagons and sturdy tricycles, and Valley Road Woodworks is one of the few manufacturers left in America that produces them. The larger tandem wagons can hold two children sitting side by side, or, if you need to haul things around your garden, the wagons will do that, too. Of interest is the Beach Wagon, which has oversized tires to make it easy to use at the beach. The company also makes a classic metal tricycle, the Valley Road Air Tire Tricycle, in red, blue, green, or pink.

Interesting Fact: Some manufacturers prefer to be represented by distributors, especially smaller workshops. The company does not have a Web site for selling purposes, nor does it sell direct to the public.

How to Find: Type the key words "Valley Road Wagon" into a search engine. This will immediately refer you to a select number of online stores that carry the wagons and the tricycles. As there are several model choices, it is recommended that you call the online stores for more detailed information.

WHITTLE TOY COMPANY, INC. ☺
600 S. Main Street, Louisiana, MO 63353
Telephone: 573-754-4033
Web site: www.woodentrain.com

Whittle Toy Company, Inc. makes wooden trains that include Mega Trains, which are large railroad cars; regular-size wooden train sets, tracks, and bridges; trucks, including school buses and post office trucks; and the Mr. Zip™ LLV (Long Life Vehicle), Amtrak™ train stations, and turntables.

Interesting Fact: Whittle Shortline Railroad™ is the number one maker of wooden toy trains in the United States and uses wood from reforested birch. This is the company that makes the famous Little Engine That Could™ train, including the engine, boxcars, and caboose.

How to Find: Please refer to the Web site for a complete listing of retail locations and online retailers. The company also has a factory store and a retail location in Missouri.

WISCONSIN WOODCHUCK ✿
3274 N. Rifle Road, Rhinelander, WI 54501
Telephone: 715-282-5953
Web site: www.wisconsinwoodchuck.com

Wisconsin Woodchuck handcrafts two separate selections of products. The first selection is scale-model collectibles that are made of beautiful hardwoods. These are signed pieces, intricate and fairly expensive. The second selection is a collection of children's toys. Unlike the expensive collectibles, there is a large selection of cars, trucks, campers, tractors, and tractor-trailers in the $2.00–$5.00 range. Somewhat more expensive items include toy buses, large and small wooden train sets, airplanes, helicopters, boats, tugs, and paddle wheelers. The toys are finished with mineral oil for safety or with nontoxic paints. In addition to the models and toys, Wisconsin Woodchuck also makes hardwood rocking cradles and an airplane rocking toy.

Interesting Fact: Chuck and Leslie Felton, the owners of Wisconsin Woodchuck, specialize in handcrafting collectible scale models that are signed, dated, and numbered.

How to Find: Orders may be placed through the Web site or by contacting the company through its customer service number.

WUNDERWORKS OF AMERICA
Wunderworks of America is located in the St. Louis, Missouri, area.
Telephone: 314-323-1530
Web site: www.wunderworkstoys.com

Wunderworks of America manufactures the Wunderwagon® in the shapes of school buses, fire engines, taxi cabs, and trains. Riding toys are available in dog and duck shapes. The typical age range is from age 2 to about age 6.

Interesting Fact: Wunderworks Toys is an American wagon and riding toymaker. The company has the unique concept of providing changeable sides to its wagons, so a child can get pulled around in a fire engine one day and a school bus the next. The wagons and riding toys are made of wood and painted in nontoxic paints.

How to Find: Orders may be placed through the Web site or by contacting the company through its customer service number.

Let's Build this Together

It seems there is so little time these days for family togetherness. Model building is a wonderful way for families to bond, whether the family spends quiet time making a dollhouse or a sailing ship, watches steam puff from an engine, or builds a tractor model in the heart of a large city. There are still wonderful American manufacturers of models for children from preschool to high school and beyond. Please see the Model Building section in the product index E under Children's Products: Model and educational kits for additional companies.

GREENLEAF DOLLHOUSES ⊛ ↑
463 Lake Road, Schenevus, NY 12155
Telephone: 800-253-7150
Web site: www.greenleafdollhouses.com

Greenleaf Dollhouses produces a wide selection of dollhouse kits and dollhouse furniture. The kits range in complexity from a Victorian home with seven gables to a haunted house to a camping trailer! The dollhouse furniture is made for every room in the house. The kits also range in price point. Obviously, hobbyists who like to collect miniatures will spend months decorating these houses, or the houses can be very simply decorated to bring joy to your child. Because they contain small pieces, these houses are not appropriate for very young children. In addition to the dollhouse kits, Greenleaf Dollhouses also makes kits for building birdhouses.

Interesting Fact: Established in 1947, Greenleaf Dollhouses is the largest dollhouse manufacturer in the world. In 2009, it should have a company store open to the public, and the company plans to offer limited-edition models in addition to the regular product line.

How to Find: Greenleaf Dollhouses may be ordered directly from the company or through an extensive retail network of stores that sell miniatures. Please call customer service for the retail store nearest you.

HOVERCRAFTMODELS.COM™
P.O. Box 2222, Windemere, FL 34786
Telephone: 240-252-1805
Web site: www.hovercraftmodels.com

Hovercraftmodels.com™ manufactures several models of radio-controlled hovercrafts. These models are obviously not intended for young children.

Interesting Fact: In 1994, Kevin Jackson, founder of Hovercraftmodels
.com™, built and demonstrated a semiscale model of the first working
Hovercraft. The model was the result of extensive research. The model
was shown at a few events and elicited a lot of interest and inquiries
from other model builders who wanted access to drawings and other
information.

How to Find: Orders may be placed through the Web site or by
contacting the company through its customer service number.

JENSEN STEAM ENGINES ↑
700 Arlington Avenue, Jeannette, PA 15644
Telephone: 800-525-5245
Web site: www.jensensteamengines.com

Jensen Steam Engines manufactures miniature steam engines and
steam power generators. For hobbyists and educators, Jensen produces
nine models of brass- and nickel-plated engines. The company also
produces cast iron models for collectors. These models are appropriate
for children ages 9 and up, obviously with parent or teacher supervision

Interesting Fact: Established in 1932, Jensen Steam Engines represents
a trip back in time. Not only is the factory unusual in that it makes
miniature engines, but many of the parts, such as the brass fittings, are
made in nearby foundries or in the shop itself. However, the more
meaningful part of the journey is steam itself. Many children, and even
some adults, may not understand that, before gasoline engines and
electrical power, it was steam that moved America. These products are
sought after for science classes and science fairs because they are as
instructional as they are fascinating.

How to Find: Orders may be placed by calling Jensen Steam Engine
customer service or by visiting the Web site.

LINDBERG MODELS®/J. LLOYD INTERNATIONAL
The company is located in the Cedar Rapids, Iowa, area.
Telephone: 319-365-5842
Web site: www.lindberg-models.com

Lindberg Models®/J. Lloyd International manufactures Lindberg® Models and Lindberg Science Kits.™ The models include unassembled anatomicals kits, missiles and spacecraft, aircraft, armor, cars and trucks, dinosaurs, historical and patriotic kits, ships, destroyers, and submarines. There are more than 200 kits available. These are unassembled plastic model kits and are not toys appropriate for young children.

Interesting Fact: J. Lloyd International has several brands that are made in the USA under its banner (see the listing under Big Wheels® in Chapter 6). The largest line in terms of variety is the Lindberg® Models and Lindberg Science Kits.™ Other brands by J. Lloyd International that are made in the USA include Tim Mee Toy®, Mighty Wheels®, Kid League®, Tootsie Toy®, and Mr. Bubbles®.

How to Find: Lindberg Models are widely available in specialty and hobby stores throughout the United States, as well as through online retailers

• •

MOORE'S FARM TOYS ↑
3695 Raiders Road, Dresden, OH 43821
Telephone: 740-754-6248
Web site: www.mooresfarmtoys.com

Moore's Farm Toys manufactures scale-model, highly detailed tractors and combines, farm implements such as sprayers and cultivators, grain trucks, tractor trailers, pickups with snow blades, flatbeds, log trailers, and many more. Please note that these models are meant for middle-school and older children as they contain many small parts. These are models and are not meant to be toys.

Interesting Fact: The founder of Moore's Farm Toys was probably born to do what he is doing. The son of a farm equipment salesman, he started collecting scale-model farm toys in 1974, around the time his own son was born, not quite knowing where it would lead. After attending a toy show in 1981, he had an idea to manufacture scale models. By 1994, demand was so great that he had to move the operation and put on help. Despite a fire in 1998, he continued his operations, and today, with several employees, his business continues to grow. Even if you live in a city, here's your chance to get close to a farm!

How to Find: Moore's Farm Toys is sold through a network of hobby shops and model retailers. If you can't find these items at your hobby store, please call customer service.

● ●

NU-CUT WOOD PRODUCTS ✾ ↑

11089 S. 2700 W, South Jordan, UT 84095
Telephone: 801-254-6366
Web site: www.martindollhouses.com

NU-Cut Wood Products produces large dollhouses and dollhouse furniture, made to fit the scale of the most popular dolls on the market. The dollhouses are in kit form and, when fully assembled, will stand higher than your preschool child. The company recently introduced My Play Kitchen, which includes full-size heirloom kitchen sets, and Action Figure City sets for kids who like to play with action figures.

Interesting Fact: Frank Martin and his wife, Bobbie, started the company about 16 years ago. The company specializes in making over-size dollhouse kits out of white birch. Please note that the dollhouses are meant for children 4 years and older. They are not meant to be climbed on.

How to Find: Orders may be placed by faxing an order or by contacting the company through its customer service number.

Puzzles and Games for All Ages

America has not lost its ability to manufacture fine puzzles and games. The games are creative, often humorous, sometimes traditional, but always reflective of the integrity of the people we interviewed.

The diversity of these companies and the products they sell is matched only by the diverse backgrounds of the owners. Some of the companies were born out of big business, or strategic planning, while other companies were started by a single person with a dream. Despite a tendency for some among us to think that products such as American-made games and puzzles have disappeared, we found the opposite to be true. American puzzles and games are winning awards for their creativity and their ability to challenge young minds.

BLISTERS™ DICE GAME

P.O. Box 716, Westborough, MA 01581
Telephone: 508-366-4091
Web site: www.blistersdicegame.com

Blisters™ **Dice Game** produces the Blisters Dice Game, a great game to take on camping trips and hikes. The company also produces Thaxx™ and the Mountain Climb™ game for children ages 5 and up.

Interesting Fact: The Blisters™ Dice Game was created by the game's inventor, Tim Novak, during a 2,000-mile walk from Georgia to Maine on the Appalachian Trail. The game was called Blisters simply because Tim's feet were covered with them by the end of the six-month hike!

How to Find: Orders may be placed directly through the Web site.

BUFFALO GAMES

220 James E. Casey Drive, Buffalo, NY 14206
The company prefers e-mail.
Web site: www.buffalogames.com

Buffalo Games manufactures made-in-America games and jigsaw puzzles. For children, there are card games such as Nacho Loco™ and Monster Maker™, jigsaw puzzles, and party games that can be played by the entire family.

Interesting Fact: Established in 1986, Buffalo Games sought to bring new and challenging games to the traditional game scene. Its first product was a double-sided jigsaw puzzle that must be built from both sides! In 1998, Buffalo Games introduced iMAgiNiff,™ a board game, which has now sold more than 1 million copies. Other games include Nacho Loco™, Monster Maker™, Bandits™, and Slap-N-Grab™. Party games include Faces™ and Ruin™.

How to Find: Buffalo Games has wide retail distribution throughout the United States. You may also order online through the Web site or call customer service for more information.

∙∙

CARROM, INC. ↑ T

218 E. Dowland Street, Ludington, MI 49431
Telephone: 231-845-1263
Web site: www.carrom.com

Carrom, Inc. manufactures children's games and furniture. The age range is from toddlers on up. Under Carrom's banner are several American-manufactured brands, including Carrom Classic Games®, Carrom Sports Table Games®, and the Drueke Board Games®. The Carrom Classics encompass old favorites such as Nok Hockey®, Shuffle Board, and Skittles; Sports Table Games include Air Hockey® and Foosball®; and Drueke Games® consist of classics such as chess, cribbage, poker, and the Shoot the Moon® games. It is worth your time to go to the Carrom Web site to appreciate the size of the product line.

Interesting Fact: An American manufacturing treasure, the Carrom Company is more than 100 years old. In fact, many collectors and antique dealers like to find old Carrom games. There is a link on the Web site that explores the collectable aspects of the Carrom product line.

How to Find: Carrom games are widely available in retail stores throughout the United States. However, you may also order the complete selection through the company Web site. Please call customer service if you need assistance.

∙∙

CEACO/GAMEWRIGHT® ✈

70 Bridge Street, Newton, MA 02458
Telephone: 800-638-7568
Web site: www.gamewright.com

Ceaco/Gamewright® manufactures a large selection of toys for specific age groups, starting at age 3, then 3–6, 6–8, and 8–10 and up. The products include all kinds of card games, dice games, and board and party games. The Web site has Gamewright® games categorized by age, so you can pick the toy most appropriate to your child's age group.

Interesting Fact: Gamewright® was founded in 1994 by two families that were seeking better games for their children. One of its best-selling games, Sleeping Queens™, was developed by a 6-year-old girl from

New Jersey. Gamewright sponsors Game Nights at various schools in conjunction with PTA/PTOs so that parents may get to see their games on a more personal level.

How to Find: Gamewright's products may be found at your local specialty toy shop, or customers can shop directly through the company Web site. Call the customer service number for more information.

. . . .

CHANNEL CRAFT, INC. ↑

P.O. Box 101, Charleroi, PA 15022
Telephone: 800-232-4FUN
Web site: www.channelcraft.com

Channel Craft, Inc. manufactures an extensive selection of authentic American toys, games, and puzzles that are as entertaining as they are educational. Some of the more popular items in the line include boomerangs, tiddly-winks, Jacks, wooden tops and spinners, yo-yos, skip ropes, travel games, and the classic tin box travel games such as Fish Pond. In addition to the products Channel Craft® makes in-house, it carries a selection of products made by craftspeople from the Appalachian region.

Interesting Fact: Dean Helfer, Jr., founded Channel Craft® more than 25 years ago, while he was still in college. The first product was a boomerang, which he would sell out of the back of a van at craft shows. He became fascinated with the toy business and turned a business school course paper into an SBA loan application. The company has so far moved twice due to expansion. Channel Craft's current location near Pittsburgh comprises three buildings where more than 70 workers manufacture and assemble toys.

How to Find: Channel Craft products are widely sold in specialty toy stores throughout the United States. If you have seen a particular product on the Web site and can't locate it, please call customer service.

. . . .

FAT BRAIN® TOYS, INC. ↑ ✈

20285 Wirt Street, Elkhorn, NE 68022
Telephone: 800-590-5987
Web site: www.fatbraintoys.com

Fat Brain® Toys, Inc. makes Dado Cubes™ and Dado Squares®, interlocking construction games suitable for children of late preschool age and older. In addition to the Dado toys, which are made in America, the company also distributes many brands, some of which are imported.

Interesting Fact: Dado Cubes™ and Dado Squares™, voted Dr. Toy Top 20 Best Childen's Products 2007, are the creation of Mark Carson, the founder of Fat Brain® Toys. Mark is the father of three children, and, when he was buying toys for his children at holiday time or for their birthdays, he wasn't feeling good about the toys that were available. He felt that many of the toys were not intellectually appropriate for his children. He wanted to find toys that would challenge them and make them think.

How to Find: Orders may be placed through the Web site or by contacting the company through its customer service number.

GRANDPA'S GAMES AND CRAFTS ↑

30 Reinig Street, Belgrade, MT 59714
Telephone: 406-539-9639
Web site: www.grandpasgamesandgifts.com

Grandpa's Games and Crafts handcrafts board games for school-age children and older. The games include Froggy; Trout Pond; Coyote; Yote, an African board game; and Nine Man's Morris, a Colonial-period game. Please remember that the small pieces that come with this game present a choking hazard for children ages 5 and under.

Interesting Fact: Chris Kyser's interest in anthropology and ethnocultural historic games led him to create a business where he makes games embraced by cultures throughout the world. He feels his games are all about families making connections, and he wants his games to serve as ways that families can spend a little quality time together in the midst of their busy daily lives. Each game comes with complete instructions, playing pieces, and a game cloth that can travel anywhere.

How to Find: You may order directly through the Web site.

GREAT AMERICAN PUZZLE COMPANY ⊛ ↑ ✈

16 S. Main Street, South Norwalk, CT 06854
Telephone: 800-922-1194
Web site: www.greatamericanpuzzle.com

Great American Puzzle Company manufactures children's puzzles ranging in size and complexity from puzzles with 20 pieces up to puzzles with more than 1,000 pieces. The vast majority of the puzzles are made in the USA. The puzzles for young children with moving parts are imported.

Interesting Fact: This woman-founded company was started more than 30 years ago and has grown in size to a line of more than 150 items.

How to Find: Orders may be placed through the Web site or can be purchased at numerous retail locations. Please call customer service if you need assistance.

JABO, INC.

2619 Dudley Avenue, Parkersburg, WV 26102
Telephone: 800-338-9578
Web site: www.jabovitro.com

Jabo, Inc. manufactures marbles for classic marble games such as Chinese checkers.

Interesting Fact: Jabo, Inc. and the company it acquired in 1992, the Vitro Agate Corporation, form the oldest marble-making facility in America. Millions of marbles are produced at Jabo's manufacturing facility for games, decorative gems, industrial usage, and collectors. The company is switching most of its production to industrial usage; however, it will maintain a small stock of marbles for games and play.

How to Find: You can call customer service for information on product availability. The company is slowly phasing out many of its classic toy marbles.

K'NEX® INDUSTRIES ☺

2990 Bergey Road, Hatfield, PA 19440
Telephone: 800-543-5639
Web site: www.knex.com

K'nex® Industries manufactures K'nex products for children from preschool to ages 9 and older. Products include Thrill Rides, tub and case sets with K'nex parts, vehicles that use wheels, and fun animals.

According to the company, K'Nex is the only building system that allows children to have a working toy after the project is completed. The company's philosophy is that children can imagine something and then build it and play with it.

Interesting Fact: The founder of the company, Joel Glickman, got his inspiration for K'Nex® while he was playing with straws at a crowded, noisy wedding. Joel began tinkering with the straws and started to think about the possibilities of connecting them into unique shapes. K'Nex has a strong commitment to guiding children to express themselves by designing and creating new forms. The company that makes K'Nex is what is known as a high-volume injection molding company. It makes products for many other American manufacturing companies. The K'Nex toy is its first toy product.

How to Find: K'nex products are widely sold in department stores and specialty toy stores and by other retailers. You may order some of the kits online. Call customer service if you need more information.

KVALE GOOD NATURED GAMES ☺ ✈

771 Parkview Avenue, St. Paul, MN 55117
Telephone: 866-254-1276
Web site: www.head1liners.com

Kvale Good Natured Games manufactures the Head1Liners game, which is appropriate for children ages 12 and up. All of the materials and labor for this game are American made. Other games on the Web site are imported.

Interesting Fact: Tony Kvale's passion as a child was to design board games or to improve on existing board games so that the entire family could play games together on camping trips and at family reunions.

How to Find: You can order directly through the Web site or call customer service for dealers nearest your location.

LUCY HAMMET™ GAMES

P.O. Box 905, Mineola, TX 75773
Telephone: 888-420-7585
Web site: www.lucybingogames.com

Lucy Hammet™ **Games** makes classic education picture bingo games that can be enjoyed by children as young as 3 years of age as well as by adults. The company is always introducing new games. The current line includes Lucy Hammet's Dinosaur Bingo™, Lucy Hammet's Bug Bingo™, and Lucy Hammet's Ocean Bingo™. New games for 2008 include Lucy Hammet's Sports Bingo™ and Lucy Hammet's Vegetable Bingo™.

Interesting Fact: Lucy Hammet was an art major before launching her company. Her motivation was that she needed to invent a game for her children while the family was on a long road trip. The games expanded from that point. Lucy has illustrated many of the games that make up the product selection.

How to Find: Orders may be placed through the Web site or by contacting the company through its customer service number.

· ·

MAMASOES, Inc. ⊛ ↑
6651 NW 23rd Avenue, Gainesville, FL 32606
Telephone: 352-376-1649
Web site: www.mamasoes.com

MaMaSoes, Inc. handcrafts wooden puzzles out of poplar and birch and makes manual-dexterity skill games and push and pull toys. The company still makes the Sjoelbak skill game and a Tic Tac Toe game.

Interesting Fact: Ria van Soestbergen, the founder of MaMaSoes, was born and raised in Holland. When she and her husband first came to the United States, they decided to produce a traditional Dutch game of skill called Sjoelbak. The game sold only moderately well. Then Ria traveled to Japan, and through a contact she made the acquaintance of a master Japanese puzzlemaker. She learned puzzlemaking skills, and, when she came back to the States, she began to offer the puzzles on her Web site. The business began to really grow from that point.

How to Find: Orders may be placed through the Web site or by contacting the company through its customer service number. The company routinely participates in crafts fairs and shows.

· ·

MARBLE KING USA, INC. ⊛
First Avenue, Parden City, WV 26159
Telephone: 800-672-5564
Web site: www.marblekingusa.com

Marble King USA, Inc. manufactures both traditional marbles in all kinds of colors and sizes and wooden marble games that are made in America. The company is also known for its flat gems, which are used for flower arrangements and candles.

Interesting Fact: Marble King® was founded in 1949 by Barry Pink and Sellers Peltier. Despite changing times, marbles and marble games are still widely played throughout the United States. Each year, the company sponsors the National Marble Tournament in Wildwood, New Jersey. Wildwood is also home to the National Marbles Hall of Fame.

How to Find: Marble King® is sold throughout the United States in specialty and independent toy stores or through the company Web site. You may also call customer service or visit the company store.

MGC CUSTOM PUZZLES ↑ ✂ ★

31 Bogue Lane, East Haddam, CT 06423
Telephone: 860-873-3093
Web site: www.mgcpuzzle.com

MGC Custom Puzzles handcrafts puzzles and wooden jigsaw puzzles for children and adults. Parents can supply the company with an image, for example the child's face or a new puppy, and the company will create a puzzle with that image. The puzzles can be made in any degree of complexity desired. The company can customize.

Interesting Fact: Mark Cappitella is a full-time puzzlemaker who has worked on customized puzzle projects as large as 8′ by 10′! Most people send Mark pictures to make into puzzles to celebrate birthdays, weddings, and anniversaries. The company also has the ability to customize special-needs puzzles, for example, for visually impaired or autistic customers.

How to Find: Please e-mail or call the company in order to get a quote on a customized wooden jigsaw puzzle.

MOON MARBLE COMPANY ✳ ⌑ ✈

600 E. Front Street, Bonner Springs, KS 66012
Telephone: 888-410-0680
Web site: www.moonmarble.com

Moon Marble Company manufactures many of the old-fashioned marble games that most people have given up for lost. These games include Storm the Castle and Knuckle Bones. Please note that these toys are not appropriate for children under the age of 3. Some toys shown on the Web site are imported. Please call customer service for more complete information.

Interesting Fact: The Moon Marble Company has been in business since 1997, teaching kids and adults how to play marbles and demonstrating marble making. It has had visitors from every state and from 35 countries. While most of the marbles the company sells are purchased from other marble makers, it still produces collectible, artisan marbles. Looking for something unusual to do with your child? Spend a day learning how to make marbles.

How to Find: You can order directly through the Web site.

··

PETERS' GROUP LTD.
P.O. Box 320, Goshen, IN 46526
Telephone: 574-534-0565
Web site: www.stackandstick.com

Peters' Group Ltd. manufactures a wood building-block construction toy in various model kits, including a cabin, Grande Villa, country barn, and castle. The kits are said to improve manual dexterity and encourage creativity. The toy is suitable for children ages 4 and older.

Interesting Fact: Andy Peters represents the third generation of fine furniture craftsmen in his family. The family has a passion and a feeling for wood. As part of the company's furniture-making process, Andy wondered how he could best put the scrap wood to good use. He started to experiment and developed the Stack & Stick® building system. As the company has grown, it has made a continuing commitment to using only recycled wood from surrounding furniture factories and lumber mills.

How to Find: Stack & Stick® products may be found at specialty retail outlets throughout the United States and in catalogs, or orders may be placed through the Web site. For the nearest retailer, please e-mail the company.

··

PUZZLEMAN TOYS, THE ✿ ✂

21050 Placer Hills Road, Colfax, CA 95713
Telephone: 530-637-5575
Web site: www.thepuzzleman.com

The Puzzleman Toys handcrafts personalized name puzzles, vocabulary and number puzzles, map puzzles, picture puzzles, and puzzles for older children and adults. The company can customize.

Interesting Fact: Husband-and-wife team Ed and Suzanne Scotten have been handcrafting puzzles for more than 20 years. The puzzle pieces are nearly half an inch thick and are painted with nontoxic, water-based paints and stains.

How to Find: In addition to sales through their Web site, the Scottens participate in several crafts shows in California, Arizona, and Nevada.

··

ROY TOY® MANUFACTURING ☺ ↑

P.O. Box 660, East Machias, ME 04630
Telephone: 207-255-0954
Web site: www.roytoy.com

Roy Toy® Manufacturing manufactures wooden log construction sets in several variations. The sets include the Original Roy Toy, Woodlinks sets so that young builders can create their own designs, fun forts and barn sets, build-and-paint sets, and the classic play sets. The packaging used in Roy Toy products is also made in America.

Interesting Fact: Established around 1930, the company made products that nurtured a generation of Depression-era builders. The Original Roy Toy set sold in toy stores for about 10 cents. When the company's founder died, his family didn't want to enter the business, and the company shuttered its doors in the 1960s. In the early 1990s, almost 30 years later, the founder's grandson brought the company back to life. The company describes Roy Toy® products as being Earth-friendly. All wood used is sustainably harvested, and dyes are nontoxic, approved food dyes.

How to Find: Roy Toys are available through online toy stores and specialty retailers or directly from the Roy Toy Web site. For more information, call customer service.

....

SERENDIPITY PUZZLE COMPANY ☺ ↑
Serendipity Puzzles is based in the Waukesha, Wisconsin, area.
Telephone: 800-891-7479
Web site: www.serendipitypuzzles.com

Serendipity Puzzle Company manufactures a full line of puzzles for children of all ages and for adults. Puzzles range in complexity from 25 pieces for school-age children through 1,500-piece puzzles for teens looking for a monumental challenge. There are numerous themes and styles, including standard puzzles with themes such as nature, cats, dogs, horses, and the outdoors; shaped puzzles without rectangular borders; double circle puzzles; large piece puzzles; round puzzles; puzzles for the entire family; children's puzzles; and puzzle décor kits, which allow the customer to make a puzzle into a permanent picture. There is also a line of religious-themed stationery for adults.

Interesting Fact: Serendipity Puzzle Company is about 8 years old. The company produces all of its puzzles using 100 percent recycled fibers, water-based inks and coatings, and recycled packaging. It has been certified by the Forest Stewardship Council and the Rainforest Alliance.

How to Find: Serendipity Puzzles are widely distributed through several retail and department store outlets. You may also buy puzzles through the Web site or through many online stores.

....

SMETHPORT SPECIALTY COMPANY ● T
51 Magnetic Avenue, Smethport, PA 16749
Telephone: 800-772-8697
Web site: www.smethporttoy.com

Smethport Specialty Company manufactures magnetic games, games for travel, wall pocket organizer charts, educational games, and board games for the entire family. The company is the creator of the classic Wooly Willy® and Hair-do Harriet® games.

Interesting Fact: An American manufacturing treasure, Smethport was founded in 1908 and has remained in Pennsylvania for more than a century. In 2005, Smethport Toys, along with the entire town of Smethport, celebrated the fiftieth anniversary of the Wooly Willy® game.

How to Find: Smethport Toys sells only to retailers. Please see the company Web site for a list of stores. If you can't find a nearby dealer or don't have a computer, call the customer service number for assistance.

STORYBOARD TOYS

429 Martin Street, Longmont, CO 80501
Telephone: 866-668-8697
Web site: www.storyboardtoys.com

Storyboard Toys manufactures the Arthouse™, an educational toy that enables children to design, construct, and then decorate a miniature space with their peers. Other models of the concept include an American horse barn, a Viking longhouse, and a Japanese home.

Interesting Fact: Founded in 2002, Storyboard Toys is the designer of Arthouse™, a unique way for children not only to design their own miniature spaces but also to create stories about those spaces and to interact with peers. The company describes this as a new play pattern.

How to Find: Orders may be placed directly through the Web site or by calling customer service.

TAG TOYS®, INC. ★

1810 S. Acacia Avenue, Compton, CA 90220
Telephone: 800-488-4824
Web site: www.tagtoys.com

Tag Toys®, Inc. manufactures toys for early learning from infancy to age 6. Depending upon the child's age, the toys will address sorting and motor skills, memory skills, numbers and counting games, and writing and spelling games. Tag Toys® also makes children's room furniture, including desks and chairs, playtables, benches, and storage units. The remainder of the toy line includes trucks, dollhouses, Noah's Ark toys, block sets, personalized items, brightly colored puzzles, and art supplies such as paint brush holders and chalk boards on easels. TAG also makes products for child or adult rehabilitation.

Interesting Fact: The stated mission of the Tag Toy® Company is to stimulate and develop intelligence in the first years of life. Founded by psychotherapists and educators in 1976 to address intellectual deficits among children with learning disabilities, the company has grown to include products for all children between ages 1 and 6. The original management team started making products in a garage; the company now occupies more than 50,000 feet of manufacturing space.

How to Find: Orders may be placed directly with the company through its Web site or by calling into customer service.

• •

TAURUS TOY COMPANY
501 3rd Street, Franklin, PA 16323
Telephone: 877-BNR-BLOK
Web site: www.taurustoy.net

Taurus Toy Company manufactures pieces that attach to popular construction toys to enable children to make a maze or course, or the pieces can be used on their own. The sets contain from 40 pieces to 150 pieces (in the Race 'n Roll™ marble race course).

Interesting Fact: The original Block-N-Roll™ toy was created in Silver Lake, New Hampshire, in 1995 by five young brothers. Unlike other popular building-block games that typically follow set designs, Block-N-Roll encourages children to use their imagination to create shapes. At the same time, the block system is compatible with other building-block games, allowing children to create all kinds of fun marble games and courses. The appropriate age is 6 and up. According to the company, Block-N-Roll has won national recognition, including an award from the Parent's Guide for Children's Media, the Dr. Toy Best Vacation Children's Products Award, and the Oppenheim Toy Portfolio Award.

How to Find: Taurus Toys can be purchased through the company Web site or through numerous retailers and online retail sites.

• •

WINNING MOVES® GAMES ✈
100 Conifer Hill Drive, Danvers, MA 01923
Telephone: 800-664-7788
Web site: www.winning-moves.com

Winning Moves® Games manufactures the Uncle Wiggily game in the USA. Other games made by the company are imported.

Interesting Fact: Winning Moves® Games makes the classic children's game Uncle Wiggily®. Uncle Wiggily's origins go back to 1910; the game is based on a series of stories by the famous children's author Howard Roger Garis. In 1916, Milton Bradley published the first Uncle Wiggily game. It is a classic American game and the forerunner of many modern games. While the game has undergone slight modification over the years, it is still very similar to the original.

How to Find: The Uncle Wiggily Game is widely available in toy stores and specialty stores throughout the United States.

ZOMETOOL, INC.®
7475 W. 5th Avenue, Lakewood, CO 80226
Telephone: 888-966-3386
Web site: www.zometool.com

Zometool, Inc.® manufactures the Zometool, a challenging game to encourage children to create and design. The Zometool is appropriate for children from age 6 and up and for adults. The product comes in several different kits, and it is possible to purchase parts as well. Because it contains small parts, this product is not appropriate for very young children.

Interesting Fact: The Zometool® came about as the result of the company's founders' fascination with the architecture of dome housing. While they knew the benefits, they also knew of the drawbacks. Nevertheless, their vision led to designs for unique playground equipment and climbers. The playground systems were introduced in 1971. In 1979, the company realized that the connecting system it had developed would make a great toy and a way for future architects to design the dome houses of the future.

How to Find: The Zometool is widely distributed throughout the United States at virtually every major retailer. If you are unable to find Zometools, please call customer service and a representative will assist you.

Fantastic American Plastic Toys

The companies listed in this part of the chapter are among the largest of all the American toy manufacturers, with product lines that are as creative as they are extensive. The mold-making and manufacturing skills required to make these products are every bit as impressive as those of the artists who work in wood or metal.

··

AMERICAN PLASTIC TOYS, INC.®

799 Ladd Road, Walled Lake, MI 48390
Telephone: 800-521-7080
Web site: www.americanplastictoys.com

American Plastic Toys, Inc.® manufactures products primarily for children between the ages of 18 months and 7 years old. The product line is extensive, and there is something for just about every child in the age range. It is important to explore the Web site. Some of the more popular toys include doll accessories such as doll strollers; baby nurseries and carriages; construction toys such as dump trucks, trucks, and tractors; wagons and riding toys; role-play sets such as play tool benches, desks, play kitchens, and laundries; kid-size plastic outdoor furniture; and plastic boats and beach toys.

Interesting Fact: Established in 1962, American Plastic Toys makes a full line of plastic children's toys in many different categories. All of its products are made in America.

How to Find: The Web site has a store locator to direct customers to the top 50 chains that carry the company's products. There are also a number of online retailers. Call customer service for additional information.

··

GREEN TOYS™, INC. ♻ ☺

912 Cole Street, San Francisco, CA 94117
Telephone: 415-839-9971
Web site: www.greentoys.com

Green Toys™**, Inc.** manufactures a miniature, 17-piece tea set, kid-size indoor gardening kits that include garden tool and pots, a 27-piece miniature cookware and dining set, and a sand play set. These toys are for preschool children and up and, because they contain small pieces, they are most appropriate for age 3 and up.

Interesting Fact: The brilliant idea behind the company comes from partners Robert von Goeben, a toy-industry executive, and Laurie Hyman, a marketing executive in the high-tech field. Green Toys™ are manufactured in the USA from curbside-collected plastic milk containers. All aspects of toy production, including manufacturing, packaging, assembly, and fulfillment, occur in California. The packaging, like the product itself, is made of recycled materials.

How to Find: Green Toys, Inc. primarily sells its products through a growing number of retailer outlets throughout or through many online stores. If you type Green Toys into a search engine, several online retailers will result.

....

LITTLE TIKES® COMPANY, THE ✈
2180 Barlow Road, Hudson, OH 44236
Telephone: 866-855-4650
Web site: www.littletikes.com

The Little Tikes® **Company** manufactures plastic toys mainly for toddlers and preschool children approximately 2–6 years of age. The majority of the product line is very large, and it is suggested that you explore the Web site in detail. Part of the product line is made in the USA: outdoor play items, which includes toddler and swing seats, Swing Along™ Castle, Climb and Slide Castle, Twin Slide Climbers, and others; playhouses, including Endless Adventures® Magic Doorbell™ Play-house, Picnic on the Patio™ Playhouse, Cambridge Cottage Playhouse, and others; ride toys, including Ride & Relax™ Wagon, Toddler Tractor & Cart, Cozy Coupe®II™ Car, Classic Sport Cycle, Push & Ride™ Racer, Team Coupe, and others; sports toys, including Just Like the Pros™ Basketball Set and others; role-play toys, including Shopping Cart and Push & Ride™ Doll Walker, among others; and furniture, including Rain-bow™ chairs, Race Car Twin Beds, Easy Store™ Play Table, rocking horses, and toy chests.

Interesting Fact: Little Tikes® manufactures about 70 percent of its products, including the ride toys, in Ohio. The products the company makes in the USA are easily found on the Web site. Other products are imported.

How to Find: The products can be found in virtually every major chain store in America. You may also order through the Web site or call customer service.

....

STEP2® COMPANY, THE, LLC ✈
10010 Aurora Hudson Road, Streetsboro, OH 44241
Telephone: 800-347-8372
Web site: www.step2.com

The Step2® Company makes a large and diverse product line of plastic toys for toddler and preschool children. The approximate age range for the toys is 2–6 years. The product line is very large, and it is suggested that you explore the Web site in detail. The Made in USA product line includes the following categories: furniture products, including folding chairs and tables, tool chest dressers, rockers, Dream Castle Convertible Beds, Lifestyle™ twin beds, fire engine toddler beds, and others; outdoor play, including the Naturally Playful® products, such as play-houses, Neat & Tidy Cottage, Lookout Tree House, Clubhouse Climber, toddler swings, and others; role-play furniture, including the Lifestyle™ Grand Walk-in Kitchen, the puppet theater, and others; and riding toys, including the Safari Wagon, Push Around Buggy, Coaster Training Bike, Zip & Zoom Pedal Car, and others.

Interesting Fact: According to the company, Step2® is the largest toy manufacturer in America that actually has manufacturing facilities in the United States. Approximately 90 percent of the product line is made in America. If you type in USA into the appropriate box on the Web site, the products will appear. Other products are imported.

How to Find: The Step2 product line can be found in virtually every major chain retailer. The Web site has a store locator, or, as few stores will carry the entire product selection, customers can order online direct from the company.

Arts and Crafts

The companies in this listing specialize in helping children to bring out their creative side. Like those in other areas of this chapter, these companies are award winners recognized for their ability to entertain and inspire children.

AMERICAN EASEL COMPANY ✿ ↑

2869 22nd Street SE, Salem, OR 97301
Telephone: 877-765-9549
Web site: www.americaneasel.com

American Easel Company manufactures children's and students' easels. It also makes easels for artists as well as for display purposes, in all price ranges.

Interesting Fact: The wife-and-husband founders of American Easel started the business in their garage in 1992. The business grew very quickly at first, but the founders intentionally slowed the company's growth until they were satisfied that the quality of the product they were producing was superior to imported products.

How to Find: Customers can contact the company and purchase the easels directly or search the Web site store locator for the nearest dealer to their location.

OMNICOR, INC./WIKKISTIX® ✿ ★

11034 N. 23rd Drive, Phoenix, AZ 85025
Telephone: 800-869-4554
Web site: www.wikkistix.com

Omnicor, Inc./Wikkistix® produces the Wikkistix® toy for children. The product is appropriate for children ages 3 and up, and kits are available in numerous themes. For example, there are kits devoted to holidays such as Halloween and Valentine's Day, educational kits such as number and alphabet sets, and kits for religious designs and craft activities. Wikkistix® may also be used for 3-D applications such as animal sculptures or for decorating gifts. Larger kits for schools or bulk packaged Wikkistix are often used in restaurants or even on airplanes because, unlike crayons or markers, the product makes no mess. Wikkistix have been used with patients receiving occupational therapy.

Interesting Fact: Wikkistix is a creative play toy made of acrylic, hand-knitting yarn containing a food-grade, nontoxic wax. There is neither latex nor any peanut or nut oil. The wax is similar to that used in lipsticks and on food products. The pieces can be stuck together to create all kinds of interesting shapes. As the "stix" are in different colors, when they are applied to a surface they form a pretty design.

How to Find: Wikkistix are widely available through several retail store chains. There is a store locator on the Web site, or you may order through online retailers.

....

PERLER® BEADS

1801 N. 12th Street, Reading, PA 19604
The company prefers e-mail.
Web site: www.perlerbeads.com

Perler® Beads manufactures interactive craft activity games for children from approximately preschool to school age. The company sells bead assortments, templates, idea books, and accessories. The designs are created by taking the beads and placing them on a template or pattern. Once the design is created, it is ironed to create a permanent picture. There are numerous kit themes, including Animal Friends, Things That Go, and Seasonal Kits, which celebrate times of the year or holidays. However, for those really creative children, it is also possible to get a blank template and large bead assortments to create a totally new design. There are also more advanced designs, which allow children to make 3-D, free-standing objects out of the beads. Because they contain small pieces, these crafts are not meant to be used by children under 3 years old. A responsible adult should do the ironing of the finished design.

Interesting Fact: According to the company, Perler Beads® won the 2007 Toy of the Year in its category from *Family Fun* magazine.

How to Find: Perler® Beads are sold at major craft, toy, and department stores. You can also order online from online retailers or go through the company Web site.

● ●

SKULLDUGGERY™

5433 E. La Palma Avenue, Anaheim, CA 92807
Telephone: 800-336-7745
Web site: www.skullduggery.com

Skullduggery™ manufactures model kits appropriate for children ages 6 and up. The modeling kits are available in many themes; some are serious, and some are just for fun. Some of these kits allow you to create fossil replicas, such as dinosaur eggs; ammonite (snail) fossils; and and saber tooth tiger teeth; and extinct and contemporary animal skulls. There is also the Cast & Paint® Signature Pitch, which allows your young baseball player to make a cast of his hand holding a base-ball, and Cast & Paint® cars, trucks, NASCAR® models, and animals.

Interesting Fact: Though the company makes many kits for individual use, its strength is its classroom science kits for up to 30 students. The kits come with teacher lesson plans and educational materials.

How to Find: There are several ways to order: by shopping at retail stores and online retail sites, through the Skullduggery Web site, by telephone or fax, or by calling customer service.

Everything Plush and Cuddly

It seems that a plush toy of some kind is always one of the first toys given to a child. It is also interesting that plush toys are often treas-ured into adulthood. Long after other toys leave us, these big and small stuffed creatures never seem to quite make it into the trash bin.

There are several American manufacturers that specialize in pro-ducing just about any kind of stuffed toy you can imagine. Please note that some of the plush toys listed in this part of the book are not intended for young children but are more for display and collection and very light play.

....

ADOPTABLE KINDERS™ BY GRANZA

P.O. Box 195096, Winter Springs, FL 32719
Telephone: 407-257-1257
Web site: www.adoptablekinders.com

Adoptable Kinders™ by Granza manufactures classic rag dolls in nearly 30 different styles, along with rag doll clothing and rag doll furniture. There are both boy and girl rag dolls and rag dolls representing various races. The company also makes Friendly Pillows™ that come in five different colors and are perfect for nap times. The company also makes software for interactive play.

Interesting Fact: Great companies like Granza, Inc. exist for moms, dads, and grandparents who lament the fact that the toys of yesteryear have all but disappeared. Granza manufactures the classic rag doll in many different styles, along with empathic pillows called Friendly Pillow™. When a rag doll is purchased for a child, its name can automatically be registered. The Web site has an "E-school," which is full of all kinds of games, puzzles, and learning tools.

How to Find: The company has an online store, and its products may be purchased directly through the Web site. If customers don't have a computer or need assistance, they may call customer service for more information.

....

BIG PLUSH® STUFFED TOYS ↑ ✈

4779 Boston Post Road, Pelham Manor, NY 10803
Telephone: 800-238-9481
Web site: www.bigplush.com

Big Plush® Stuffed Toys makes plush toys in all kinds of animal shapes and in many different colors, along with toys in several seasonal themes. Please note that not all of the company's products are made in the USA. Go to the Web site and refer to the section devoted to stuffed animals made in the USA.

Interesting Fact: Big Plush®, based in Brooklyn, New York, can trace its origins to the 1970s. The founder spent the first part of his career managing a stuffed-toy factory in New York. When the factory was forced out of business by a rise in imported products, he was undaunted and started his own company. Business has been steadily growing ever since. Big Plush® makes the largest stuffed toys you have ever seen. In fact, some of its stuffed toys, such as bears, can be up to 8' in height, and it made a lovable snake that is more than 30' long! It ships its plush animals all over the world.

How to Find: Orders may be placed through the Web site or by contacting the company through the customer service number.

COTTON MONSTER™ ❀ ☺ ✂

Cotton Monster is an online business located in the Seattle, Washington, area.
The company prefers e-mail.
Web site: www.cottonmonster.com

Cotton Monster™ handcrafts unique plush animals in the form of different breeds of monsters that are partly works of art and partly toys that are made to inspire the imagination. The monsters are lovable and not scary, but, at the same time, they should not be given to children under 3 years of age because they contain small pieces. All of the fabric used in Cotton Monster products has been recycled. There is limited production. The company can customize.

Interesting Fact: Jennifer Strunge, the founder of Cotton Monster™, has always had an interest in creating art outside of itself. She doesn't want her fun creations to be admired just for the sake of art but wants them to be given to older children for light play or for interaction such as "tea parties" or for simply having an imaginary friend to talk to when no one else is around. First and foremost, Jennifer is an artist who loves to work with plush and to make people happy with her unexpected and whimsically shaped pieces.

How to Find: Cotton Monster is an online store, and the unique plush toys can be ordered directly through the Web site.

E. WILLOUGHBY BEAR COMPANY ⊛ ✂

2 Star Road, Elizabeth, ME 04107
Telephone: 207-767-4183
Web site: www.ewbears.com

E. Willoughby Bear Company handcrafts one-of-a-kind teddy bears. Each bear takes on a different personality. The orphan bears are very popular. Please note that, though it is tempting to give these bears to small children, they will probably be appreciated by older children who are starting to like to collect stuffed animals. Each bear takes on a life of its own and is certainly not made from a cookie cutter design. There is limited production.

Interesting Fact: Anne Crenshaw, the owner of E. Willoughby, is an artist who loves to make bears. Her work has been featured in numerous books and magazines, and she has won many awards.

How to Find: These are customized stuffed bears. Please inquire by phone or e-mail.

FORT CLOUDY ⊛ ✈

Fort Cloudy is located in the Seattle, Washington, area.
Telephone: 443-695-2458
Web site: www.fortcloudy.com

Fort Cloudy handcrafts the unique plush toy for toddlers Ninja Fetus™ and has expanded into applique designs for tee shirts and snappies. The hilarious plush toys are completely handcrafted in the USA. The tee shirts and snappies are hand decorated in the USA but may currently use imported blank clothing. Limited production.

Interesting Fact: Sarah, the founder of Fort Cloudy, is fortunate to have a mom who is the owner of a quilting shop. Sarah found herself fascinated by the process of quilting, and, being a photographer and artist, she began to experiment making plush toys and applique designs.

How to Find: Orders may be placed directly with the company through the Fort Cloudy Web site.

KATHY'S KREATIONS ⊛ ↑

The company is located in the Camp Verde, Arizona, area.

Telephone: 602-547-8760

Web site: www.kathyskreations.com

Kathy's Kreations handcrafts numerous stuffed animals including dogs, cats, farm animals, and all kinds of exotics. As these items are shaped by hand, no two are ever alike.

Interesting Fact: Founded in 1982, Kathy of Kathy's Kreations has made a career out of making realistic-looking stuffed animals. A keen interest in nature coupled with a fine art background provided the expertise required to choose the line, shape, and detail necessary to capture the essence of each animal. The animals are not meant to be typical play toys; rather, they are realistic reproductions of the actual animal. They are meant to be displayed or cuddled by older children as part of a stuffed-animal collection but are not appropriate for infants or toddlers. The animals are so realistic that they have been used as props in plays and movies.

How to Find: Orders may be placed directly through the Web site or by calling customer service.

MY PAPER CRANE ⊛

P.O. Box 863, Waynesboro, PA 17268

The company prefers e-mail.

Web site: www.mypapercrane.com

My Paper Crane handcrafts unique plush objects ranging from foods to items with faces and personalities. Any child who collects stuffed toys will appreciate these pieces. Note that some of the plush objects are more suited for older children and light play or even display. Because of the small pieces on some designs, these stuffed toys are not suitable for children under 3 years of age.

Interesting Fact: Heidi Kenney is an artist who specializes in making unique but kid-friendly plush objects. She began her Web site as a place to keep photos of the things she was making. The business has grown to the point where her designs have found their way to international as well as domestic markets. These are not your ordinary plush toys and may include shapes ranging from pieces of toast to plush-toy birthday cakes to plush-toy bathroom fixtures.

How to Find: The widest selection of My Paper Crane products may be found online through the Web site. However, there is also a store locator on the Web site.

· ·

STUFFINGTON BEAR FACTORY™ ✿ ✂ ⬚

2302 East Thomas Road, Phoenix, AZ 85016
Telephone: 602-225-9513
Web site: www.stuffington.com

Stuffington Bear Factory™ manufactures a huge selection of stuffed animals in many sizes, colors, and shapes. Some of these animals are bears (of course) in many colors, horses, lambs, rabbits, cats, owls, monkeys, frogs, lions, and reindeer. The company also makes clothes and accessories for stuffed animals. Stuffington Bear ™ dresses bears for special occasions, such as graduations and weddings. Stuffington Bear offers factory tours.

Interesting Fact: Stuffington Bear Factory™ is one of the few stuffed-animal factories in the USA. It has been in business since 1959. Not only are its stuffed animals made in the USA, but so are all the materials that it uses to make its products. Aside from manufacturing, it offers fun educational tours of its facility, as well as an interactive retail store where customers can stuff their own furry friend.

How to Find: Orders may be placed directly through the Web site or by calling customer service.

· ·

SUNSHINE TEDDY BEARS ✿ ✂

Sunshine Teddy Bears is based in the Indianapolis, Indiana, area.
Telephone: 317-222-4121
Web site: www.sunshineteddybears.com

Sunshine Teddy Bears handcrafts collectible, keepsake teddy bears. No two bears are alike, and no two outfits are alike. The clothes on the bears are vintage. Even if you aren't about to purchase one of these teddys, you must look at the Web site to see the selection and the cast of characters. The artist is happy to give her bears a name of your choosing. There is limited production. Allow at least two weeks for delivery.

Interesting Fact: Dawn Hornig started her teddy bear company in 1992, after making a bear for a friend. According to Dawn, each Sunshine Teddy Bear is hand sewn from a variety of fur colors and styles and is fully jointed. Sunshine Teddy Bears are available dressed or undressed; each bear's clothing is as unique as each bear, and no two are ever dressed alike.

How to Find: Call customer service to ensure availability of the bear you desire, or place an order through the Web site.

• •

VERMONT TEDDY BEAR® ⌑
6655 Shelburne Road, Shelburne, VT 05482
Telephone: 800-829-BEAR
Web site: www.vermontteddybear.com

Vermont Teddy Bear® manufactures a selection of stuffed bears suitable for small children, as well as Occupation bears for older children and grown-ups. For older children and teens, there are graduation bears and sports bears such as cheerleader bears, soccer bears, and snowboarder bears. According to the company, the bears are 100 percent child safe when naked! The Occupation bears may have small pieces and are not suitable for infants or toddlers. There is a new baby bear for new moms.

Interesting Fact: Vermont Teddy Bear® was founded shortly after John Sortino discovered that all of the stuffed animals he had for his baby son were made overseas. He wondered why there weren't more American stuffed toys. He and his wife began sewing bears, and they eventually had enough to sell from a cart at a farmer's market. He immediately sold out. People started to ask him if he could ship the bears elsewhere. Within a short time, the idea of the Bear Gram™ was born.

How to Find: Orders may be placed through the Web site, or customers may contact the company through the customer service number.

Just Plain Fun

There are some toy companies whose products defy an exact classification. They can be simple fun or add to exercise. They can be a kind of arts and crafts game, bring out fantasy, or simply help childen play together.

....

AEROBIE, INC.
744 San Antonio Road, Palo Alto, CA 94303
Telephone: 350-493-3050
Web site: www.aerobie.com

Aerobie, Inc. manufactures the Aerobie® Pro Ring , the Aerobie® Aero Spin™ Yo-Yo, the Aerobie® Squidgie Ball™, and several other flying rings and boomerangs in the USA. Other products may be imported.

Interesting Fact: The Aerobie® was the creation of Alan Adler, an engineer with a passion for the aerodynamics of sailing. In the early 1980s, Mr. Adler became convinced he could improve upon the other flying ring toys of that era. His first design would go on to become the Aerobie® Pro-Ring. By the way, the Aerobie® holds the world record for the longest throw of any object that doesn't require mechanical assistance, such as a propellor.

How to Find: There is a store locator on the Aerobie, Inc. Web site for your convenience. The products are widely available in the sporting goods departments of large chain retailers.

....

ARROWCOPTER® ✿
P.O. Box 1807, Hollister, CA 95024
Telephone: 831-634-0145
Web site: www.arrowcopter.com

Arrowcopter® manufactures a flying toy that is launched. It comes in sets of one or two copters, as well as another model that flashes in the dark for night flying. Because of the skills required and the presence of some smaller parts, the Arrowcopter is not appropriate for children under the age of 3.

Interesting Fact: The Arrowcopter was invented in the late 1960s. It is a unique toy that allows the child to launch the propellor into the air like an arrow; it then falls to Earth like a helicopter. According to the company, the propellor can go as high as 300 feet before gently falling to the ground. At one time, Arrowcopter was one of the most popular toys in America, but, with the advent of the computer, interest fell off. Now, as parents realize the value of fun outdoor play, the Arrowcopter is again gaining in popularity.

How to Find: The Arrowcopter is best purchased through your local independent toy store, kite store, or hobby and crafts store.

....

BLU TRACK®

1116 E. 7th Street, Pella, IA 50219
Telephone: 641-780-1892
Web site: www.blutrack.com

Blu Track® manufactures a dual-lane racing system for 1/64th-scale racing cars, along with the accessories for creating race tracks with all kinds of different possibilities. The company places great emphasis on keeping the assembly simple so that children of all ages can easily assemble it.

Interesting Fact: While Randy Belding, the founder of Blu Track®, was in purchasing for a major corporation, he did a lot of travel. When on a business trip, he was reflecting as to why his son had grown so bored with a race track set. Randy realized that the two of them had more fun putting it together than playing with it, so Randy devised a new kind of track that had unlimited possibilities, and Blu Track® was born.

How to Find: You may purchase the Blu Track® racing system through the company Web site or do an online search for retailers that carry the products.

....

EDEN KAZOO COMPANY T ⚽ ⌑

8703 S. Main Street, Eden, NY 14057
Telephone: 716-992-3960
Web site: www.edenkazoo.com

Eden Kazoo Company manufactures kazoos in different models, including a French horn kazoo, a trumpet kazoo, and a trombone kazoo. For the executive in your life, there is even a 24-karat-gold-plated kazoo!

Interesting Fact: It is hard to put the kazoo in a toy category. It is equally difficult not to smile when someone is playing a kazoo! The

Original American Kazoo Company was reorganized and established in 1916 and is now the only metal kazoo factory in North America. Its museum highlights history and amusing trivia and shows step by step the way kazoos are made. According to the company, this is one of the few working museums left in the United States. The company welcomes factory tours. The kazoo-making equipment is the same equipment that was installed in 1907.

How to Find: Call customer service for help and information on purchasing kazoos. There is a company store with a full kazoo selection.

··

FINGA ZINGA®/EVUS-ARTISAN, INC. ✽
The company is located in the Sanford, Florida, area.
The company prefers e-mail.
Web site: www.fingazinga.com

Finga Zinga®/Evus-Artisan, Inc. Finga Zinga™ manufactures two types of the Finga Zinga™ action skill toy. One version is all wood with attached ends, and the other glows when used with glowsticks, which are available in five different colors. The nine current colors of the Finga Zinga™ were named by school children in a contest and include Atomic Tangerine (neon orange), My Little Leprechaun (dark green), and GloWorm (glow-in-the-dark).

Interesting Fact: Lynn Tierney, inventor of Finga Zinga™, claims her inspiration for this unique toy came from a dream about Johnny Depp! The Finga Zinga™ is an action skill toy composed of a hollow shaft, which holds a glowstick, and two colorful end pieces. The toys can be tossed, caught, or juggled.

How to Find: Finga Zingas™ are available through the company Web site. There are also specialty retailers and gift services throughout the United States that carry the product.

··

KIMMEL GNOMES ✽ ✂
1324 Shephard Street, Sturgis, SD 57785
The company prefers e-mail.
Web site: www.kimmelgnomes.com

Kimmel Gnomes handcrafts ceramic gnomes in all shapes, sizes, and characters, as well as toadstools, frogs, and other gnome accessories. These are keepsakes made by the only true ceramic gnome maker in America. They will bring joy to your child and your garden for many years to come. There is limited production.

Interesting Fact: Children love gardens. Children also like fantasy and making up stories. It is a wonderful thing for kids to see seeds sprout into plants. It is even more wonderful to know that a friend is always watching over their flowers. Candice Kimmel fell in love with gardens and gnomes when she was a little girl living in Wales. When she moved to America, she brought her love of gnomes and toadstools and garden fantasy with her. A talented artist and potter, Candice makes gnomes and other fantasy characters in a little hidden cottage (honest) in South Dakota.

How to Find: Orders may be placed directly with the company through its Web site or by calling customer service.

· ·

PEERLESS PLASTICS, INC. O ✈

510 Willow Street, Farmington, MN 55024
Telephone: 800-458-9595
Web site: www.peerlessplastics.com

Peerless Plastics, Inc. manufactures many different styles and colors of play mats, both folding and nonfolding. The nonfolding mats are available in assorted colors, and there is a selection of peg mats that allow for easier storage. The folding mats, such as the heavy-duty Kinder mat and the Daydreamer™ mat, are meant for nap times. Please note that these mats are frequently used in educational settings for drawing, napping, or light play, and they are also appropriate for home use. The company also manufactures the Mat Bus™ mat cart to store multiple mats. Other products in the line are imported.

Interesting Fact: Based in Farmington, Minnesota, Peerless Plastics has been in business for more than 50 years.

How to Find: Peerless Plastics does not sell direct to the public but sells through educational products distributors. Call the company for the name of the nearest educational products distributor, or search online by typing Peerless Plastics into a search engine.

....

PLAY CLAY FACTORY ✿

The company is located in the Lamar, Colorado, area.
Telephone: 800-925-2529
Web site: www.playclayfactory.com

Play Clay Factory manufactures a selection of colored play doughs
packaged in various-sized containers. The doughs are available in
several fruit scents such as Pineapple Punch, Grape Bubble, and Pink
Lemonade.

Interesting Fact: This company is an invention of a mother of four
children and several grandchildren. The invention was the result of
necessity, as the founder's husband had been out of work for six weeks.

How to Find: Orders may be placed directly through the Web site or by
calling customer service.

....

TERRAPIN TOYS™ ✿ ↑

P.O. Box 11565, Eugene, OR 97440
Telephone: 800-774-3875
Web site: www.terrapintoys.com

Terrapin Toys™ manufactures Mary's Softdough™ in all kinds of
versions, including scented dough, glow-in-the-dark dough, and glitter
dough, in addition to the original. The company recently came out with
cookie cutter accessories. When stored in its container, Softdough will
last up to a year. Recommended for children ages 3 and up.

Interesting Fact: Mary Newell, the founder of Terrapin Toys™, never
intended to go into the toy business. In college, she had a part-time job
at a daycare center and decided to make a modeling dough for the
children. The dough was a big hit, and she took the product to an
outdoor farmer's market, where it generated a lot of excitement. After
college, she thought she would get a real job and do something
different, but the dough product was becoming so popular that she
turned it into a business.

How to Find: The company's products are available in retail locations
or may be purchased through the Web site. Please call customer service
for further information.

TOOBEE® ↑

P.O. Box 166, Sussex, WI 53089
Telephone: 262-246-8480
Web site: www.toobee.com

Toobee® manufactures the Toobee, a unique flying toy that is about the weight of a marshmellow.

Interesting Fact: Toobee® is a flying can that was developed by aeronautical engineers. When thrown, the Toobee rises or curves depending on the spin that's put on the product. The world record throw is almost 300 feet. According to the company, 100 percent of the profits are donated to children's charities.

How to Find: Orders may be placed through the Web site or by contacting the company through their customer service number.

TORI TAKO, INC. ⊛ ✈

P.O. Box 18183, Salt Lake City, UT 84118
Telephone: 888-232-6947
Web site: www.toritako.com

Tori Tako, Inc. manufactures metal spinners and Jack kites. Jack kites measure up to 60" from wing tip to wing tip, and they are made in the shapes of birds. When Jack Kites are flown, the wind beats the wings, and the kite moves just like a bird. Spinners are in a fixed location, and, as the wind moves them, they almost appear to be kaleidoscopes. Other products are imported.

Interesting Fact: Tori Tako's entire company is built on wind! It has a large selection of kites, banners, spinners, and other elements that have fascinated small and big children over the centuries. Please be advised that certain products shown on the Web site are imported.

How to Find: Orders may be placed through the Web site or by contacting the company through the customer service number.

WORLD'S GREATEST BATH BOATS ⊛ ✂

2735 65th Avenue, Princeton, MN 55371
Telephone: 763-389-3517
Web site: www.bathboats.com

World's Greatest Bath Boats handcrafts handmade bath boats out of Wisconsin basswood. The bath boats are often given as gifts for births, weddings, and even retirements. Customers can call in or e-mail interesting facts about the person receiving the boats, and the company will personalize the boats with those facts.

Interesting Fact: Dana McDill made the first bath boat for his newborn son in 1971. It turned out so well that he decided to go to street fairs with his wife, Mary, to sell bathboats from a cart. He has since sold thousands of boats. While some people collect Dana's bath boats, most give them to their children for the bathtub.

How to Find: Orders may be placed through the Web site or by contacting the company through the customer service number.

••

YACKLEBALL®   ❀ ✂
369 S. Main Street, Troutman, NC 28166
Telephone: 704-528-1130
Web site: www.yackleball.com

Yackleball® manufactures the Yackleball® in its regular size, in a smaller or junior size, and in a night version. In 2009, the company is scheduled to make a similar product for pets. The company has the ability to custom imprint.

Interesting Fact: The inspiration for Patricia Littwin's invention, the Yackleball®, grew out of her wish to improve the motor skills of one of her children. She drew a puffy X shape and realized she had the makings of a new throwing toy that virtually any child could master. Ms. Littwin has been widely featured in the media as an example of American entrepreneurship. Yackleball® products are manufactured in the USA.

How to Find: You may order the Yackleball® online through the Web site, or there is a store locator for your convenience.

Outdoor Play

Both creative play and exercise seem to come from the swing sets and other outdoor games that are found in our backyards and schoolyards. The American manufacturing companies in this list make swing sets and outdoor play equipment for a wide range of budgets and needs.

....

CEDARWORKS® ✄

799 Commercial Street, Rockport, ME 04856
Telephone: 800-GO-CEDAR
Web site: www.cedarworks.com

CedarWorks® manufactures swing sets in many different styles. While the Serendipity series requires a lot of room and has numerous design elements, the Revelry series has much smaller elements that can stand alone and has a much simpler design. The company can customize.

Interesting Fact: Founded in 1981 in Rockport, Maine, and owned by the Brown family, CedarWorks® describes its product as America's premium swing set. Custom made from northern white cedar, the swing sets are available in many styles and configurations. CedarWorks' product line has grown from two basic climbing structures to five play system product lines with 15 structures and numerous accessories. Swing sets are made to meet each customer's specific needs.

How to Find: The company Web site is set up to allow the customer to view sample swing sets that are already fabricated, or you can design a custom set online. Please call customer service for assistance.

....

FLEXIBLE FLYER® T

100 Tubb Avenue, West Point, MS 39773
Telephone: 888-350-3015
Web site: www.flexible-flyer.com

Flexible Flyer® manufactures swing sets in various sizes and styles, as well as hobby horses.

Interesting Fact: An American manufacturing treasure, the company has been in business since 1889. Flexible Flyer® is America's largest manufacturer of hobby horses. Each horse is hand painted.

How to Find: Virtually every major retail chain carries some of the Flexible Flyer swing sets. Call customer service, or contact Flexible Flyer through the Web site for information on dealers in your area.

. . . .

PHONY PONY TIRE SWING ☺ ⌗

4704 E. Highway 92, Lakeland, FL 33801
Telephone: 800-300-7484
Web site: www.cowhorncountry.com

Phony Pony Tire Swing manufactures the Phony Pony Tree Swing in several different colors. In addition to the swing, the company also sells swing accessories.

Interesting Fact: The company uses recycled automobile tires to make its swings. It uses tires without steel belts to promote safety. The swings can hold up to 250 pounds, and this is important, as more than one child will frequently ride. The swings are primarily designed for children ages 2–10 years.

How to Find: The Phony Pony Tire Swing is available through the company's Web site. Customers may also visit the company store, in Lakeland, Florida.

. . . .

PLAY NATION PLAY SYSTEMS, INC.®

480 Cobb Parkway, Marietta, GA 30060
Telephone: 800-445-PLAY
Web site: www.playnation.com

Play Nation Play Systems, Inc.® manufactures wooden swing sets and playhouses in redwood, cedar, and pine. Some of the accessories may be imported.

Interesting Fact: The Play Nation Play System® uses California redwood and western red cedar as they are natural alternatives to preserved lumber.

How to Find: Swing sets and playhouses are sold through specialty retailers throughout the United States. Please call customer service for assistance in locating a dealer.

. . . .

PLAYWORLD SYSTEMS, INC. ® ↑

1000 Buffalo Road, Lewisburg, PA 17837
Telephone: 800-233-8404
Web site: www.playworldsystems.com

Playworld Systems is a commercial manufacturer of swing sets for parks and recreation departments, schools, and other organizations. The Play Designs® products are for children ages 2–5 years; the Play World™ products are for children ages 5–12 years. Although this company's products are typically sold to schools or parks because of their price, they have been sold to private homeowners, as well, and that is why the company is being included in this part of the chapter.

Interesting Fact: Starting its life in the late 1950s as a machine shop, Playworld Systems® is a family-owned business that is now in its third generation.

How to Find: Customers who wish to talk to a sales representative may visit the Web site and fill out the sales rep locator.

SPRING SWINGS & MORE ✈

2000 Avenue P, Riviera Beach, FL 33404
Telephone: 561-845-6966
Web site: www.springswings.com

Spring Swings & More manufactures outdoor equipment for children from ages 3 to teens. The Fun Ride™ products run along a cable, while the Spring Swing™ attaches to a swing motion. The Fun Ride™ and the Spring Swing™ are manufactured in the USA. Parts either are all domestically sourced or may contain imported parts. Other products are imported.

Interesting Fact: Spring Swings & More is a specialty toy manufacturer of outdoor, backyard residential play products. Established more than 20 years ago, the company has created lasting, durable, and safe backyard and residential playground toys.

How to Find: The products may be found at major toy retailers throughout the United States or through online retailers, or they may be purchased through the company Web site.

SWING 'N SLIDE®

1212 Barberry Drive, Janesville, WI 53545
Telephone: 800-888-1232
Web site: www.swing-n-slide.com

☆
Made Here, Baby!

Swing 'n Slide® manufactures ready-to-assemble (RTA) swing sets with different options and styles and in different price ranges. The RTA Wood Complete™ kits come in four different models; the No-Cut™ RTA kits have everything a customer needs except the 4 × 4 lumber beams and come in two models; the Custom™ RTA kits come in eight different models.

Interesting Fact: Swing 'n Slide® introduced the first rock-climbing wall for residential use, in 1999.

How to Find: Swing 'n Slide products are carried by all of the major hardware chains, as well as by numerous independent retailers. The Web site has a store locator. If you can't find a store near to you, please call customer service.

••

YARD CANDY
Yard Candy is an online store located in Oxford, PA.
Telephone: 610-998-9510
Web site: www.yardcandy.com

Yard Candy manufactures sandboxes out of cedar or poly-lumber, depending upon the model. The Comfort Sandbox has two padded benches; there is also a deluxe model with a roof, an octagon-shaped sandbox, and an ingenius sand table that doubles as a picnic bench. Covers are available for all sandboxes.

Interesting Fact: Yard Candy specializes in making several different models of sandboxes and a unique sand table. The sand table comes to you mostly assembled, and the sandboxes are all pre-cut for easy assembly with full directions.

How to Find: Yard Candy is set up as an online business. A customer service number is provided for your information. The company states that the shipping charges are nominal to any part of the country.

Child Safety and Toy Safety Resource Guide

It is important for parents and guardians to have the most up-to-date information on the toys, apparel, and other products they are buying for their children. It is also essential for all of us to be aware of child safety issues, whether we are parents, relatives, teachers, or coaches.

The following list should help those who wish to find resources on product safety, child safety, childproofing a home, new children's products, and product recommendations or recalls.

Some of the organizations we list are quite specific in their missions, while others are simply fun and entertaining; they represent government, industry groups, commercial ventures, and parents who simply want to reach out to one another. If you fear that you may have a product in your household that might have been recalled, we suggest that your first stop should be the U.S. Consumer Product Safety Commission, which appears in these listings.

New organizations, blogs, and Web sites devoted to products and the general topic of child safety are constantly springing up these days. Please think of these resources as your starting point. Some of these sites have a lot of blogging activity, so it will be relatively easy for you to discover other new and interesting resources.

American Academy of Pediatrics (AAP)
Web site: www.aap.org
Telephone: 847-434-4000

☆
Appendix

The **American Academy of Pediatrics** Web site contains general information on children's health from newborns to age 21. Start your search by typing in a keyword such as "children's toys." The Web site will direct you to recent papers covering the subject. Parents, please note: the AAP cannot answer specific questions about your child's health. You should always consult your pediatrician.

American National Safety Institute (ANSI)
Web site: www.ansi.org

The mission of the **American National Safety Institute** is to oversee the creation and use of thousands of norms and guidelines that directly impact businesses in nearly every sector of American manufacturing. This is the organization that helps set important product standards that safeguard your child. Though parts of the Web site are quite technical, by doing a search on the site, parents can find several interesting lay articles on topics. For example, typing the keywords "Lead in Children's Toys" will reveal several articles and issues on that topic.

American Specialty Toy Retailing Association (ASTRA)
Web site: www.astratoy.org
Telephone: 800-591-0490

The **American Specialty Toy Retailing Association** is the trade organization for independent toy manufacturers and the toy trade. However, as a valuable public service, the Web site contains useful buying guides and interesting topics for parents. The ASTRA site also has retail toy store listings, as well as the organization's choices for best products of the previous year. The product selections include imported as well as American-made products.

Babyproofingdirectory.com
Web site: www.babyproofingdirectory.com

This is a useful Web site to help make parents aware of the babyproofing services that are available throughout the United States, and it gives parents tips for a do-it-yourself babyproofing plan.

There are also outdoor safety and travel safety tips, as well as features such as "Toy Safety for Tots."

Babyzone®
Web site: www.babyzone.com

Babyzone® offers information on child safety for parents and guardians of children from babies through to teens. Topics include information on babyproofing your home, children's toy recalls, and car-seat safety.

Center for Disease Control and Prevention (CDC)
Web site: www.cdc.gov
Telephone: 800-311-3435

The Center for Disease Control and Prevention site has many relevant papers and articles under the banner "Health and Safety Topics." By typing in a keyword, for example, "Toy Safety," you can locate a number of informative references. Some of these articles may be technical; however, others are quite informative and are easy to read.

Child Safety Network (CSN)
Web site: www.csn.org

The **Child Safety Network**, while not addressing issues such as toy or product safety, is focused on protecting children from online predators, abduction, abuse, and many other childhood dangers.

Consumer Federation of America (CFA)
Web site: www.consumerfed.org
Telephone: 202-387-6121

The **Consumer Federation of America** is a policy organization that advocates on behalf of consumers. It does an extensive amount of research and education. By typing keywords such as "Child Safety" or "Toys" into the Web site search, you can find interesting facts, papers, and presentations on the topic that interests you.

Consumer Reports
Web site: www.consumerreports.org

Consumer Reports is one of the nation's leading authorities on testing and ranking products. The publication is very well known and often provides us with a third-party voice when we make a buying decision. Under the "Babies and Kids" tab, there are ratings and reviews of hundreds of toys and other children's products.

Dr. Toy
Web site: drtoy.com

"**Dr. Toy**" is also known as Stevanne Auerbach, Ph.D., who for more than 30 years has been considered one of the nation's leading experts on the topic of play. The Dr. Toy Web site is loaded with information on toys and games and covers virtually every aspect of the toy industry. Dr. Auerbach lists recommendations for what she considers the top toy products. Please note that some of the toys recommended may be imported.

KidsHealth®
Web site: www.kidshealth.org

According to the Web site, **KidsHealth®** is the largest and most-visited Web site on the Internet providing doctor-approved health information. There are many interesting articles written for parents on how to choose safe toys, on recent toy recalls, and on how to childproof your home.

iVillage Total Health Network
Web site: www.parenting.ivillage.com

The iVillage Web site may best be thought of as an online community. Parents are able to ask for and receive feedback on many important social and health issues. Parents or guardians may join numerous discussion groups. Among numerous topics relating to children, this Web site contains information on toy safety, which parents may find a very useful resource.

Mom Blogs, The
Web site: www.themomblogs.com

The Mom Blogs is a directory of hundreds of "Mommy" blogs from all over North America. Some of the blogs specifically contain reviews of new baby products. While the information is subjective, it is extremely valuable for parents to compare and contrast their experiences with certain products and children's-products companies or simply to discuss parenting issues in a free-form conversation.

National Network for Childcare (NNCC)
Web site: www.nncc.org

The **National Network for Childcare** Web site is devoted to assisting childcare professionals in helping to better safeguard children under their supervision. There is a comprehensive listing of articles and publications on all aspects of child safety.

National Safety Council® (NSC)
Web site: www.nsc.org

The **National Safety Council®** emphasizes education to help parents to better address the safety issues that affect their children. Children's safety issues range from teenage driving to serious aspects of infant safety, such as the proper use and installation of car seats and issues and solutions related to lead-based paint.

Oklahoma State University, Environmental Health & Safety Department
Web site: www.pp.okstate.edu

The state universities are often great resources; they offer noncommercial Web sites that provide information solely for the purposes of education and public service. Oklahoma State University has an "Environmental Health & Safety" tab that addresses children's and consumer issues. By entering keywords such as "Holiday Safety," "Safe Toys," or "Holiday Toy Checklists," parents can find many fine articles on those topics.

☆
Appendix

Oppenheim Toy Portfolio
Web site: www.toyportfolio.com

The **Oppenheim Toy Portfolio** was created by Stephanie and Joanne Oppenheim, child development experts and widely published authors. The Oppenheims frequently appear on network television, where they educate parents on topics such as play and the entire topic of toys. The Web site contains a treasure of information on children's toys and games, with reviews of hundreds of American-made and imported children's toys. The toy categories are broken down by age group. The Oppenheim Toy Portfolio offers its top product picks for the previous year. Please see Chapter 7 for an interview with Stephanie and Joanne Oppenheim.

Parenthood.com
Web site: www.parenthood.com

Parenthood.com is a commercial site that describes itself as an online parenting resource. The Web site contains extensive information on important health and safety-related issues for parents of kids from the infant years through teenagers. By typing keywords such as "Toy Safety Shopping Tips" or simply "Child Safety," you will find several worthwhile features.

Parents.com
Web site: www.parents.com

Parents.com is the site for *American Baby*, *Parents*, and *Family Circle* magazines. The site contains a wealth of information about all aspects of childrearing, good hygiene, and child safety. There are numerous references to the best toys for children, general toy safety, and infant safety issues. These references can be accessed simply by typing keywords such as "Toys" or "Toy Safety" into the Web site.

Safer Child, Inc.
Web site: www.saferchild.org

Safer Child is a nonprofit children's safety resource based in Spokane, Washington. The Web site contains many links to information on all aspects of child safety, for example, car-seat safety and the proper way to buy and use sporting goods equipment for children.

Toy Industry Association™, Inc. (TIA)
Web site: www.toyassociation.org
Telephone: 212-675-1141

The **Toy Industry Association** Web site is primarily intended for toy producers, toy importers, and the toy trade. The Web site is also used by toy safety testing laboratories, toy designers, and safety consultants. As you might imagine, the Web site contains industry-specific information; however, there is excellent general reading on topics such as toy safety, playing with your child, and the organization's choice for best toy products for the previous year. The selection may include imported as well as American-made products.

Toy-tma.com
Web site: www.toy-tma.com

This Web site contains toy information, toy reviews, and comments for parents and toy hobbyists on a wide variety of issues relating to toys and play.

University of Maryland Medicine
Web site: www.umm.edu
Telephone: 800-492-5538

This Web site contains a wealth of information on children's health. Among the many topics covered in the Children's Health Guide is information on how to find a safe toy.

University of Minnesota
Web site: www.extension.umn.edu

Another excellent university resource, the University of Minnesota Web site has a great deal of information on the topic of child safety.

Many of the articles are exclusive to the site and range in scope from features on improving one's parenting skills to farm equipment safety.

U.S. Consumer Product Safety Commission (CPSC)
Web site: www.cpsc.gov
Recall Hotline: 888-655-8484

The **Consumer Product Safety Commission** is the organization "charged with protecting the public from unreasonable risks of serious injury or death from more than 15,000 types of consumer products under the agency's jurisdiction." It is the CPSC that is responsible for determining if a children's product should be recalled because of a potentially dangerous design flaw or other problem. The CPSC Web site has the most up-to-date information on recalls, as well as archives of products recalled in the recent past.

U.S. Department of Health & Human Services
Web site: www.healthfinder.gov

The U.S. Department of Health and Human Services maintains this excellent Web site in order to assist consumers in finding information on the overall topic of health. The site gathers information on topics from health care complaints to faulty products to policies regarding medical programs. By typing in keywords such as "Toy Safety" or "Lead in Products," you can find information from many different sources.

United States National Library of Medicine, National Institutes of Health
Web site: www.nlm.nih.gov
Telephone: 888-FIND-NLM

The National Library of Medicine has extensive resources on topics such as child safety, choking hazards, car-seat safety, and how to inspect toys. By typing in keywords such as "Toy Safety" or "Child Safety," you can retrieve information from many different sources.

WebMD

Web site: www.webmd.com

WebMD is a popular Web site for people of all ages to use as a health reference. Many articles are generated by the site itself in the WebMD *Health News* features. By entering a keyword such as "Toys" or "Toy Safety," you can locate important features on those topics.

American Manufacturing Treasures

This listing honors those American manufacturing companies that, despite all odds, have been making products for children for more than a century.

Amana Woolen Mill, Amana, Iowa (Blankets), est. c. 1845

Carrom, Inc., Ludington, Michigan (Games), est. 1889

Colgate Juvenile Products, Atlanta, Georgia (Mattresses), est. 1907

Eden Kazoo Company, Eden, New York (Kazoos), est. 1907

Faribault Mills, Faribault, Minnesota (Blankets), est. 1865

Flexible Flyer, West Point, Mississippi (Swing Sets, Hobby Horses), est. 1889

Holgate Toys, Bradford, Pennsylvania (Toddler & Preschool Toys), est. 1789

Johnson Woolen Mills, Johnson, Vermont (Children's Clothes), est. 1842

Little River Windsors, Berwick, Maine (Furniture), est. c. 1805

Louisville Slugger, Louisville, Kentucky (Baseball Bats), est. 1884

Old Town® Canoes and Kayaks, Old Town, Maine (Water Sports), est. 1898

Round House™ Manufacturing Company, Oklahoma (Overalls), est. 1903

Simmons Kids®, Atlanta, Georgia (Mattresses), est. 1870

Smethport Specialty Company, Smethport, Pennsylvania (Children's Games), est. 1908

Vermont Tubbs, Brandon, Vermont (Furniture), est. 1840

Whitney Brothers Educational Toys, Keene, New Hampshire (Educational Furniture), est. 1904

American Manufacturing Companies Founded, Co-Founded, or Owned by Women

The number of American manufacturing companies run by women is impressive. These women are proud of their companies; more than that, they are proud of the safety and quality of their products.

A Wish Come True
Aero Tech Designs, Inc.
Amana® Woolen Mill
Amenity™, Inc.
American Easel
Appalachian Baby Design
Arrowcopter®
Babies 'N Bows
Baby Beau & Belle
Baby Burpees
Baby Go Retro®
Baby Knits and More
Baby Nay®
Baby's First Ball
Bahama Bob's Apparel
Bailey Boys, Inc., The
Bean Bag City
Beary Basics™
Bébé Chic, Inc.®
Bébé Monde, Inc.

Belle Bags
Belle Organic Baby Carrier
Belle Pearl™
Bercot Children's Wear
BetterLiving–Sun Aire™ Products
Big Bellies Bibs™
Bitty Braille
Black Mountain Apparel™
Blankets by Carol
Bold Mary
Bossy Baby
Brag-e-let's®
Brahms-Mount Textiles
Brighton Pavilion®/Jane Keltner
    Collections
Buchmann's Toy Maker Shop
Buddy's Jeans®
Bum Genius™
Bumkins® Finer Baby Products
Camden Rose

Caroline & Company™
Cat's Pajamas®, The
Cayden Creations
Ceaco/Gamewright®
Chloe Emma Designs
Cindy's Throws
Clairebella, Inc.
Cloth & Needle
Colonial Braided Rug Company
Conversion Products, Inc.
Cool Clothing, USA
Cornbag Critters
Cornpatch Creations
Cotton Caboodle
Cotton Monkey
Cotton Monster™
Cover Play Yard®
Cow Track Creations
Crescent Moon™ Snowshoes
Crib Rock® Couture
Cubby Hole Toys
Custom Made for Kids™
D and Me Wood Toys
DCM Products
Diapees & Wipees®
Dittany Baby
Doodletown™ Toys, Inc.
Downtime™ Baby
E. Willoughby Bear Company
Eden Kazoo Company
Eden's Bouquet
Eight3One™
EmBears
Esperanza Threads
EZ 2 Love®
Fairy Finery™
Finga Zinga®/Evus-Artisan, Inc.
Focoloco
Footwear by Footskins®
Fort Cloudy
Fortune Tee
Garden Kids™
Glenna Jean Manufacturing
Go Mama Go Designs
GoZo USA™
Great American Puzzle Company
Green Babies

Green Toys™, Inc.
Greenleaf Dollhouses
Hand Picked Pumpkin™
Happy Panda® Baby
Heart of Vermont™
His Idea Crafts
Holy Lamb Organics
Honeysuckle Dreams
Hotslings®
Hoy Shoe Company, Inc.
Imagination Creations®
Itasca Moccasin
Iza-bella, Inc.
Jackson Kayak
Jen Jen Kids
Johnson Woolen Mills®
Jonti-Craft®, Inc.
Joy Carpets
Kaiya Eve™ Couture
Kandle Kids Wear
Kathy's Braided Rugs
Kathy's Kreations
Kid's & Pets Furniture
Kimmel Gnomes
Kiwi Industries
Klu™ Mountain Outerwear
Kumquat Baby
La Petite Fee™/Nstyle Designs
Lauri® Toys
Leachco™, Inc.
Liliputians NYC
Lilipad Studio
Little Capers, Inc.
Little Colorado™, Inc.
Little Gems Jewelry
Little Giraffe, Inc.
Little Mass
Little Miss Liberty Round Crib Co.™
Lollipop Zen™
Lots 2 Say Baby
LucasWorks™
Lucy Hammet™ Games
M Group, The/Bamboosa®
Mad River Rocket™ Sled Company, Inc.
Malina, Inc.
MaMaSoes, Inc.
Maple Landmark of Vermont, Inc.

Companies Committed to Green or Organic Manufacturing

The number of American children's product manufacturers that make their products from organic materials or recycle materials or dedicate their manufacturing facilities to "green," sustainable practices is growing with every passing year. In this index, we list companies that have made the move to "green," with many more to come.

A Natural Home
Allagash Wood Products, Inc.
Amenity™, Inc.
American Apparel®
American Recycled Plastic, Inc.
Animals and Arks
Appalachian Baby Design
Belle Organic Baby Carrier
Bossy Baby
Bum Genius™
Bumkins® Finer Baby Products
Camden Rose
Chuck Roast, Inc.,
Cindy's Throws
Clothes Made from Scrap, Inc.
Colonial Braided Rug Company
Community Playthings
Cotton Caboodle
Cotton Monkey

Cotton Monster™
Crescent Moon™ Snowshoes
Crib Rock® Couture
Dittany Baby
Duc Duc™
Earth Wear® Organic Cotton Originals
Eco Tots™
Eight3One™
Esperanza Threads
Flagship Carpets
Focoloco
Garden Kids
Green Babies
Green Toys™, Inc.
Hand Picked Pumpkin™
Heart of Vermont™
Holy Lamb Organics
Honeysuckle Dreams
Hotslings®

American Children's Products Manufacturers Listed by State

We are proud to have 46 states represented in *Made Here, Baby!*

ALABAMA
Under the Green Roof

ARKANSAS
Better Living–Sun Aire™ Products
Mohawk Canoes
Whimsy Woods Children's Furniture

ARIZONA
Binky Couture®
Bumkins® Finer Baby Products
Kathy's Kreations
ME4Kidz™, Inc.
Omnicor, Inc./Wikkistix®
Solar Eclipse®
Stuffington Bear Factory

CALIFORNIA
Aerobie, Inc.
Amenity™, Inc.
American Apparel®
Arrowcopter®
Baby Burpees
Baby Nay®
Beary Basics™
Bébé Monde, Inc.
Bottle Blankie™, Inc.
Cat's Pajamas®, The

Charlie Rocket
City Threads, Inc.
Cohort® Skateboards
Cool Clothing, USA
Cool Sofa
Corsican Furniture Company
Cover Play Yard®
Cow Track Creations
Crib Rock® Couture
Fold-a-Goal®
Fortune Tee
Green Toys™, Inc.
Heartwood Arts
Jen Jen Kids
Kaiya Eve™ Couture
Kokatat Watersports Wear
Kumquat Baby
Lambs & Ivy®
Life Kind Products™
Little Capers, Inc.
Little Gems Jewelry
Little Giraffe®, Inc.
Little Mass
Little Miss Liberty Round Crib Co.™
Malina
Matilda & Company™
Meg Dana & Company
My Blankee™, Inc.

ILLINOIS
Bean Products
Calutech®, Inc.
Creative Frontier, The/Retract-A-Gate®
Cubby Hole Toys
Custom Made for Kids™
Hand Picked Pumpkin™
La Petite Fee™/Nstyle Designs

INDIANA
Bercot Children's Wear
Bernhaus Furniture
Eco Tots™
Peters' Group Ltd.
Steffy Wood Products
Sunshine Teddy Bears
Three Weavers
Train Tables Online, Inc.

IOWA
Amana® Woolen Mill
Blu Track®
Dodger Industries
Lindberg Models®/J. Lloyd International
Original Big Wheel®, The/J. Lloyd
    International
Slick Sugar™

KANSAS
Moon Marble Company
Soark® Running Apparel

KENTUCKY
Louisville Slugger®

LOUISIANA
Sanders Handcrafted Toys

MAINE
Allagash Wood Products, Inc.
Belle Pearl™
Brahms-Mount Textiles, Inc.
CedarWorks®
Conversion Products, Inc.
E. Willoughby Bear Company
Knockabout Toys

Little River Windsors
Old Town® Canoe & Kayak
Penobscot Bay Porch Swings
Roy Toy® Manufacturing
Taurus Toy Company

MARYLAND
Honeysuckle Dreams
Kathy's Braided Rugs
Mr. Bobbles Blankets
Red Prairie, The
Salisbury Pewter

MASSACHUSETTS
Baby's First Ball
Barnstable Bat, Inc.
Blisters™ Dice Game
Brag-e-let's®
Ceaco/Gamewright®
Exergen Thermometer
Focoloco
Guillow's
Kidioms™
Mylec, Inc.®
Nanny Gram™
Quality Fleece
Skateluge™
Sterlingwear of Boston™, Inc.
Winning Moves® Games

MICHIGAN
American Plastic Toys
Camden Rose
Carrom, Inc.
Lindenwood, Inc.
Mon Amie
Poof-Slinky, Inc.
Rochelle Furniture Company
Roebuck Studio
TC Sports, Inc.

MINNESOTA
Battle Lake Outdoors™
Beka, Inc.
Doodletown™ Toys, Inc.
Fairy Finery™
Faribault Mills™

Footwear by Footskins®
Heartland Sports Manufacturing
Itasca Moccasin
Jonti-Craft®, Inc.
Kvale Good Natured Games
Loll Designs
My Green Closet
North States Industries, Inc.
Peerless Plastics, Inc.
Riedell® Shoes, Inc.
Round Belly Clothing
Weenonah
World's Greatest Bath Boats

MISSISSIPPI
American Made Fitness Equipment, LLC®
Buddy's Jeans®
Flexible Flyer®

MISSOURI
Bum Genius™
Children's Factory, The
Hoy Shoe Company, Inc.
Modest Apparel, Inc.
Ozark Mountain Kids
Wee Ones, Inc.
Whittle Toy Company, Inc.
Wunderworks of America

MONTANA
Celery Furniture
Cindy's Throws
D and Me Wood Toys
Grandpa's Games and Crafts

NEBRASKA
Fat Brain™ Toys, Inc.
Needak® Soft Bounce™ Rebounders

NEVADA
Lollipop Zen™

NEW HAMPSHIRE
Chuck Roast, Inc.,
Hampshire Pewter
Oak Designs, Inc.
Whitney Brothers Educational Toys

NEW JERSEY
Bébé Chic, Inc.®
Berg Furniture
My Goodness Duds
Patch Kraft® Original Designs

NEW MEXICO
Kiwi Industries
Northstar Toys

NEW YORK
Animals and Arks
Austin Air Systems, Ltd.
Big Plush Stuffed Toys
Bitty Braille
Buchmann's Toy Maker Shop
Buffalo Games
Community Playthings®
Don Edwards Wooden Toy Works
Downtime™ Baby
Duc Duc™
Eden Kazoo Company
EmBears
Green Babies
Greenleaf Dollhouses
Havlick Snowshoe
Joseph Abboud™
Liliputians NYC
Newberry Knitting
Sassy Scrubs®
Tough Traveler®

NORTH CAROLINA
Belle Bags
Britax™ USA
Charles Craft
Colonial Braided Rug Company
Eagle USA, Inc.
Huggage
Marpac Corporation
Neat Solutions, Inc.
Patsy Aiken Designs
Rockin' Choppers
Texas Jeans®
Wood Designs
Yackleball®

OHIO
A Natural Home
Amish Valley Oak
Bean Bag City
Drifter Bags
Esperanza Threads
Lehman's, Inc.
Little Tikes® Company, The
Mission Time Designs
Moore's Farm Toys
My Little Blankie
Naturepedic®
Step 2 Company, LLC, The
U.S. Wings®

OKLAHOMA
Childwood Baby Cradles & Rocking
    Horses
Leachco™, Inc.
DCM Products
Round House™ Manufacturing Co.
Serendipiti-Do-Da
Wee-Boos, LLC

OREGON
American Easel Company
Aqua Jogger®
Bike Friday®
Carpets for Kids®
Colorgrown Clothing, Inc.
Columbia Knit
Garden Kids™
Jump Rope Store
My Precious Kid™
Outside Baby
Pacific Rim Woodworking
Peri Ponchos
Poppywood Toys
Preemie Yums©/Nu Baby
Queen Bee Creations™ & Chickpea
    Baby™
Soft Star Shoes
Terrapin Toys™
Wild Zoo, Inc.™

PENNSYLVANIA
A Wish Come True

Aero Tech Designs, Inc.
Babies 'N Bows
Berlin Wagons
Big Bellies Bibs™
Channel Craft, Inc.
Cloth & Needle
Cornbag Critters
EZ 2 Love®
Holgate Toys®
Jensen Steam Engines
K'nex® Industries
Lauri® Toys
My Paper Crane
Perler® Beads
Playworld Systems
Rethreds, Inc.
Smethport Specialty Company
Valley Road Woodworks
Wonderboy®, Inc.
Xootr LLC
Yard Candy

RHODE ISLAND
Old Fashioned Blocks
Rug Factory Store

SOUTH CAROLINA
A.S. Tees
M Group, The/Bamboosa®

SOUTH DAKOTA
Kimmel Gnomes

TENNESSEE
Adams USA
Bahama Bob's Apparel
Brighton Pavilion®/Jane Keltner
    Collections
Caroline & Company™
Diamond Gusset Jeans, Inc.
Earth Wear® Organic Cotton Originals
His Idea Crafts
Jackson Kayak
L.C. King Manufacturing
Legend Fitness®
Mason Corporation
Oreck Corporation

American-Made Children's Products

This cross-reference will make it easier to find all of the companies making a particular type of product. To recommend a company to be included, contact us at www.madeherebaby.com.

Baby Products: Traveling with Baby (includes slings, pouches, carriers, car seats, and accessories)
Belle Organic Baby Carrier
Britax™ USA
Cornpatch Creations
Cover Play Yard®
Dittany Baby
GoZo USA™
Hotslings®
iBert, Inc.
Leachco™, Inc.
ME4Kidz™, Inc.
My Blankee™, Inc.
My Karma Baby™
My Precious Kid™
Neat Solutions, Inc.
New Native® Baby
Peanut Shell®, The
Prince Lionheart®
Rockin' Baby Slings
Solar Eclipse®
Sweet Fletcher Designs
Tough Traveler®
U.S. Sheepskin

Zolo Wear®

Baby Products: Diaper bags, diapers, wipes, and diaper storage
Bailey Boys, Inc., The
Bum Genius™
Bumkins® Finer Baby Products
Clairebella, Inc.
Diapees & Wipees®
Fortune Tee
GoZo USA™
Mon Amie
New Native® Baby
Ozark Mountain Kids
POSH™ by Tori
Prince Lionheart®
Queen Bee Creations™ & Chickpea Baby™
Rethreds, Inc.
Round Belly Clothing
Sweet T Baby
Tough Traveler®

Baby Products: Baby keepsakes of all kinds
Animals and Arks

Index E

Amenity™, Inc.
Appalachian Baby Design
Baby's First Ball
Bailey Boys, Inc., The
Beary Basics™
Bébé Chic, Inc.®
Blankets by Carol
Brahms-Mount Textiles, Inc.
Childwood Baby Cradles & Rocking Horses
Cindy's Throws
Clairebella, Inc.
Colgate Juvenile Products
Colorgrown Clothing, Inc.
Corsican Furniture Company/ corsican.com™
Cover Play Yard®
Earth Wear® Organic Cotton Originals
Eden's Bouquet
Esperanza Threads
Faribault Mills™
Glenna Jean Manufacturing
Go Mama Go Designs
Heart of Vermont™
Holy Lamb Organics
Honeysuckle Dreams
Hugg-A-Planet®
Jen Jen Kids
Lambs & Ivy®
Lehman's, Inc.
Life Kind Products™
Little Giraffe®, Inc.
Little Miss Liberty Round Crib Co.™
M Group, The/Bamboosa™
Mon Amie
Mr. Bobbles Blankets
My Blankee™, Inc.
My Goodness Duds
My Little Blankie
Naturepedic®
New Native® Baby
Ozark Mountain Kids
Patch Kraft® Original Designs
Quality Fleece
Robbie Adrian™
Round Belly Clothing

Sage Creek U.S.A., Inc./Sage Creek Naturals®
Simmons Kids®
Snug Fleece Woolens®
SOS From Texas
Sweet T Baby
Three Weavers
Topnotch4kids
Twinkle Baby®
U.S. Sheepskin
Vivetique™, Inc.

Baby Products: Baby clothing
A Natural Home
A.S. Tees
American Apparel®
American Joe™ Authentic American Apparel
Babies 'N Bows
Baby Beau & Belle
Baby Go Retro®
Baby Knits and More
Baby Nay®
Bahama Bob's Apparel
Bailey Boys, Inc., The
Beary Basics™
Bébé Chic, Inc.®
Bébé Monde, Inc.
Bercot Children's Wear
Binky Couture®
Bitty Braille
Black Mountain Apparel™
Bossy Baby
Camden Rose
Charles Craft
Charlie Rocket
Chuck Roast, Inc.,
Cloth & Needle
Clothes Made from Scrap, Inc.
Colgate Juvenile Products
Colorgrown Clothing, Inc.
Cotton Caboodle
Cotton Monkey
Cow Track Creations
Crib Rock® Couture
Dittany Baby
Downtime™ Baby

Earth Wear® Organic Cotton Originals
Eden's Bouquet
Eight3One™
Esperanza Threads
Fortune Tee
Garden Kids™
Go Mama Go Designs
Green Babies
Hand Picked Pumpkin™
Happy Panda® Baby
Holy Lamb Organics
Iza-bella
Jen Jen Kids
Kandle Kids Wear
Kidioms™
Kiwi Industries
Klu™ Mountain Outerwear
Kumquat Baby
Lambs & Ivy®
Liliputians NYC
Little Giraffe®, Inc.
Little Mass
Lollipop Zen™
M Group, The/Bamboosa™
Matilda & Company™
Mon Amie
Mountain Sprouts®
Mouseworks, The
My Blankee™, Inc.
My Goodness Duds
My Vintage Baby™
Nanny Gram™
Neptune Zoo™
New Native® Baby
Original Flap Happy®, The
Outside Baby
Ozark Mountain Kids
Panhandle Babies™
Patsy Aiken Designs
Peanut Shell®, The
Preemie Yums©/Nu Baby
Red Prairie, The
Robin's Hoods™ by Nature & Design
Round Belly Clothing
Sage Creek U.S.A., Inc./Sage Creek
    Naturals®
Serendipiti-Do-Da

Slick Sugar™
Solar Eclipse®
SOS From Texas
Sweet T Baby
Toni Tierney Children's Clothing
Topnotch4kids
Tra la la, Inc.
U.S. Sheepskin
Wild Childwear

**Baby Products: Toys, plush toys, and
    dolls**
Appalachian Baby Design
Baby's First Ball
Bébé Chic, Inc.®
Camden Rose
EmBears
EZ 2 Love®
Fort Cloudy
Honeysuckle Dreams
Hugg-A-Planet®
Lots 2 Say Baby
Maple Landmark of Vermont, Inc.
Northstar Toys
Ozark Mountain Kids
Salisbury Pewter
Stuffington Bear Factory
Sunshine Teddy Bears
Turner Toys, Inc.
Twinkle Baby®
U.S. Sheepskin

**Baby Products: Nursing and feeding,
    including bibs, burp cloths,
    keepsakes, nursing wear, and nursing
    pillows**
A Natural Home
A.S. Tees
Baby Burpees
Baby Nay®
Beary Basics™
Big Bellies Bibs™
Bottle Blankie™, Inc.
Bumkins® Finer Baby Products
Caroline & Company™
Cayden Creations
Charles Craft

Clairebella, Inc.
Cotton Monkey
Earth Wear® Organic Cotton Originals
Esperanza Threads
Fortune Tee
Green Babies
Hampshire Pewter
Holy Lamb Organics
Jen Jen Kids
Kumquat Baby
Leachco™, Inc.
Lots 2 Say Baby
Metal Morphosis®
Mon Amie
My Blankee™, Inc.
Neat Solutions, Inc.
New Native® Baby
Ozark Mountain Kids
Peanut Shell®, The
Prince Lionheart®
Round Belly Clothing
Salisbury Pewter
Simply Tiffany Taite™
SOS From Texas
Sweet T Baby
Woodbury Pewter
World's Greatest Bath Boats
Zenoff Products, Inc.

**Baby and Children's Products: Booties,
    footwear, and socks**
Beary Basics™
Charles Craft
Eden's Bouquet
Esperanza Threads
Footwear by Footskins®
Hoy Shoe Company, Inc.
Itasca Moccasin
Nanny Gram™
Okabashi Brands, Inc.
Piper Sandals™
Principle Plastics/Sloggers®
Rethreds, Inc.™
Soft Star Shoes
Spanx® by Sara Blakely®
U.S. Sheepskin
Wee Ones, Inc.

Wheelhouse Designs
Wigwam Mill, Inc.

**Children's Products: Clothing for
    toddlers and preschoolers**
American Apparel®
American Joe™ Authentic American
    Apparel
Appalachian Baby Design
Babies 'N Bows
Baby Beau & Belle
Baby Go Retro®
Baby Knits and More
Baby Nay®
Bahama Bob's Apparel
Bailey Boys, Inc., The
Beary Basics™
Bébé Monde, Inc.
Bercot Children's Wear
Binky Couture®
Bitty Braille
Black Mountain Apparel™
Bold Mary
Bossy Baby
Calico Closet
Camden Rose
Charles Craft
Charlie Rocket
Chuck Roast, Inc.,
City Threads, Inc.
Cloth & Needle
Clothes Made from Scrap, Inc.
Columbia Knit
Cornpatch Creations
Cotton Caboodle
Cow Track Creations
Crib Rock® Couture
Dittany Baby
Earth Wear® Organic Cotton Originals
Eden's Bouquet
Eight3One™
Esperanza Threads
Fairy Finery™
Focoloco
Fortune Tee
Garden Kids™
Green Babies

American Apparel®
American Joe™ Authentic American
  Apparel
Baby Knits and More
Bahama Bob's Apparel
Bailey Boys, Inc., The
Bercot Children's Wear
Bitty Braille
Black Mountain Apparel™
Buddy's Jeans®
Charlie Rocket
Chuck Roast, Inc.,
Cloth & Needle
Clothes Made from Scrap, Inc.
Columbia Knit
Cool Clothing, USA
Crib Rock® Couture
Fairy Finery™
Focoloco
Garden Kids™
Imagination Creations®
Johnson Woolen Mills®
Klu™ Mountain Outerwear
L.C. King Manufacturing
Little Capers, Inc.
M Group, The/Bamboosa™
Mouseworks, The
My Green Closet
Newberry Knitting
Original Flap Happy®, The
Panhandle Babies™
Patsy Aiken Designs
Polka Dot Market
Quality Fleece
Red Prairie, The
Robin's Hoods™ by Nature & Design
Round House™ Manufacturing Co.
Sassy Scrubs®
Slick Sugar™
Sterlingwear of Boston™, Inc.
Texas Jeans®
Tutti Bowling Wear
Wheelhouse Designs
Wigwam Mill, Inc.

Children's Products: Jeans for boys and
  girls
American Joe™ Authentic American
  Apparel

Buddy's Jeans®
Charlie Rocket
Diamond Gusset Jeans, Inc.
L.C. King Manufacturing
Liliputians NYC
Round House™ Manufacturing Co.
Texas Jeans®

Children's Products: Jewelry for children
  and moms
Belle Pearl™
Brag-e-let's®
Chloe Emma Designs
La Petite Fee™/Nstyle Designs
Little Gems Jewelry
Simply Tiffany Taite™

Children's Products: Outdoor furniture
Allagash Wood Products, Inc.
American Recycled Plastic, Inc.
Conversion Products, Inc.
Little Colorado™, Inc.
Loll Designs
Penobscot Bay Porch Swings
Whimsy Woods Children's Furniture
Yard Candy

Children's Products: Indoor furniture,
  room decorations, mattresses, and
  bedding
A Natural Home
Amenity™, Inc.
American Recycled Plastic, Inc.
Amish Valley Oak
Bean Bag City
Bean Products
Beka, Inc.
Berg Furniture
Bernhaus Furniture
Brighton Pavilion®/Jane Keltner
  Collections
Buchmann's Toy Maker Shop
Carpets for Kids®
Celery Furniture
Chickory Wood Products
Cindy's Throws
Community Playthings®

☆
American-Made Children's Products

Colonial Braided Rug Company
Flagship Carpets
Joy Carpets
Kathy's Braided Rugs
Rug Factory Store

Children's Products: Sports and fitness clothing and swimwear
Adams USA
Aero Tech Designs, Inc.
Bailey Boys, Inc., The
City Threads, Inc.
Cool Clothing, USA
Dodger Industries
Eagle USA, Inc.
Imagination Creations®
Kokatat Watersports Wear
Original Flap Happy®, The
Patsy Aiken Designs
Prieto Sports
Race Ready®
Rethreds, Inc.
Soark® Running Apparel
Solar Eclipse®
Trenway Textiles
Tutti Bowling Wear
Wigwam Mill, Inc.

Children's Products: Fitness equipment
American Made Fitness Equipment, LLC®
Aqua Jogger®
Fold-a-Goal®
Heartland Sports Manufacturing
Legend Fitness®
Needak® Soft Bounce™ Rebounders
TC Sports, Inc.

Children's Products: Sports activities of all kinds
Aerobie, Inc.
American Made Fitness Equipment, LLC®
Barnstable Bat, Inc.
Bean Products
Children's Factory, The
Cohort® Skateboards
Crescent Moon™ Snowshoes
Fold-a-Goal®

Havlick Snowshoe
Heartland Sports Manufacturing
Jackson Kayak
Jump Rope Store
Louisville Slugger®
Mad River Rocket™ Sled Company, Inc.
Mohawk Canoes
Mountain Boy Sledworks
Mylec, Inc.®
Needak® Soft Bounce™ Rebounders
Old Town® Canoes and Kayaks
Peanut Shell®, The
Peerless Plastics, Inc.
Poof-Slinky, Inc.
Redfeather Snowshoes®
TC Sports, Inc.
Wenonah Canoe
Wiffle Ball, Inc., The
Xootr LLC
Yackleball®

Children's Products: Anything on wheels for play or fitness
American Plastic Toys, Inc.®
Beer City Skateboards
Berlin Wagons
Bike Friday®
Cohort® Skateboards
Little Tikes® Company, The
Mason Corporation
Original Big Wheel®, The/J. Lloyd International
Poof-Slinky, Inc.
Riedell® Shoes, Inc.
Sacrifice Skateboards
Skate One Corporation
Skateluge™
Step 2 Company, LLC, The
Valley Road Woodworks
Wunderworks of America
Xootr LLC

Children's Products: Water sports
Aqua Jogger®
Jackson Kayak
Kokatat Watersports Wear
Mohawk Canoes

Children's Products: Arts and crafts products and kits

American Easel Company
Beka, Inc.
Community Playthings®
Grandpa's Games and Crafts
Greenleaf Dollhouses
Jonti-Craft®, Inc.
Lauri® Toys
Omnicor, Inc./Wikkistix®
Peanut Shell®, The
Perler® Beads
Play Clay Factory
Popular Poplar Toys
Skullduggery™
Tag Toys®, Inc.
Terrapin Toys™

Children's Products: Plush toys and dolls

Adoptable Kinders™ by Granza
Bébé Chic, Inc.®
Big Plush Stuffed Toys
Cotton Monster™
E. Willoughby Bear Company
EmBears
Fort Cloudy
Honeysuckle Dreams
Hugg-A-Planet®
Kathy's Kreations
Lehman's, Inc.
My Paper Crane
Ozark Mountain Kids
Stuffington Bear Factory
Sunshine Teddy Bears
Sweet Blossom Boutique
Under the Green Roof
Vermont Teddy Bear®

Children's Products: Children's toys

Adoptable Kinders™ by Granza
Aerobie, Inc.
American Plastic Toys, Inc.®
Animals and Arks
Arrowcopter®
Babies 'N Bows
Berlin Wagons

Big Plush Stuffed Toys
Blu Track®
Buchmann's Toy Maker Shop
Camden Rose
Carrom, Inc.
Channel Craft, Inc.
Chickory Wood Products
Children's Factory, The
Childwood Baby Cradles & Rocking Horses
Community Playthings®
Cotton Monster™
Cubby Hole Toys
D and Me Wood Toys
Don Edwards Wooden Toy Works
Doodletown™ Toys, Inc.
Eden Kazoo Company
EmBears
EZ 2 Love®
Fat Brain™ Toys, Inc.
Finga Zinga®/Evus-Artisan, Inc.
Fort Cloudy
Green Mountain Blocks
Green Toys™, Inc.
Greenleaf Dollhouses
Paul K. Guillow, Inc.
Heartwood Arts
His Idea Crafts
Holgate Toys®
Hotslings®
Huggage
Jensen Steam Engines
John Michael Linck—Toymaker
Jonti-Craft®, Inc.
Jump Rope Store
Just Kids Stuff
K'nex® Industries
Knockabout Toys
Lauri® Toys
Lehman's, Inc.
Lindenwood, Inc.
Little Colorado™, Inc.
Little Tikes® Company, The
Maple Landmark of Vermont, Inc.
New Native® Baby
Northstar Toys
NU-Cut Wood Products

Children's Products: Outdoor play, including swing sets

Children's Products: Special needs

Index

Index

☆
Index

☆
Index

☆
Index

☆

Index